THE RIGHT WING INDIVIDUALIST TRADITION IN AMERICA

The Right Wing Individualist Tradition in America

Advisory Editors:

Dr. Murray N. Rothbard,
Polytechnic Institute of Brooklyn
Jerome Tuccille,
New School for Social Research

SOCIETY WITHOUT GOVERNMENT

THE MARKET FOR LIBERTY
Morris and Linda Tannehill

SOCIETY WITHOUT COERCION
A New Concept of Social Organization
Jarret B. Wollstein

Arno Press & The New York Times
New York • 1972

Reprint Edition 1972 by Arno Press Inc.

The Market for Liberty Copyright © 1970 by Morris and
   Linda Tannehill
Reprinted by permission of Morris and
   Linda Tannehill
Society Without Coercion Copyright © 1969 by the
   Society for Rational Individualism
Reprinted by permission of the Society for
   Rational Individualism

LC# 74-172235
ISBN 0-405-00440-0

The Right Wing Individualist Tradition in America
ISBN for complete set: 0-405-00410-9
See last pages of this volume for titles.

Manufactured in the United States of America

THE MARKET FOR LIBERTY

MORRIS *AND* LINDA TANNEHILL

Copyright © 1970 by Morris and Linda Tannehill
P. O. Box 1383
Lansing, Michigan 48904

All rights reserved.
First Printing, March, 1970

TABLE OF CONTENTS

Acknowledgments iv

PART I—The Great Conflict 1
   Chapter 1. If We Don't Know Where We're Going..... 2
               2. Man and Society 6
               3. The Self-Regulating Market 16
               4. Government—An Unnecessary Evil 32

PART II—A Laissez-Faire Society 43
   Chapter 5. A Free and Healthy Economy 44
               6. Property—The Great Problem Solver 54
               7. Arbitration of Disputes 65
               8. Protection of Life and Property............ 77
               9. Dealing With Coercion 88
              10. Rectification of Injustice 101
              11. Warring Defense Agencies and
                   Organized Crime 109
              12. Legislation and Objective Law 116
              13. Foreign Aggression 126
              14. The Abolition of War 136

PART III—How Do We Get There? 149
   Chapter 15. From Government to Laissez Faire.......... 150
              16. The Force Which Shapes the World......... 160

Acknowledgments

The authors wish to express their gratitude to Skye d'Aureous and Natalee Hall for numerous ideas and suggestions (including Mr. d'Aureous' ideas on data banks for intellectual property, educational TV, and the interest of insurance companies in medical and drug safety); to Roy A. Childs, Jr., for several philosophical arguments against statism; and to Anthony I.S. Alexander for the concept of monetary reparations for coercive injustices and the idea that justice consists of rectifying the injustice insofar as is humanly possible, the idea that property ownership is the solution to pollution problems, the idea that Ayn Rand's "competing governments" argument against anarchy is actually a devastating argument against government, and for many hours of fruitful discussion.

PART I

THE GREAT CONFLICT

"Since late Neolithic times, men in their political capacity have lived almost exclusively by myths."—Dr. James J. Martin

1
If We Don't Know Where We're Going . . .

If we don't know where we're going, chances are we won't get there!

Our world is increasingly stirred with dissatisfaction. Myriads of people on every continent are whispering or shouting or writing or rioting their discontent with the structures of their societies. And they have a lot to be dissatisfied with—poverty which increases in step with increasingly expensive anti-poverty programs, endlessly heavier burdens of taxation and regulation piled on by unmindful bureaucrats, the long death-agonies of meaningless mini-wars, the terrible, iron-fisted knock of secret police . . .

Youth are especially dissatisfied. Many long to turn the world upside down, in hopes that a better, freer, more humane society will emerge. But improvements in man's condition never come as a result of blind hope, pious prayers, or random chance; they are the product of knowledge and thought. Those who are dissatisfied must discover what sort of being man is and, from this, what kind of society is required for him to function most efficiently and happily. If they are unwilling to accept this intellectual responsibility, they will only succeed in exchanging our present troubles for new, and probably worse, ones.

An increasing number of people are beginning to suspect that governmental actions are the cause of many of our social ills. Productive citizens, on whom the prosperity of nations depends, resent being told (in ever more minute detail) how to run their business and their lives. Youth resent being drafted into involuntary servitude as hired killers. The poor are finding, to their bitter disappointment, that government can bleed the economy into anemia but that all its grandiose promises and expensive programs can do nothing but freeze them in their misery. And everyone is hurt by the accelerating spiral of taxes and inflation.

Nearly everyone is against *some* governmental actions, and an increasing number want to cut the size of government anywhere from slightly to drastically. There are even a few who have come to believe that it is not just *certain* governmental activities, nor even the size of the government, but *the very existence of government* which is causing the problems. These individuals are convinced that if we want to be permanently free of government-caused ills we must get rid of government itself. Within this broad anti-statist faction, there are plenty of "activists" who march or protest or just dream and scheme about means of bringing part or all of the governmental system crashing down.

Although these anti-authoritarian individuals have taken a firm and well-justified stand *against* the injustice of government, few of them have an explicitly clear idea of what they are *for*. They want to tear down the old society and build a better one, but most of them hold only hazy and contradictory ideas of *what* this better society would be like and what its structure should be.

But if we have no clear idea of what our goals are, we can hardly expect to achieve them. If we bring our present authoritarian system crashing down around our ears withour formulating and disseminating valid ideas about how society will operate satisfactorily without governmental rule, all that will result is confusion, ending in chaos. Then people, bewildered and frightened and still convinced that the traditional governmental system was right and necessary in spite of its glaring flaws, will demand a strong leader, and a Hitler will rise to answer their plea. So we'll be far worse off than we were before, because we will have to contend with both the destruction resulting from the chaos and a dictator with great popular support.

The force which shapes men's lives and builds societies is not the destructive power of protests and revolutions but the productive power of rational ideas. Before anything can be produced—from a stone axe to a social system—someone must first have an idea of what to aim for and how to go about achieving it. Ideas must precede all production and all action. For this reason, ideas are the most powerful (though often the most underestimated) force in man's world.

This is a book about an idea—the discovery of what kind of society man needs in order to function most efficiently and happily . . . and how to achieve that society. It is a book about freedom—what it really is and implies, why man needs it, what it can do for him, and how to build and maintain a truly free society.

We are not envisioning any Utopia, in which no man ever tries to victimize another. As long as men are human, they will be free to choose to act in an irrational and immoral manner against their fellows, and there will probably always be some who act as brutes, inflicting their will upon others by force. What we are proposing is a system for dealing with such men which is far superior to our present governmental one—a system which makes the violation of human liberty far more difficult and less rewarding for all who want to live as brutes, and downright impossible for those who want to be politicians.

Nor are we proposing a "perfect" society (whatever that is). Men are fallible, so mistakes will always be made, and there will never be a society of total equity. Under the present governmental system, however, blunders and aggressive intrusions into the lives of peaceful individuals tend to feed on themselves and to grow automatically, so that what starts as a small injustice (a tax, a regulation, a bureau, etc.) inevitably becomes a colossus in time. In a truly free society, blunders and aggressions would tend to be self-correcting, because men who are free to choose will not deal with individuals and firms which are stupid, offensive, or dangerous to those they do business with.

The society we propose is based on one fundamental principle: *No man or group of men*—including any group of men calling themselves "the government"—*is morally entitled to initiate* (that is, to start) *the use of physical force, the threat of force, or any substitute for force* (such as fraud) *against any other man or group of men.* This means that no man, no gang, and no government may morally use force in even the smallest degree against even the most unimportant individual so long as that individual has not himself initiated force.[1] Some individuals *will* choose to initiate force; how to deal with them justly occupies a major part of this book. But, although such aggressions will probably never by fully eliminated, rational men can construct a society which will discourage them rather than institutionalizing them as an integral part of its social structure.

Of course, our knowledge of what a truly free society would be like is far from complete. When men are free to think and produce, they innovate and improve everything around them at a startling rate, which means that only the bare outlines of the structure and functioning of a free society can be seen prior to its actual establishment and operation. But more than enough can be reasoned out to prove that a truly free society—one in which the initiation of force would be dealt with justly instead of institutionalized in the form of a government—is feasible. By working from what is already known, it is possible to show in general how a free society would operate and to answer fully and satisfactorily the common questions about and objections to such a society.

---

[1] The terms "initiated force" and "coercion" are used to include not only the actual initiation of force but also the threat of such force and any substitute for force. This is because a man can be coerced into acting against his will by threats or deprived of a value by force-substitutes, such as fraud or theft by stealth, just as surely as he can by the actual use of physical force. The threat of force is intimidation, which is, itself, a form of force.

If We Don't Know Where We're Going . . .

For years men with plans to improve society have debated the merits and demerits of various kinds and amounts of government, and they have argued long and heatedly over how much freedom was desirable or necessary to provide for the needs of man's life. But very few of them have tried to clearly identify the nature of government, the nature of freedom, or even the nature of man. Consequently, their social schemes have not been in accordance with the facts of reality and their "solutions" to human ills have been little more than erudite fantasies. Neither the futile and time-worn panaceas of the Establishment, nor the "God and country" fervor of the Right, nor the angry peace marches of the Left can build a better society if men do not have a clear, reality-based, non-contradictory idea of what a better society is. If we don't know where we're going, we won't get there.

It is the aim of this book to show where we are (or should be) going.

2
Man and Society

In all of recorded history, men have never managed to establish a social order which didn't institutionalize violations of freedom, peace, and justice—that is, a social order in which man could realize his full potential. This failure has been due to the fact that thinkers have never clearly and explicitly understood three things—namely, 1—the nature of man, 2—what kind of society this nature requires for men to realize their full potential, and 3—how to achieve and maintain such a society.

Most self-styled planners and builders of societies haven't even considered that man might have a specific nature. They have regarded him as something infinitely plastic, as the product of his cultural or economic milieu, as some sort of identity-less blob which they could mold to suit their plans. This lack of realization that man has a specific nature which requires that he function in a specific way has given rise to floods of tears and blood . . . as social planners tried to wrench man apart and put him back together in a form they found more to their liking.

But because man *is*, he *is something*—a being with a specific nature, requiring a specific type of society for his proper functioning as a human being. Since Darwin, scientific research has been steadily uncovering evidences of evolution which show the development of the nature of the human animal. In order to survive, men had to acquire certain behavioral knowledge and capacities—for instance, the knowledge that voluntary cooperation is good and the capacity to stop clubbing each other. Most men conduct their lives according to this knowledge and, when left alone, get along quite well. Social planners have always been among the most ignorant about man's nature. Evidence that man has a specific biological nature which cannot be remolded to suit society-builders continues to mount,[1] but political rulers continue to ignore it. If men are to be happy and successful, they must live in harmony with the requirements of their nature. What, then, are the essentials of man's nature?

---
[1]See *TERRITORIAL IMPERATIVE* and *AFRICAN GENESIS*, by Robert Ardrey, and *THE NAKED APE*, by Desmond Morris.

Life is given to man, but the means to sustain his life are not. If a man is to continue living, he must in some way acquire the things he needs to sustain his life, which means that either he or someone else must produce these things. There is no environment on earth where man could exist without some sort of productive effort, and there is no way he could be productive without using his mind to decide what to produce and how to produce it. In order to survive, *man must think*—that is, he must make use of the information provided by his senses. The more fully and clearly he uses his mind, the better he will be able to live (on both the physical, including the material, and the psychological levels).

But thinking is not an automatic process. Man may expend a little or a lot of mental effort to solve his problems, or he may just ignore them and hope they'll go away. He may make it a policy to keep his mind fully aware and always to use it as effectively as he can (whether he is a genius or a dimwit), or he may drift through life in an unfocused mental haze, playing ostrich whenever he sees something that would require mental effort and commitment. The choice to think or not to think is his, and it is a choice which every man must make.

Because man must initiate and maintain the process of thinking by an act of choice, no one else can force him to think or do his thinking for him. This means that *no man can successfully run another man's life*. The best thing one man can do for another is not to prevent him from enjoying the benefits of his thinking and productive work, nor to shield him from the bad effects of refusing to think and produce.

Life is given to man, but the knowledge of how to sustain that life is not. Man has no automatic knowledge of what is good or bad for him, and he needs this knowledge in order to know how to live. If he is to have a full and happy life, he needs a blueprint to show him what is pro-life and what is anti-life and to guide his choices and actions. Such a blueprint is a code of morality—a chosen guide to action. If a man wants his morality to further his life instead of crippling it, he must choose a morality which is in harmony with his evolved nature as a sensing, thinking being.

Choosing effective guides to action is not a matter for blind faith or reasonless whim; it requires clear, rational thought. Therefore, one's morality shouldn't be a set of dos and don'ts inherited from one's parents or learned in church or school. It should be a clearly thought-out code, guiding one toward pro-life actions and away from anti-life actions. "The purpose of morality is . . . to teach you to enjoy yourself and live."² A rational morality doesn't say, "Don't do this because God (or society, or legal authorities, or tradition) says it's evil." It *does* say, "Only if you act according to your reason can you have a happy, satisfying life."

In any code of morality, there must be a standard—a standard by which all goals and actions can be judged. Only life makes values meaningful . . . or even possible—if you're dead you can't experience any values at all (and without values, happiness is impossible). So, for each man who values living, his own life is his moral standard (death, the negation of all values, is the only alternative "standard"). Since each man's own life is his objective standard, it follows that whatever serves or enhances his life and well-being is good, and whatever damages or destroys it is wrong. In a rational morality—one designed to further each individual man's life and happiness, whatever is pro-life is moral and whatever is anti-life is immoral. By "life" is not meant merely man's physical existence but all aspects of his life as a sensing, thinking being. Only by rational thought and action can a man's life be lived to its fullest potential, producing the greatest possible happiness and satisfaction for him.

Man has only one tool for getting knowledge—his mind, and only one means to know what is beneficial and harmful—his faculty of reason. Only by thinking can he know what will further his life and what will harm it. For this reason, choosing to think is man's most powerful tool and greatest virtue, and refusing to think is his greatest danger, the surest way to bring him to destruction.

Since man's life is what makes all his values possible, morality means acting in his own self-interest, which is acting in a pro-life manner. There is nothing mystical or hard to understand about right and wrong—a rational morality makes sense. Traditional morality, teaching that each man must devote a part of his life, not primarily for his own good, but for God or the State or "the common good," regards man as a sacrificial animal. Today, many are recognizing this doctrine for what it is—the cause of incalculable human carnage, and a morality or life is gradually replacing it. A rational morality is a morality of self-interest—a pro-life morality.

The only way for a man to know what will further his life is by a process of reason; morality, therefore, means acting in his *rational* self-interest (in fact, no other kind of self-interest exists, since only that which is rational is in one's self-interest). Sacrifice (the act of giving up a greater value for a lesser value, a non-value, or a dis-value) is always wrong, because it is destructive

---
²From John Galt's speech in Ayn Rand's *ATLAS SHRUGGED.*

of the life and well-being of the sacrificing individual.[3] In spite of traditional "moralities" which glorify "a life of sacrificial service to others," sacrifice can never benefit anyone. It demoralizes both the giver, who has diminished his total store of value, and the recipient, who feels guilty about accepting the sacrifice and resentful because he feels he is morally bound to return the "favor" by sacrificing some value of his own. Sacrifice, carried to its ultimate end, results in death; it is the exact opposite of moral, pro-life behavior, traditional "moralists" to the contrary notwithstanding.

A man who is acting in his own self-interest (that is, who is acting morally) neither makes sacrifices nor demands that others sacrifice for him. There is no conflict of interest between men who are each acting in his own self-interest, because it is not in the interest of either to sacrifice for the other or to demand a sacrifice from the other. Conflicts are produced when men ignore their self-interest and accept the notion that sacrifice is beneficial; sacrifice is *always* anti-life.

In summary: man, by his nature, must choose to think and produce in order to live, and the better he thinks, the better he will live. Since each man's own life makes his values possible, chosen behavior which furthers his life as a thinking being is *the moral*, and chosen behavior which harms it is *the immoral*. (Without free choice, morality is impossible.) Therefore, rational thought and action and their rewards, emotional, physical, and material, are the whole of a man's self-interest. The opposite of self-interest is sacrfiice which is always wrong because it's destructive of human life.[4]

Any society in which men can realize their full potential and live as rational and productive human beings must be established in accordance with these basic facts of man's nature. It must be a society in which each man is left unmolested, in which he is free to think and to act on his ideas . . . without anyone else trying to force him to live his life according to *their* standards. Not only must each man be free to act, he must also be free to fully enjoy the rewards of all his pro-life actions. Whatever he earns in emotional joy, material goods, and intellectual values (such as admiration and respect) must be completely his—he must not be forced against his will to give up any of it for the supposed benefit of others. *He must not be forced to sacrifice,* not even for "the good of society."

---
[3] If a mother goes without a new dress to buy a coat for her child whom she loves, that is not a sacrifice but a gain—her child's comfort was of more value to her than the dress. But if she deprives herself and the child by giving the money to the local charity drive so that people won't think she's "selfish," *that is a sacrifice*.
[4] For a much fuller development of objective ethics, see Chapter 1, "The Objectivist Ethics," of THE VIRTUE OF SELFISHNESS, by Ayn Rand. While Miss Rand is at present confused in the area of politics, her explanation of ethics is, by and large, very good.

To the extent that a man isn't free to live his life peacefully according to his own standards and to fully own whatever he earns, he is a slave. Enslaving men "for the good of society" is one of the most subtle and widespread forms of slavery. It is continually advocated by priests, politicians, and quack philosophers who hope, by the labor of the enslaved, to gain what they haven't earned.

A society in which men can realize their full potential must be one in which each man is free to act in his self-interest according to the judgment of his own mind. The only way a man can be compelled against his will to act contrary to his judgment is by the use or threat of physical force by other men. Many pressures may be brought to bear on a man, but unless he is compelled by physical force (or the threat of force, or a substitute for force) to act against his will, he still has the freedom to make his own choices. Therefore, the one basic rule of a civilized society is that no man or group of men is morally entitled to *initiate* (to *start*) the use of physical force, the threat of force, or any substitute for force (such as taking something from another person by stealth) against any other man or group of men.

This doesn't mean that a man may not defend himself if someone else initiates force against him. It does mean that he may not *start* the use of force. To *initiate* force against anyone is *always* wrong, because it compels the victim to act contrary to his own judgment. But to defend oneself against force by retaliating with counter-force is not only permissible, it is a moral imperative whenever it is feasible, or reasonably safe, to do so.[5] If a man really values his values, he has a moral obligation *to himself* to defend them—not to do so would be sacrificial and, therefore, self-destructive. The difference between initiated force and retaliatory force is the difference between murder and self-defense. (Pacifists who have consistently refused to defend themselves when attacked have frequently been killed—the belief in pacifism is anti-life.)

As long as a man doesn't initiate force, the actual goals and interests which he chooses to pursue don't control the free choice or threaten the goals of anyone else. It doesn't matter whether a man goes to church every day or advocates atheism, whether he wears his hair long or short, whether he gets drunk every night or uses drugs or stays cold sober, whether he believes in capitalism or voluntary communalism—so long as he doesn't reach for a gun . . . or a politician . . . to compel others to live as he thinks they should. As long as men mind their own business and don't initiate force against their fellow men, no one's life-style is a threat to anyoue else.

---

[5]Retaliatory force is defensive, not coercive, in nature; coercion is initiated force, the threat to initiate force—which is intimidation, or any substitute for initiated force.

When a man initiates force against another man, he violates his victim's rights. *A right is a principle which morally prohibits men from using force or any substitute for force against anyone whose behavior is non-coercive.* A right is a moral prohibition; it doesn't specify anything with regard to *what* actions the possessor of the right may take (so long as his actions are non-coercive)—it morally prohibits others from forcibly interfering with any of his non-coercive actions. For example, a beachcomber has the right to life; this right says nothing of what the beachcomber may do with his life—it says only that no one else may forcibly interfere with his life so long as he doesn't initiate force or fraud against them. Suppose, however, that the beachcomber does initiate force against a cab driver and does $100 worth of damage to the taxicab. In order to rectify the injustice, the beachcomber must pay the cabbie $100. The beachcomber does not, then, have the right to whatever part of his life and/or property that is required to make reparations to the cabbie (the cabbie has a just claim to it). Suppose, further, that the beachcomber will not willingly pay the $100; the cabbie is no longer morally prohibited from using force against the beachcomber to collect what is now rightfully his. The beachcomer, by his initiation of force against and to the detriment of another man, has alienated himself from the right to that part of his life which is required to pay his debt.[6] Rights are *not* inalienable, but only the possessor of a right can alienate himself from that right—no one else can take a man's rights from him.

Each person has a right to his own life, which means that each person is a self-owner (assuming that his behavior has been and is non-coercive). Because a man has a right to own his life, he has the same right to any part of that life. Property is one part of a man's life. Material goods are necessary to sustain life, and so are the ideas which a man generates. So, man invests his time in generating ideas and in producing and maintaining material goods. A man's life is made up of time, so when he invests his time in material or intellectual property (ideas) he is investing parts of his life, thereby making that property an extension of his life. The right to property is part of the right to life. There is no conflict between property rights and human rights—property rights *are* human rights.

Another aspect of man's life is his freedom of action. If a man is not free to use his mind, his body, and his time in any action he wishes (so long as he doesn't initiate force or fraud), he is in some degree a slave. The right to liberty, like the right to property, is an aspect of the right to life.

---

[6]This subject will be discussed in greater detail in Chapter 10, "Rectification of Injustice."

All rights are aspects of the right to life, which means that each man has the right to every part of *his own* life. By the same token, he is not morally entitled to any part of another man's life (assuming the other man has not initiated force or fraud against him). Any "right" which violates someone else's rights is no right at all. There can be no such thing as a right to violate a right, or rights would be meaningless. A man has the right to *earn* a decent living, but he does not have the right to a decent living if it must be provided by force out of someone else's earnings. That is, he has no right to enslave others and force them to provide his living—not even if he does so by getting the government to pass a law taxing others to make payments to him. Each individual is the owner of his own life . . . and no one else's.

Rights are not a gift of God or of society; they are the product of the nature of man and of reality. If man is to live a productive and happy life and realize his full potential as a human being, he must be free from coercion by other men. The nature of man demands that he must have values and goals in order to live—without them, human life is impossible. When a man is not free to choose his own goals, he can't act on the feedback from his behavior and so he can't correct his errors and live successfully. To the extent that a man is forcibly prevented by others from choosing his own values and goals, he is a slave. Slavery is the exact opposite of liberty; they cannot coexist.

Rights pertain only to individual men. There is no such thing as minority rights, States' rights, "civil" rights, or any other form of collective rights. The initiation of force against the collective is really the initiation of force against the individuals of which the collective is composed, because the collective has no existence apart from the individuals who compose it. Therefore, there are no collective rights—there are only the rights which every individual has to be free from the coercive actions of others.

Morally, each man owns himself, and he has the right to do anything which does not violate another man's right of self-ownership. The only way a right can be violated is by coercion. This is why society in harmony with the requirements of man's nature must be based on the rule of non-initiation of force—it must be a laissez-faire society.

Laissez faire means "let people do as they please," meaning, let everyone leave others alone to do as they choose. A laissez-faire society is a society of non-interference—a mind-your-own-business, live-and-let-live society. It means freedom for each individual to manage *his own* affairs in any way he pleases . . . not just in the realm of economics but in every area of *his life*. (If he restricts his behavior to *his own* affairs, it is obvious that he cannot initiate the use of force against anyone else.) In a laissez-faire society, no man or group of men would dictate anyone's life-style, or force them to pay taxes to a State bureaucracy, or prohibit them from making any voluntary trades they wanted.

There will likely never be a society completely free from the initiation of physical force by some men against others, because men can act irrationally if they choose to. A laissez-faire society is not a Utopia in which the initiation of violence is impossible. Rather, it is a society which does not *institutionalize* the initiation of force and in which there are means for dealing with aggression justly when it does occur.

Can men ever achieve a laissez-faire society? Many people have an unshakable conviction that anything so "ideal" could never become a practical reality. They can't explain why they're so sure of this; they just *feel* an unreasoned "certainty" that it must be so. What is behind this reasonless "certainty" that the good (liberty) is unachievable? The answer lies in the inverted "morality" of tradition—altruism.

Altruism is the philosophical doctrine which holds that anything which is done out of concern for the welfare of others is good but that it is evil if motivated by concern for self. Some variation of this doctrine has been a basic part of nearly all of the world's religions and philosophies for man's entire history. One of the most common of religious tenets is that selfishness is evil and that only a selfless concern for the needs of others will win favor with God and man. Sacrifice is held to be among the greatest of virtues, simply because the beneficiaries of the sacrifice are others and the loser is self. It isn't hard to see one of the reasons for the long-standing prominence of altruistic doctrines—religious and political leaders can collect much more substantial offerings and taxes from people whom these leaders succeed in convincing that it is their moral duty to give as much as possible in sacrificial service to others than they can from people who live for their own rational self-interest. This "something for nothing" doctrine—altruism—is the moral ideal of human parasites.

Altruism is an inverted morality, a "morality" of death. It teaches man that his interests are opposed to the interests of everyone else and that the only "moral" thing he can do is to sacrifice his interests. This means that whatever is practical and beneficial for a man is "immoral," and conversely, that whatever is "moral" for him is impractical and destructive of his values. To the extent that a man is committed to some version of altruism, he can be either practical and immoral or moral and impractical—he cannot be both moral *and* practical at the same time . . . and his self-respect and honesty hang in the balance.

This artificial dichotomy between the moral and the practical splits man in two and sets him against himself. To the extent he makes himself worthy to live (by sacrificing his values), he makes himself unable to live; to the extent he makes himself able to live (by keeping and using his values), he makes himself unworthy to live. No man can fully practice such a code—if he did, it would kill him. For those who accept a "morality" based on altruism, their only protection from this belief is *hypocrisy;* they give it lip-service but practice it only so far as it is religiously and socially required to keep up a good front. This is the cause of most of the hypocrisy in our culture. Altruism makes hypocrisy necessary in order to live.

A society full of hypocrisy is headed for the crematorium. The moral/practical dichotomy not only necessitates hypocrisy, it also gives all the advantages to evil, since the good is, by virtue of its goodness, incurably impractical for life on earth. If the evil and the practical are one and the same, then evil must always win. According to the altruist philosophy, evil holds all the cards and man can hope for very little improvement in his life or in his society.

Of course, people who hold the moral/practical dichotomy seldom consciously realize what they believe. They just know that whatever is right and good seems somehow unworkable, at least on any major scale. The idea of a laissez-faire society—that is, a society of non-interference—leaves them unmoved because it seems so impractical.

But the "morality" of altruism is exactly opposite to the facts of man's nature. In reality, the only thoughts and actions which are in man's self-interest are rational ones, and there is never any conflict of interest between men who are behaving rationally. Sacrifice harms not only the man who makes the sacrifice but also the man who accepts it; it is, therefore, inevitably detrimental. Acting in one's rational self-interest is always right, so the moral and the practical are simply two sides of the same coin. Since moral actions are inherently practical and pro-life, immoral actions are always impractical and anti-life. Evil—i.e., anti-life behavior—is, by its nature, weak and can only survive by the support good men can be misled into giving it. It follows, therefore, that a laissez-faire society *is* both practical and attainable.

If a laissez-faire society *is* attainable, why haven't men established one before now? The answer is that essentially good people have prevented it by their unwitting support of slavery. The majority of people throughout history have accepted the idea that it was both proper and necessary for some men to coercively rule over others. Most of these people weren't basically bad, and probably only a few of them have had a lust for power. But they have held a terribly wrong idea which has caused them to support a social system that institutionalizes slavery and violence. It is this idea—that it is proper and/or necessary for some men to coercively govern others, which is *the idea of government*—that has prevented the establishment of a laissez-faire society and which has been responsible for incalculable human suffering and waste in the form of political and religious persecutions, taxes, regulations, conscription, slavery, wars, despotisms, etc., etc. To achieve a laissez-faire society, it is only necessary to enable enough people to change this idea in their minds. All that is required for the *defeat* of evil is that good men stop their unwitting support of it.

There is a great and growing conflict in our world between those who want to be free and those who want to rule (together with those who want to be ruled). This great conflict has been taking shape for centuries, but the vast majority of people have never understood what it was all about because they haven't seen that the issue was *freedom* versus *slavery*. Because they have believed that men must be governed, most people have been, however, unwittingly and apathetically on the side of slavery. Until recently, no more than a tiny handful of individualsts have realized what freedom means and how necessary it is for man's happiness and well-being.

The great conflict between freedom and slavery, though it has taken many forms, finds its main expression in a conflict between two powerful and opposing human institutions—the free market and government. The establishment of a laissez-faire society depends on the outcome of the war between these two institutions—a war whose most crucial battles are fought on the field of ideas.

3
The Self-Regulating Market

Government bureaucrats and their allies among the currently influential opinion-molders have made a practice of spreading misinformation about the nature of a free market. They have accused the market of instability and economic injustice and have misrepresented it as the origin of myriads of evils from poverty to "the affluent society." Their motives are obvious. If people can be made to believe that the laissez-faire system of a free, unregulated market is inherently faulty, then the bureaucrats and their cohorts in classrooms and editorial offices will be called in to remedy the situation. In this way, power and influence will flow to the bureaucrats . . . and bureaucrats thrive on power.

The free-market system, which the bureaucrats and politicians blame so energetically for almost everything, is nothing more than individuals trading with each other in a market free from political interference. Because of the tremendous benefits of trade under a division of labor, there will always be markets. A market is a network of voluntary economic exchanges; it includes all willing exchanges which do not involve the use of coercion against anyone. (If A hires B to murder C, this is not a market phenomenon, as it involves the use of initiated force against C. Because force destroys values and disrupts trade, the market can only exist in an environment of peace and freedom; to the extent that force exists, the market is destroyed. Initiated force, being destructive of the market, cannot be a part of the market.)

Trade is an indispensible means of increasing human well-being. If there were no trade, each person would have to get along with no more than what he could produce by himself from the raw materials he could discover and process. Obviously, without trade most of the world's population would starve to death, and the rest would be reduced to a living standard of incredible poverty. Trade makes a *human* existence possible.

When two people make a trade, each one expects to gain from it (if this were not so, the trade wouldn't be made). And, if each trader has correctly estimated how much he values the things being

The Self-Regulating Market

traded, each does gain. This is possible because each person has a different frame of reference and, therefore, a different scale of values. For example, when you spend 30¢ for a can of beans, you do so because the can of beans is more valuable to you than the 30¢ (if it weren't, you wouldn't make the purchase). But, to the grocer, who has 60 cases of canned beans, the 30¢ is more valuable than one can of beans. So, both you and the grocer, acting from your different frames of reference, gain from your trade. In any trade in which the traders have correctly estimated their values and in which they are free to trade on the basis of these values without any outside interference, both buyer and seller must gain.

Of course, if some outside influence—such as a gangster or a politician—prohibits the traders from doing business or forces them to trade in a manner which is unacceptable to one or both, either the buyer or the seller (or both) will lose. This happens whenever laws control prices, quality of goods, time and place of purchase (liquor laws), shipment of goods over borders (interstate commerce, tariffs, international trade restrictions), or any other aspect of trade. Only a voluntary trade can be a completely satisfactory trade.

Money is used because it makes trading easier and increases the number and type of trades possible. If you wanted to get rid of a motorcycle and to get in exchange a six months supply of groceries, three pairs of pants, several records, and a night on the town with your girlfriend, you'd find it pretty hard to make the trade without the use of money as a medium of exchange. By using money, you can sell that motorcycle to anyone who will buy it and use the cash to buy whatever you want. Because the use of money makes it no longer necessary for the buyer to have an assortment of the exact goods the seller wants, many more and better trades can be made, thus increasing the satisfaction of everyone.

Money also acts as the means of calculating the relative worth of various goods and services. Without money, it would be impossible to know how many phonographs a car was worth, or how many loaves of bread should be exchanged for the service of having a tooth pulled. Without a standard medium of exchange to calculate with, the market couldn't exist.

To the extent that voluntary trade relationships are not interfered with (prohibited, regulated, taxed, subsidized, etc.), the market is free. Since governments have always made a practice of interfering with markets, and indeed depend on such interferences in the form of taxes, licenses, etc., for their very existence, there has never been a sizable and well-developed market which was totally free.

The United States of America, though theoretically a free country, suffers from an almost unbelievable amount of market regulation.[1] Though often called a capitalistic country, the U.S.A. actually has a mixed economy—a mixture of some government-permitted "freedom," a little socialism, and a lot of fascism. Socialism is a system in which the government owns and controls the means of production (supposedly for "the good of the people," but, in actual practice, for the good of the politicians). Facism is a system in which the government leaves nominal ownership of the means of production in the hands of private individuals but exercises control by means of regulatory legislation and reaps most of the profit by means of heavy taxation. In effect, facism is simply a more subtle form of government ownership than is socialism. Under fascism, producers are allowed to keep a nominal title to their possessions and to bear all the risks involved in entrepreneurship, while the government has most of the actual control and gets a great deal of the profits (and takes none of the risks). The U.S.A. is moving increasingly away from a free-market economy and toward fascist totalitarianism.

It is commonly believed and taught, particularly by those who favor the present "Establishment," that the market must have external controls and restraints placed upon it by government to protect helpless individuals from exploitation. It is also held that governmental "fine tuning" is needed to prevent market instability, such as booms and busts. A vast amount of governmental action is based on the theory that the market would speedily go awry without regulation, causing financial suffering and economic havoc.

When politicians and so-called economists speak of "regulating the market," what they are actually proposing is legislation *regulating people—preventing* them from making trades which they otherwise would have made, or *forcing* them to make trades they would not have made. The market is a network of trade relationships, and a relationship can only be regulated by regulating the *persons* involved in it.

An example of government regulation of the market is "price control." A price is the amount of money (or other value) which sellers agree to take and buyers agree to give for a good or a service. A price isn't a conscious entity and couldn't care less what level it is set at or what controls it is subjected to. But the buyers and sellers care. It is *they* who must be controlled if the price is to be held at an artificial level. Price control, like all other political controls and regulations imposed on the market by legislative force, is . . . *people control!*

---

[1] See *TEN THOUSAND COMMANDMENTS,* by Harold Fleming; 1951; PRENTICE-HALL, INC., N.Y.

The Self-Regulating Market

Of course, such people-regulation can only be imposed by the initiation of the threat and use of physical force. If people were willing to trade in the manner prescribed by the government planners, they would already have been doing so and the market-regulating "services" of the planners would be unnecessary. Only by forcing unwilling buyers and sellers to act differently from what they would have if left free can government regulate or "fine tune" the economy.

This initiation of force against peaceful buyers and sellers inevitably causes them to act against their best interests, or at least what they believe to be their best interests. When they act against their interests, they inevitably suffer a loss of value. It is a commonly held myth that government bureaucrats know far better than the rest of us "how things ought to be run," so that it is actually good for the public as a whole if some people are forced to act against their selfish interests. But this myth of "the wise government planner" ignores two important facts. First, you are in a far better position to know how to manage your affairs, including your business and professional life, than is some far-off, politically selected bureaucrat. And this truth is just as applicable to every other person operating honestly and peacefully in the market, especially those whose market transactions are extremely complex and important. You may make mistakes in your market dealings, but the bureaucrat's isolation from direct and immediate information about your situation and his lack of a strong personal interest in your affairs absolutely guarantee that he will make a lot more and bigger mistakes, even if he's honestly trying to help. Besides, when a bureaucrat makes a mistake in regulating your affairs, he doesn't receive any feedback, in the form of economic losses, to alert him to his error. You receive all the feedback, but you aren't in a position of control, so you can't correct the error.

The second important fact ignored by the myth of "the wise government planner" is that the individuals who are being forced by government regulation to act against their interests are a part of the very public which is supposed to benefit from these governmental controls. Therefore, a loss of value by those who are controlled is also a loss of value for "the public." And, because a market consists of a network of highly interconnected relationships, a loss to any person dealing in the market tends to diffuse to those doing business with him, and from them to their business contacts, etc.

For example, suppose the government were to pass a law requiring all washing machines in laundromats to have a washing cycle at least 45 minutes long, to protect customers from insufficiently washed clothes. The laundromat owners, being unable to serve as many customers per washing maching as before, would take in less money. This would prevent them from buying more and newer washers and driers, which would hurt the manufacturers of these products, who would then be unable to buy as much steel and porcelain, etc., etc. At the other end of the line, the customers of laundromats would also be hurt as a shortage of available washing machine time developed, due to the original 45-minute regulation plus the laundromat owners' inability to buy new machines and replace wornout ones. (At this point, some government bureaucrat is sure to call for federal action to deal with the crisis in the laundromat industry caused by "the excesses of an unregulated market!")

In this way, people who were naturally already doing business in the most profitable way, for both seller and buyer (remember, we're talking about a free, competitive market), are forced by government regulation of the market to act differently, which causes them losses. Advocates of government regulation usually accept the idea of imposing some losses on those who are regulated, but they fail to take into account the fact that those losses will inevitably diffuse throughout the economy like ripples spreading in widening circles over a pond. They also fail to recognize that a society with government regulation is dangerous to every individual person, because anyone may be the next victim, directly or indirectly, of government controls.

But even though government regulation of the market necessitates the initiation of force and causes widespread losses, many people still feel it is necessary to force some sort of order on the seeming chaos of the market. This belief stems from a complete misunderstanding of the way in which the market functions. The market is not a jumble of distorted and unrelated events. Instead, it is a highly complex but orderly and efficient mechanism which provides a means for each person to realize the maximum possible value and satisfaction commensurate with his abilities and resources. A brief examination of the workings of the market will illustrate this point. (A complete proof of it would require several hundred pages of economic analysis.[2])

The price of any good on the market (including such things as a doctor's fees and the rates of interest on borrowed money) is determined by the supply of the good available relative to the demand for it.[3] Within the limits of available resources, the supply is controlled by the demand, since producers will produce more of a good in order to increase their profits when customers demand more and

---

[2]For a most excellent treatise on economic principles, see Murray N. Rothbard's 2-Vol. *MAN, ECONOMY, AND STATE* (D. Van Nostrand Company, Inc.).

[3]The belief that prices are set by the cost of production is erroneous. Actually, in the context of the total market, the prices of the various factors of production are determined by the return which their products are expected to earn. For a complete analysis of this subject, see Dr. Rothbard's *MAN, ECONOMY, AND STATE*.

The Self-Regulating Market

are thus willing to spend more for it. So it is consumer demand which really calls the tune in a *free* market.

Consumer demand is the aggregate result of the economic value-judgments of all the individual consumers. Thus, it is the values of individuals, expressed through their demand for various products, which cause the market to be what it is at any given time.

The price of any good on the market will tend to be set at the point where the supply of that good (at that price) is equal to the demand for it (at that price). If the price is set below this equilibrium point, eager buyers will bid it up; if it is set above, the sellers will bid it down until it reaches equilibrium. At the equilibrium price, all those who wish to buy or sell at that price will be able to do so without creating surpluses or shortages. If, however, the price is artificially lowered by a government price-control, more buyers will be attracted while sellers will be unwilling to sell, creating a shortage with its attendant problems of rationing, queues, and black markets. On the other hand, if government sets the price higher than the equilibrium price, there will be a surplus of the good, bringing financial ruin to those who are unable to sell their excess stock. A specialized example of this occurs in the labor market whenever government (or government-privileged unions) forces a minimum wage higher than the equilibrium wage, leading to a surplus of labor and so causing unemployment problems and an increase in poverty (and this is only one way in which government causes unemployment and poverty).

Thus, the market has a built-in self-regulating mechanism which continually adjusts the price of products (and, similarly, their quantity and quality) to the supply of available resources and to the amount of consumer demand. It works like a complex signal system, visible to all and reliable *if not interfered with*. The signals are given by consumer value choices. They are transmitted to the sellers (businessmen and entrepreneurs) by means of profit and loss. A profit tells the businessman that consumers are pleased with his product and that he should continue or even increase the level of production. A loss shows him that not enough consumers are willing to buy his product at the price he is asking, so he should either lower his price or redirect his money and effort into some other line of production.

This signal system keeps the market constantly moving toward equilibrium even as new data enter and upset the previous balance. For example, suppose that Eastern Electric begins manufacturing a newly invented TV tube which shows the picture in three dimensions. As consumers hear of the new 3D TV (via news reports and advertising), demand for it skyrockets. The number of 3D TVs

Eastern Electric can produce is limited, so the large demand and small supply result in an extremely high price and high profit margins for Eastern Electric. But this same high profit, which may seem at first to be an instance of market imbalance and unfairness, is the signal which moves the market toward equilibrium. Eastern Electric's high profits stimulate other firms to do research on 3D TV so that they may enter the field with new and better models and share in the profits. Soon, half a dozen firms are selling competing 3D TVs and the increased supply satisfies the demand. This brings the price down until high profits disappear and earnings in the 3D TV industry are about the same, percentagewise, as in every other industry. At this point, new firms stop entering the field, as there is nothing more to attract them. The whole market levels off and, barring another new input of data, remains stable. Thus, when the market is unhampered, any new input of data immediately sends out profit or loss signals which set in motion factors which maintain market equilibrium. The market is a self-regulating mechanism. (It should be noted that the high initial profit realized from a new product is also a just process in which the innovator is rewarded for his investment of time, money, and mental labor.)

Individual self-interest is the basis for the whole market system, which is why it works so well. The consumer acts in his self-interest when he buys things at the lowest prices and with the best quality he can find. The producer acts in his self-interest in trying to make the highest profit possible. Both consumer and producer attempt to profit from their market transactions; if either side didn't expect to gain, no trade would take place. This double utilization of the profit motive results in maximum consumer satisfaction and rewards entrepreneurial efficiency.

Government effects the economy in three major ways—1) by taxation and spending, 2) by regulation, and 3) by control of money and banking. Taxation is economic hemophilia. It drains the economy of capital which might otherwise be used to increase both consumer satisfaction and the level of production and thus raise the standard of living. Taxing away this money either prevents the standard of living from rising to the heights it normally would or actually causes it to drop. Since productive people are the only ones who *make* money, they are the only ones from whom government can get money. Taxation must necessarily penalize productivity.

Some people feel that taxation really isn't so bad, because the money taken from the "private sector" is spent by the "public sector," so it all comes out even. But though government spends tax money, it never spends this legally plundered wealth the same way as it would have been spent by its rightful owners, the taxpaying vic-

The Self-Regulating Market

tims. Money which would have been spent on increased consumer satisfaction or invested in production, creating more jobs and more products for consumers, may be used instead to subsidize welfare recipients, controlling their lives and, thus, discouraging them from freeing themselves in the only way possible—through productive labor. Or it may be used to build a dam which is of so little value to consumers and investors that it would never have been constructed without the force of government intervention. Government spending replaces the spending which people, if free, would do to maximize their happiness. In this way, government spending distorts the market and harms the economy as much or more than taxation.

If taxation bleeds the economy and government spending distorts it, governmental regulation amounts to slow strangulation. If a regulation requires businessmen to do what consumer desires would have caused them to do anyway, it is unnecessary. If it forces businessmen to act against consumer desires (which it almost always does), it harms the businessman, frustrates the consumer, and weakens the economy—and the confused consumer can usually be propagandized into blaming the businessman. By forcing businessmen to act against consumer desires, government regulation increases the cost of the regulated products (which, in our present economy, includes just about everything) and so lowers living standards for everyone and increases poverty.

Government regulation not only hurts the poor indirectly, by raising prices, but directly as well, by denying them opportunities to move up and out of their poverty. Suppose a black man who couldn't get a decent job decided to support his family by making sandwiches and selling them to the men on local construction projects. First, he would have to apply, in proper legal language and procedure, for licenses and permissions from all the branches and departments of government which required them. He would probably need licenses from city and state, permitting him to make sales. Then he would have to be regularly inspected and certified under pure food and drug laws. If he managed to comply with all this without going broke or giving up in despair, he would still be faced with the problem of keeping extensive records to enable the city, state, and Federal tax collectors to take part of his earnings and to be sure he paid his "fair share." This would require an extensive knowledge of bookkeeping, which he probably wouldn't have. Suppose he decided to hire his brother-in-law, who knew a little bookkeeping, to keep his records. Then he would have to comply with all the laws which harass other employers, including income tax and social security deductions from his employee's earnings, sales tax, minimum wage laws, and working condition standards. With such powerful barriers to success, no wonder the poor get poorer!

Not only does government regulation prevent enterprising individuals from going into business for themselves, it also helps freeze many employees into an 8-to-5 grind unnecessarily. There are a large and increasing number of jobs in our automated world which require, not that a specified set of hours be put in at an office, but that a certain amount of work be accomplished, regardless of how long it takes or where it is done. As long as an employee in this kind of job gets his work done, it shouldn't matter to the company if he does it in one hour a day and works only in his own kitchen between the hours of 2 and 3 a.m. And yet, employers, caught in the fascism of government regulation and red tape, become increasingly inflexible and insist that employees put in an 8-hour day, even if five of those hours are spent sitting at a desk doing nothing but trying to look busy. Without government regulation, businesses would be freer to innovate and would have to compete harder for labor, due to the economic boom created by freedom. This would mean much less rigid working conditions for employees.

Economic freedom is important to large businesses, but it's just as important to the ordinary man in the street, to the poor man, to the college student. In the long run, busybody regulations, usually aimed at helping special interest groups, harm everyone.

Add to this the disaster of governmental monetary control, with its inevitable inflation, depressions, balance of payments problems, gold drains, unsound currencies, and eventual monetary breakdowns and one begins to realize how much damage governmental meddling does to the marvelously efficient and productive mechanism of the market, and how much higher the standard of living would be if the market were free. In view of the poverty created by government's interferences with the economy, governmental anti-poverty programs would be laughable if they weren't so tragic.

Any governmental interference with the market, no matter how well-meaning, distorts the market and misdirects the vital signals, which misdirection further distorts the market and prevents it from moving toward stability. Government bureaucrats' "fine tuning" of the economy resembles the activities of a bunch of lunatics, armed with crowbars, "adjusting" the workings of an automated electronics plant.

The unregulated market has often been accused of creating unemployment, and the poverty of the masses in England during the Industrial Revolution is cited as an example. But the market's critics fail to point out that the poor were in an even worse condition before the Industrial Revolution when the infant mortality rate was almost 75% and periodic famines swept the land, killing off the "excess population."[4]

As a free market matures into full industrialization, the productivity of workers increases (due to increasing investment in capital goods—that is, the tools of production) so that workers' incomes rise. This is because *the only source of prosperity is value-production.* Production depends on tools—the more and better tools with which the worker is equipped, the greater his productive capacity. Industries continually improve the tools (machines) their workers use in an effort to increase production and profits. The workers' wages then rise as industries bid against each other for labor. In a free market, wages would rise because management's increased investment in tools increased the productivity of workers. Powerful unions and costly strikes would be unnecessary, since wages would always rise to market level (which is the highest level the employer could afford to pay).

Along with the rise in wages in a market free of government strangulation, unemployment drops until there is employment for everyone who wants to work. Labor is and always has been relatively less abundant than both people's demands for goods and the natural resources necessary to fill these demands. This will hold true unless and until we reach a point of overpopulation where the supply of labor exceeds the supply of raw materials, at which point there will be mass starvation. This means that (barring massive overpopulation) there will always be enough jobs in a well-developed free market.[5]

Unemployment in a fully developed industrial society is a sign of an unhealthy economy, weakened by government parasitism. The major cause of unemployment is government's interferences with the economy, minimum wage rates being a particular example. All of government's activities siphon money out of the market, leaving less to hire workers and pay them good wages. Having injured labor by injuring the market, government poses as the friend of labor and "helps" by imposing minimum wage requirements (either directly by legislation or indirectly by giving strongly preferential treatment to labor unions.) Since business has only so much capital which can be allocated to wages, when wage rates are artificially set above market level, the balance must be kept by laying off the least productive workers. This creates a class of jobless poor who

---

[4]See the article, "The Effects of the Industrial Revolution on Women and Children," by Robert Hessen, in Ayn Rand's *CAPITALISM: THE UNKNOWN IDEAL* (published in paperback by The New American Library, Inc., N.Y.).

[5]While overpopulation is a theoretical possibility, it isn't the immediate menace it is usually pictured to be. As Robert Heinlein pointed out in his science fiction novel, *THE MOON IS A HARSH MISTRESS,* the earth isn't overpopulated, it's just badly mismanaged . . . by politicians.

are supported by government welfare. It also decreases the amount of goods that can be produced, which increases their price and so lowers the standard of living for everyone.

Instead of government being recognized as the culprit, automation has frequently gotten the blame. But automation can't cut down on the total number of available jobs, simply because there is no limit to people's economic wants. No matter how many wants are filled by machines, there will still be an unlimited number of new wants left unfilled. Automation doesn't reduce the number of jobs, it merely rearranges the pattern of demand for labor, as, for example, from the industry which is being automated to the industry which is manufacturing the automated machinery. If automation were as dreadful as its foes assert, we would be wise to scrap all steamshovels in favor of hand shovels . . . or, better yet, teaspoons, to be assured of "full employment!"

The unregulated market has also been accused of the miseries of the "affluent society." Poverty and unemployment are the products of government intervention, but the free market certainly *is* responsible for affluence. If critics object to market-provided comforts and conveniences, they are quite free to do heavy labor with crude implements from dawn to dusk, sleep on a dirt floor, and suffer a high mortality rate . . . so long as they don't try to impose their way of "life" on more sensible people.

One of the reasons the bureaucrats frequently give for governmental tinkering with the economy is that if the market were left alone it would alternate between inflation and depression, or boom and bust. But just what is it that causes this dreaded "business cycle"—is this instability intrinsic in the market, or is there some external cause?

Suppose that a counterfeiter succeeded in flooding a small town with worthless bills. The inflow of new "money" would cause an artificial prosperity—a boom. Townspeople, with plenty of money on their hands, would invest heavily in new and speculative ventures. But as soon as the boom had run its course, it would become apparent that the economy couldn't support these new ventures. New businesses would fold, investors lose their money, unemployment skyrocket—a bust would have set in.

In a business cycle, the government plays much the same role as that counterfeiter. A business cycle begins when the currency is inflated because money substitutes (paper "money," coins made of low-value metal, such as the "sandwich" coins, etc.) are pumped into the economy. These money substitutes are, in reality, substitutes for nothing, since they are not backed by real monetary value (such as gold and silver); they are, therefore, worthless or very nearly so.

The Self-Regulating Market

It is government which issues currency and government which inflates the supply of money substitutes.[6] The government-inflated currency stimulates an artificial boom which misdirects the market's signal system. Entrepreneurs, thinking they are more prosperous than they really are, make malinvestments and overinvestments. The boom breaks when the nature and extent of the malinvestment is discovered. The ensuing depression is actually the market's only means of recovering from the inflation-caused malinvestment.[7] Thus, the business cycle, which has so often been blamed on laissez-faire capitalism, is actually the cold steel of the knife of government intervention in the market's vitals—free trade[8].

In spite of the fact that the free market is completely self-regulating, and that government intervention is the cause rather than the cure of market imbalance, many still fear a totally unregulated market. They contend that a free market would promote the economic exploitation of helpless individuals by powerful interest groups. It isn't enough, they feel, for individuals to be free of force and fraud—they must also be defended against the selfish predations of "Big Business," monopolies, cartels (which are actually tentative monopolies), and the rich in general. These economic bugaboos are all similar and can all be dispelled by examining the most extreme of them—monopoly.

When market freedom is advocated, one thought which springs to many minds is the fear of unchecked monopolies running amuck, trampling the rights of "the little fellow" and ruthlessly driving any would-be competitors to the wall. It is widely held that without strict government control such monopolies would proliferate and virtually enslave the economy.

Theoretically, there are two kinds of monopoly—market monopoly and coercive monopoly. A coercive monopoly maintains itself by the initiation of force or the threat of force to prohibit competition, and sometimes to compel customer loyalty. A market monopoly has no effective competition in its particular field, but it can't prevent competition by using physical force. A market monopoly can't gain its ends by initiating force against anyone—its customers, competitors,

---

[6]Banks may also inflate by holding only fractional reserves against demand deposits—for example, by making loans against checking accounts. If they weren't protected by special laws, however, banks could not indulge in fractional reserves, because this practice is too risky. In a totally free market, any bank which did not hold 100% reserves would be driven out of business by its more financially wise and sound competitors.

[7]The depression phase of the business cycle may be postponed for a long time by continued inflation, but such a policy only makes the inevitable depression more catastrophic when it does occur.

[8]See the minibook, *DEPRESSIONS: Their Cause and Cure,* by Murray N. Rothbard (Published by Constitutional Alliance, Inc., Box 836, Lansing, Mich. 48904).

or employees—because it has no legal power to compel people to deal with it and to protect itself from the consequences of its coercive actions. The initiation of force would frighten away business associates and alarm customers into seeking substitute products, doing without altogether, or, in the case of entrepreneurs, setting up a competing business to attract other dissatisfied customers. So the initiation of force by a market monopoly, far from helping it to attain its ends, would give it a quick push onto the short, downhill road to oblivion.

Because it does not initiate force, a market monopoly can only attain its monopoly status by excellence in satisfying consumer wants and by the economy of its product and/or service (which necessitates efficient business management). Furthermore, once it has attained this monopoly position, it can only hold it by continuing to give excellent service at economical prices (and the freer the economy, the more this rule holds true). If the managers of the monopoly become careless and raise their prices above market level, some other entrepreneur will see that he can undersell them and still make tremendous profits and will immediately move to enter their field. Then their potential competition will have become actual competition.[9] Large and well established companies are particularly likely to offer such competition, since they have large sums to invest and prefer to diversify their efforts into new fields in order to have a wide financial base. In a free society, where large companies were not plundered of what bureaucrats like to think of as their "excess profits" via heavy taxation, any monopoly which raised its prices above market level or became careless about the quality of its service would be virtually creating its own competition—competition too strong for it to drive out. As is always the rule in an unhampered market, the illness would create its own cure—the market is self-regulating.

Not only are market monopolies no threat to anyone, the whole concept of monopoly, as commonly held, is in error. A monopoly is supposed to be a business which has "exclusive control of a commodity or service in a given market, or control that makes possible the fixing of prices and the virtual elimination of free competition."— Webster A market monopoly cannot prevent competition from entering its field because it cannot use coercion against would-be com-

---

[9]From 1888 to 1940, Alcoa had a total monopoly on the manufacture of aluminum in the U.S.A. It maintained this monopoly by selling such an excellent product at such low prices that no other company could compete with it. During its monopoly period, Alcoa reduced aluminum prices from $8 to 20¢ a pound (!) and pioneered hundreds of new uses for its product. The book, TEN THOUSAND COMMANDMENTS, by Harold Fleming, describes the action the government took against this "ruthless monopoly" which had been guilty of maintaining its monopoly status by continual and successful efforts to satisfy its customers.

The Self-Regulating Market

petitors, and thus it can never have that "exclusive control . . . that makes possible the fixing of prices." Nor can such a monopoly be said to be free of competition, even while it has exclusive control of its market—its product must still compete for the consumer's money with every other good and service. For example, suppose a manufacturer of travel trailers has a complete monopoly over the travel trailer industry. He still must compete for the "recreation dollar" with the motel industry, and, in a broader sense, with the manufacturers of pleasure boats, swimming pools, table tennis sets, etc. Nor does his competition end there. Because the consumer may choose to spend his money for something other than recreation, our travel trailer monopolist must compete indirectly with refrigerator companies, clothing manufacturers, colleges, etc., ad infinitum. There is no industry so basic that a monopolist in that industry could manage "the virtual elimination of free competition." Even the steel industry must compete in the building materials field with lighter metals, wood, plastic, concrete, brick, and now even newly developed glass products.

In considering the concept of monopoly, it is also useful to remember that it is not the absolute size of the firm which counts, but the size of the firm relative to its market. In the 1800s, the little country grocery store had a far firmer control of its market than does the largest chain of big-city supermarkets today. Advances in ease and economy of transportation continually decrease the *relative* size of even the most giant firm, thus making even temporary market monopoly status vastly more difficult to attain. So the free market moves toward the elimination, rather than the encouragement, of monopolies.[10]

Since a market monopoly can never eliminate free competition or fix prices in defiance of the law of supply and demand, it actually bears no resemblance at all to the common notion of "the ruthless and uncontrolled monopoly" so many people have been taught to fear. If the term "market monopoly" can have any meaning at all, it can only be understood as a company which has gained a position as the only supplier of its particular good or service because customer-wants are well satisfied and its prices are so low that it is not profitable for competitors to move into that particular field. Its monopoly position will most likely not be permanent, because eventually someone else will probably "build a better mousetrap" and go into competition with it. But during the period of its market power, it is never free of competition or of the law of supply and demand in regard to prices.

---

[10]Rogge, Benjamin A., Long Playing Record Album #9, *IS ECONOMIC FREEDOM POSSIBLE?* The Foundation for Economic Education, N.Y.

It is easy to see that a market monopoly, because it cannot initiate force, poses no threat to either individual persons who deal with it or to the economy as a whole; but what about a coercive monopoly?

A coercive monopoly has exclusive control of a given field of endeavor which is closed to and exempt from competition, so that those controlling the field are able to set arbitrary policies and charge arbitrary prices, independent of the market. A coercive monopoly can maintain this exclusive control which prohibits any competition only by the use of initiated force. No firm which operated in a free-market context could afford the initiation of force for fear of driving away its customers and business associates. Thus, the only way that a business firm can sustain itself as a coercive monopoly is through government intervention in the form of special grants of privilege. Only government, which is itself a coercive monopoly, has the power to force individuals to deal with a firm with which they would rather not have anything to do.

The fear of ruthless, uncontrolled monopolies is a valid one, but it applies only to coercive monopolies. *Coercive monopolies are an extension of government, not a product of the free market.* Without governmental grants of special privilege, *there could be no coercive monopolies.*

Economic exploitation by monopolies, cartels, and "Big Business" is a non-existent dragon. In a well-developed market which is free of government interference, any advantage gained from such exploitation will send out signals calling in competition which will end the exploitation. In a free market, the individual always has alternatives to choose from, and only physical force can compel him to choose against his will. But the initiation of force is not a market function and cannot be profitably employed by firms operating in an unregulated market.

Force, in fact, is penalized by the free market, as is fraud. Business depends on customers, and customers are driven away by the exploitation of force and fraud. The penalizing of force and fraud is an inherent part of the self-regulating mechanism of the free market.

The market, if not hampered by government regulation, always moves toward a situation of stability and maximum consumer satisfaction—that is, toward equilibrium. Government intervention, far from improving society, can only cause disruptions, distortions, and losses, and move society toward chaos. The market is self-regulating—force is not required to make it function properly. In fact, the imposition of initiated force is the only thing which can prevent the market from functioning to the maximum possible satisfaction of all.

The Self-Regulating Market 31

If men aren't free to trade in any non-coercive way which their interests dictate, they aren't free at all. Men who aren't free are, to some degree, slaves. Without freedom of the market, no other "freedom" is meaningful. For this reason, the conflict between freedom and slavery focuses on the free market and its only effective opponent—government.

4
Government—An Unnecessary Evil

Because the weight of governmental power has such influence on the structure and functioning of any society, ideas concerning social organization have typically centered on the structure of the proposed society's government. Most "social thinkers," however, have taken government as a given. They have debated over the particular form of government they wished their ideal societies to have but have seldom attempted to examine the nature of government itself. But if one doesn't know clearly what government is, one can hardly determine what influences governments will have on society.

Government is a coercive monopoly which has assumed power over and certain responsibilities for every human being within the geographical area which it claims as its own. A coercive monopoly is an institution maintained by the threat and/or use of physical force—the *initiation* of force—to prohibit competitors from entering its field of endeavor. (A coercive monopoly may also use force to compel "customer loyalty," as, for example a "protection" racket.)

Government has exclusive possession and control within its geographical area of whatever functions it is able to relegate to itself, and it maintains this control by force of its laws and its guns, both against other governments and against any private individuals who might object to its domination. To the extent that it controls any function, it either prohibits competition (as with the delivery of first class mail) or permits it on a limited basis only (as with the American educational system). It compels its citizen-customers by force of law either to buy its services or, if they don't want them, to pay for them anyway.

While it is obvious that any government must hold a monopoly over at least some activities (e.g., lawmaking) within its geographical territory in order to govern at all, some thinkers have held that a "properly limited" government would not initiate force and would, therefore, not be a *coercive* monopoly. The government thus envisioned would be restricted to what its advocates consider to be minimum essential governmental functions, such as the defense of life, liberty, and property against both domestic and foreign aggression (police and military), arbitration of disputes (courts), and the administration of justice (courts and penal system).

A few of these advocates of limited government have realized that taxation is theft (theft being the act of taking the rightful property of another by force, stealth, or deceit) and have attempted to insure against governmental initiation of force by forbidding their theoretical governments to levy taxes—any taxes. But not only are their systems of voluntary government support rather hazy and unconvincing, even if such a non-taxing government could be made to work, governmental initiation of force would still not have been eliminated. A government, in order to be a government rather than simply another business firm in an open market with actual or potential competition, must maintain a monopoly in those areas which it has pre-empted. In order to insure its continued existence, this monopoly must be coercive—it must prohibit competition. Thus, government, in order to exist as a government at all, must initiate force in order to prohibit any citizen(s) from going into business in competition with it in those fields which it claims as exclusively its own.

If it could be proved to businessmen that those "basic governmental functions" of protection and defense of person and property, arbitration of disputes, and rectification of injustice could be performed very satisfactorily by private, free-market businesses (and this book will prove that they can), any supposedly non-coercive, limited government would be faced with a crucial dilemma. Either it would have to initiate force to prevent free enterprise from entering its "market(s)" or free enterprise would push government out of "business" and, hence, out of existence. As will be shown, government is unavoidably inefficient and expensive. If government didn't compel its citizens to deal with it (by maintaining itself as a coercive monopoly), the free market could offer really effective services, efficiently and at lower prices, and the government would lose all its "customers."

Government is, and of necessity must be, a coercive monopoly, for in order to exist it must deprive entrepreneurs of the right to go into business in competition with it, and it must compel all its citizens to deal with it exclusively in the areas it has pre-empted. Any attempt to devise a government which did not initiate force is an exercise in futility, because it is an attempt to make a contradiction work. Government is, by its very nature, an agency of initiated force. If it ceased to initiate force, it would cease to be a government and become, in simple fact, another business firm in a competitive market. Nor can there be any such thing as a government which is partially a free-market business, because there can be no compromise between freedom and brute force. Either an organization is a business, maintaining itself against competition by excellence in satisfying customer wants, or it is a gang of thieves, existing by brute force and preventing competition by force when it can do so. It can't be both.[1]

Further, since government is not a *market* monopoly, it can only be a *coercive* monopoly—no third alternative exists.

The prohibition of competition on which government depends for its existence is an aggressive interference with the free market and forms the basis for all the other many interferences with the market of which government has been guilty. Since government must infringe the right of free trade in order to exist, how can it be expected to refrain from other interferences with the market and the rights of its citizen-subjects?

People who grow up amid the "democratic traditions of the West" are apt to feel that this governmental initiation of force and disruption of the market is justifiable as long as the government is one which is "chosen by the people through the democratic process of free elections." They feel that under a democratic government, whatever the government does is done "by ourselves, to ourselves" and is, therefore, permissible. But the fallacy of this notion is readily apparent when one considers the people of the democratic country as individuals, rather than as insignificant fragments of a collective whole.

The belief that the people of a democracy rule themselves through their elected representatives, though sanctified by tradition and made venerable by multiple repetitions, is actually mystical nonsense. In any election, only a percentage of the people vote. Those who can't vote because of age or other disqualifications, and those who don't vote because of confusion, apathy, or disgust at a Tweedledum-Tweedledummer choice can hardly be said to have any voice in the passage of the laws which govern them. Nor can the individuals as yet unborn, who will be ruled by those laws in the future. And, out of those who do "exercise their franchise," the large minority who voted for the loser are also deprived of a voice, at least during the term of the winner they voted against.

---

[1] As an example of this attempt to marry government and business, a few well-meaning souls have proposed that government should avoid forcing its citizens to deal with it by making citizenship a matter of contract, so that only those who wished to buy governmental services need do so. But such a government, if it were to remain a government, would still have to initiate force to prohibit competition or it would lose its monopoly. In effect, it would be saying to the individual in its territory, "You do not have to buy the protection you need from the government, but the government will not allow you to buy it from anyone else." The freedom from governmental coercion offered by this "voluntary" government would be meaningless.

But even the individuals who voted and who managed to pick a winner are not actually ruling themselves in any sense of the word. They voted for a man, not for the specific laws which will govern them. Even all those who had cast their ballots for the winning candidate would be hopelessly confused and divided if asked to vote on these actual laws. Nor would their representative be bound to abide by their wishes, even if it could be decided what these "collective wishes" were. And besides all this, a large percentage of the actual power of a mature democracy, such as the U.S.A., is in the hands of the tens of thousands of faceless appointed bureaucrats who are unresponsive to the will of any citizen without special pull.

Under a democratic form of government, a minority of the individuals governed select the winning candidate. The winning candidate then proceeds to decide issues largely on the basis of pressure from special-interest groups. What it actually amounts to is rule by those with political pull over those without it. Contrary to the brainwashing we have received in government-run schools, democracy—the rule of the people through their elected representatives—is a cruel hoax!

Not only is democracy mystical nonsense, it is also immoral. If one man has no right to impose his wishes on another, then ten million men have no right to impose their wishes on the one, since the initiation of force is wrong (and the assent of even the most overwhelming majority can never make it morally permissible). Opinions—even majority opinions—neither create truth nor alter facts. A lynch mob is democracy in action. So much for mob rule.

The very word "government" means some men governing—ruling over—others.[2] But to the degree that men are ruled by other men, they exist in slavery. Slavery is a condition in which one is not allowed to exercise his right of self-ownership but is ruled by someone else. Government—the rule of some men over others by initiated force—is a form of slavery. To advocate government is to advocate slavery. To advocate *limited* government is to put oneself in the ridiculous position of advocating *limited* slavery.

To put it simply, government is the rule of some men over others by initiated force, which is slavery, which is wrong.

Those who maintain that government is an institution which holds monopoly on the use of retaliatory force (in a given geographical area) carefully omit to mention what kind of monopoly such an institution would be, and for obvious reasons. To claim that a

---

[2]The concept of "a government of laws, not of men" is just as mystical and meaningless as democracy. Laws must be written and enforced by men. Therefore, a "government of laws" *is* a government of men.

government is a *market* monopoly is patently absurd, since competition must be prohibited; with competition, it would not be a monopoly, and, therefore, it would not be a government (according to *their* "definition"). If they admit that government is a coercive monopoly, they could not fail to see that they were advocating an institution which is inherently evil and that to advocate that which is wrong is, itself, evil. It is perfectly clear that every government which ever existed, including today's governments, has maintained its existence by initiated aggression against its citizen-subjects and, further, could not continue to exist without such aggression which violates human rights. To claim, therefore, that government holds a monopoly on the use of retaliatory force is to surrender to and condone initiated force; an institution of initiated force can hardly, by any stretch of rational imagination, hold a monopoly on the use of retaliatory force. Such a notion is worse than absurd, as it helps to maintain the idea that government is good.

Government, being a coercive monopoly, must maintain its monopoly position by the initiation of force, which requires that government be a repository of power. Because of this concentration of power, it is held that some restraint must be put on government to prevent it from riding roughshod over its citizens. Since government is a monopoly with which its citizens must be forced to deal, it can allow no competition which would furnish external restraints, as there are with free-market institutions. Any outside force strong enough to effectively check the power of government would destroy its monopoly position. Restraints must, therefore, be internal, in the form of so-called checks and balances. But any system of governmental checks and balances is necessarily large, unwieldy, and expensive, which puts a far heavier burden on those who must support it than its functions would warrant (even if one overlooks the fact that governmental functions are coercive).

Further, a position with even a small amount of power over others is attractive to men who want to wield power over others. A rational man—a productive man with a high degree of self-esteem—will have no desire for such power; he has more interesting and rewarding things to do with his life (and he abhors slavery . . . of any kind). But a man who has failed to set and reach productive goals, a man who has never done anything worthwhile by his own standards, will often seek to disguise his feelings of inadequacy by taking a position of power in which he can experience the pseudo-self-esteem of telling others how to live their lives. So government, by its very nature, tends to attract the worst of men, rather than the best, to its ranks. Even if a government were started by the best of men with the best of intentions,[3] when the good men died off and the good intentions wore off, men with a lust for power would take over and work ceaselessly to increase government influence and authority (always for the "public good," of course!).

Because government attracts the type of men who desire power over others, no system of checks and balances can keep government permanently limited. Even with an extremely strict constitution, it is impossible to impose limitations which some other men cannot eventually find a way to get around. The best that can be hoped for from constitutional checks and balances is to limit the government for a longer period of time than has yet been achieved. The U.S.A. holds the record to date—around two centuries . . . to degenerate to a mixture of fascism and socialism, a new brand of sophisticated totalitarianism.

It has been said that the price of liberty is eternal vigilance. But such vigilance is a constant non-productive expenditure of energy, and it is grossly unreasonable to expect men to keep expending their energy non-productively out of "unselfish idealism." There is no area of the free market which requires the constant vigilance of the entire population to keep it from going awry. We would all be shocked and indignant if we were admonished to give such attentions to, say, the dairy industry in order to have our milk delivered unsour.

Government consists of men who govern, or rule over, others by initiated force. This means that government inevitably sets men against each other as each interest group seeks to be among the rulers, or at least on good terms with the rulers, instead of among the ruled. Such conflict between interest groups is most pronounced in a democracy, because in a democracy the course of government is determined largely by pressure groups who have special pull and/or can deliver votes and money. Each pressure group fights to gain control of the government long enough to force the passage of legislation favoring it or crippling its opponents. The constant and inevitable political warfare makes each interest group a threat to anyone outside itself and prompts otherwise non-aggressive groups to pressure the government for legislation favorable to them, as an act of self-defense if for no other reason. Thus, government creates a situation in which each man must fear everyone who belongs to a different interest group or has a different life-style. Black people fear suppression by whites, while whites are apprehensive about blacks gaining "too much" power. Middle-class, middle-aged, "straight" people dread the day when young hippies will be old enough and

---

[3]We do not, of course, concede such a possibility. We use this argument only for the purpose of illustration.

strong enough to seize power and force legislation favoring the "hip" culture. Hippies, meanwhile, resent the "straight" life-style which the present laws attempt to force on them. It's labor vs. management, urbanites vs. suburbanites, tax-payers vs. tax-consumers, in an endless, costly, and totally unnecessary battle. Without government, no one would need to fear that someone else's group would gain the upper hand and use the power of law to force its will on him. People of vastly different occupations, interests, and life-styles could live peacefully together, because none would be capable of using a politician to threaten the others. It is the power of government which causes most of the strife between various groups in our society.

Governments have always found it necessary to use force against both their own citizens and other governments. This isn't surprising when one realizes that any government can continue to exist only by maintaining a monopoly in its area of operations and that it can only maintain this monopoly permanently by the use of force. Wars and repressions are an inevitable by-product of government—they are simply the coercive monopoly's normal reaction to external and internal threats to its position. The more areas within its boundaries a government seeks to monopolize (that is, the more totalitarian it is), the more repressions it will have to use against its citizens, and the more bloody and violent these repressions will be. The more areas outside its boundaries a government seeks to control (that is, the more imperialistic it is), the more wars it will have to engage in, and the more prolonged and destructive these wars will be. Some governments are far more totalitarian and imperialistic than others and are, consequently, more cruel and bloody. But every government must initiate force because every government is a coercive monopoly. Wars and repressions are inevitable so long as governments continue to exist. The history of governments always has been, and always will be, written in blood, fire, and tears.

In addition to all the rest of its defects, the structure of any government is incurably arbitrary and, therefore, without reason. Any institution which is not a part of the free market and, therefore, not subject to the rules of the market, must be set up and operated on the basis of arbitrary rules and thus cannot be just and reality-oriented. Private business is guided by reality in the form of the market. A successful entrepreneur operates his business in accordance with the law of supply and demand and so has reality-centered reasons for the decisions he makes. But government is outside the market, unguided by the realities of the market, and thus can only be operated by arbitrary decisions. The truth of this can be seen when one honestly tries to determine just how the institution of government should be implemented (which also explains why few advocates of liberty have attempted this impossible task). For example, how should judges be chosen—by election or appointment? If elected, to what terms and by what electorate (local, state, or national)? Bipartisan or non-partisan designation? If appointed, by whom and with what controls? What are the rules for voting, who decides what they shall be, and what are the objective criteria for such decisions? Arguments over such matters are both endless and fruitless, because there are no non-arbitrary answers.

For a private business, the primary purpose of its existence is to make profits (which it can only do by pleasing its customers). Profit is the "success signal" for any businessman operating in a free market—the signal which tells him he is succeeding in the job of satisfying his customers. When a businessman begins to suffer losses, he knows he has made mistakes and that consumers are dissatisfied with his product or service. The profit signal unerringly guides businessmen toward those actions which produce the most consumer satisfaction.

But a government is a "non-profit," extra-market organization, maintaining itself, not by willing exchange, but by the forcible seizure of goods (taxation). The success signal for a politician or bureaucrat is not profit, but *power*. A government official succeeds, not by pleasing customers, but by increasing his sphere of control over the lives of others. This is why each politician struggles so hard to win elections, pass dozens of new laws, and increase the amount of patronage he has to give out. This is why each gray and faceless bureaucrat toils incessantly to increase the size, powers, and budget of his department, and the number of men working under him. The power signal unerringly guides government officials toward those actions which produce the most control over other men.

Private enterprise maintains and expands itself by continually offering people things they want. Government maintains and expands itself by depriving people of things they want, by means of forcibly seizing their goods (taxation) and forcibly preventing them from trading and living as they choose (regulation). Thus, private enterprise continually *increases* the prosperity and well-being of its customers, while government continually *decreases* the prosperity and well-being of its citizens.

But worse than anything else it does to its citizens is the fact that government cannot avoid forcibly sacrificing the just interests of at least some of them. Any government must make decisions and act on them, since it could claim no justification for its existence if it did nothing at all. Theoretically, the leaders should always act "in the interest of the people" because it would be immoral to impose on the people actions which were contrary to their interests. But, since not all the individuals who make up "the people" will find the same things to be in their interest, it follows that at least some of them must have proper, just interests which are different from or even in opposition to the supposed "public interest." This means that some citizens (those without political influence) must sacrifice their interests, hopes, ambitions, and even property and lives to further the "national interest." Since people should not and usually do not give up such values willingly, any group not based on totally voluntary membership must employ coercion to force the sacrifices which its leaders and rulers consider to be in the group's interest.

Limiting a government to the functions of protection and arbitration would lessen the sacrifices demanded of the citizens but could never eliminate them. The wastefulness of checks and balances and the inefficiency of an organization beyond the reach of competition makes governmental services far costlier and less effective than those provided by business. Thus, being forced to buy "protection services" from government is certainly a sacrifice. Any government, if it is to remain a government, must hold its monopoly status by coercion, which means it must force sacrifices on its citizens.

Every individual person has the responsibility to discover what his interests are and to work toward their achievement. When government takes some of this responsibility away from the individual, it must also take away some of his freedom of action—i.e., it must violate human rights. Further, when government forces an individual to act against his proper interests, it is forcing him to act against his own rational judgment. Such an action, in effect, puts the opinions and whims of others between a man and his perception of reality and, thus, compels him to sacrifice his basic tool of survival—his mind!

Government has always been a ball-and-chain holding back human progress and welfare. This shackle was bad enough in primitive times when life was relatively simple. In a complex society with a complex technology and nuclear weapons, it is suicidal idiocy. Government is simply inadequate to the complexities of modern life, a fact which is becoming increasingly apparent in the blundering ineptitude of governmental "solutions" to social problems, the perennial confusion and contradictions in governmental policies, and the successive breakdown of governmental programs. Government, at best, is a primitive anachronism which the human race outgrew somewhere around the time when men moved out of their caves, and which we should have dispensed with long ago.

The majority of people firmly believe that we must have a government to protect us from domestic and foreign aggression. But government is a coercive monopoly which must demand sacrifices from its citizens. It is a repository of power without external check and cannot be permanently restrained. It attracts the worst kind of men to its ranks, shackles progress, forces its citizens to act against their own judgment, and causes recurring internal and external strife by its coercive existence. In view of all this, the question becomes not, "Who will protect us from aggression?" but "Who will protect us from the governmental 'protectors'?" The contradiction of hiring an agency of institutionalized violence to protect us from violence is even more foolhardy than buying a cat to protect one's parakeet.

In view of the real nature of government, why have the majority of men throughout history accepted and even demanded it? Perhaps the most obvious reason is that the vast majority of men have not developed much ability to generate or even to accept new ideas, particularly those radically different from the familiar ones comprising the cultural status quo. There have been governments as far back as recorded history reaches, and to picture, with some detail, how we would manage without one requires more mental effort than many of the people are willing to expend. Besides, that which is new, strange, and unknown is frightening, and it's more comfortable to push the whole matter out of one's consideration by simply declaring that it wouldn't work anyway ("You Wright brothers will never get that contraption off the ground!").

Government officials have used every possible tool to convince people that government is necessary. One of their most effective weapons has been government supported education, which brainwashes the young into patriotism before they are capable of judging for themselves and creates a class of pro-State intellectuals, whose ideas create a pro-State populace. Another trick has been to invest government with tradition and pomp and to identify it with "our way of life" so that to be against government is seen as being against everything which is familiar, noble, and good.

Another factor contributing to the acceptance of government is that a great number of people have a nagging, and usually unadmitted, fear of self-responsibility—of being thrown completely on their own resources. This goes far deeper than just the knowledge that with no government there would be no welfare checks or plush bureaucratic jobs. It is a deep fear of the responsibility and risk of having to make one's own decisions and accept the consequences, with no ultimate authority to appeal to for guidance and to blame in case of failure. This is the reason for such cries as "We must have strong leadership in this time of crisis," "We need new and better leaders," and "God, give us a leader!" People who fear responsibility find it easier to call for leaders, even when those leaders may become tyrants, than to accept the risk and effort of looking for solutions to the problems that beset them (remember the "Heil Hitler" patriotism of Nazi Germany and the horror and atrocities it led to). Without a government to furnish this leadership, such people would feel hopelessly lost and adrift.

But even with all this, the majority of people might have accepted the idea of a government-free society long ago if they hadn't been sold the notion that the only alternative to government is choas. Government may be evil, they feel, but, after all, it's a necessary evil.

Aside from the fact that there no necessary evils, when one considers all the chaos governments have caused with their violations of men's liberty, arbitrary interferences with the market, and wars for plunder and power, the assumption that government prevents chaos appears more than a little ridiculous. The free market is quite capable of preventing chaos, and would do so without violating men's liberty or carrying on wars of aggression . . . as this book will demonstrate. The actual choice is not government versus chaos, but the chaotic rigidity generated by governmental aggressions versus the peaceful, evolutionary progress which naturally results from free men trading in an open market.

Government isn't a necessary evil—it's an unnecessary one.

PART II

A LAISSEZ-FAIRE SOCIETY

"Liberty—the mother, not the daughter, of order."—Proudhon

5
A Free and Healthy Economy

Imagine a feudal serf, legally bound to the land he was born on and to the social position he was born into, toiling from dawn to dusk with primitive tools for a bare subsistence which he must share with the lord of his manor, his mental processes enmeshed with fears and superstitions. Imagine trying to tell this serf about the social structure of the Twentieth Century America. You would probably have a hard time convincing him that such a social structure could exist at all, because he would view everything you described from the context of his own knowledge of society. He would inform you, no doubt with a trace of smug superiority, that unless each individual born into the community had a specific and permanently fixed social place, society would speedily deteriorate into chaos.

In a similar way, telling a Twentieth Century man that government is evil and, therefore, unnecessary, and that we would have a far better society if we had no government at all, is likely to elicit polite skepticism . . . especially if the man is not used to thinking independently. It is always difficult to picture the workings of society different from our own, and particulary a more advanced society. This is because we are so used to our own social structure that we tend to automatically consider each facet of the more advanced society in the context of our own, thus distorting the picture into meaninglessness.

Many undesirable conditions which people take for granted today would be different in a society totally free of government. Most of these differences would spring from a market liberated from the dead hand of government control—both fascist and socialist—and thus able to produce a healthy economy and a vastly higher standard of living for everyone.

In any society, unemployment is the product of government intervention in the market. A society free of government would have no unemployment problem. Labor, being scarcer than resources, would be in demand, and everyone who wanted a job could have one. When faced with a demand for labor produced by new pros-

44

perity and soaring sales, industry would be eager to hire minority group members, institute on-the-job training for the uneducated, set up plant nurseries for mothers of small children, hire the handicapped, etc., to tap every source of competent labor. Wages would be high because businesses could keep what bureaucrats call their "excess profits" and invest them in machinery to increase the productivity of their labor (and wages are determined by productivity).

There will always be large differences in the amount of income earned by different people, but in a free-market society there would be no class of jobless, hopeless poor as we have today. Instead of being abandoned to starve in a government-less society, the poor would at last be given all the opportunity and help they needed to raise themselves out of their poverty.

Of course, there will always be people temporarily or permanently unable to support themselves due to extreme mental or physical handicaps, financial bad fortune, or other causes. Such people would be helped by private charities, as there would be no government dole. Gathering enough money to help them would present no problem—we have never suffered from a lack of people willing to go into the business of collecting and dispensing charitable funds, and the people of this semi-free nation, even with over a third of their income looted by taxation, have been wealthly enough to be generous to scores of charities each year. Private charity is vastly more economical and efficient than government welfare, since it is in a much better position to distinguish those deserving of help from phonies who just want a free ride, and to dispense its funds accordingly. This practical superiority derives from the moral fact that private charity is based on voluntary contributions while government welfare payments come out of monies confiscated at the point of a legal gun from productive taxpayers.

Many people feel that charity would break down, however, when faced with the task of educating children without government schools. They believe that there could never be enough charity to take care of all the children whose parents neglected or were unable to send to school. Such an opinion is the result of failing to consider the context of a free society.

It has already been shown that poverty is a result of government interference in the economy, and that a modern industrial society need have no poverty as we understand it. This means that, while lower income people would certainly have to do without other desirable goods in order to educate their children, they would not be in the position of having no money at all to spare for schooling. Furthermore, when parents knew that there was no government to pick up the tab for them, they would be likely to think twice before taking on the responsibility of having a greater number of children than they could adequately care for and educate. With birth control devices free of hampering prescription laws and their manufacturers free to advertise in the mass media, family size among the poorly educated lower income groups could be expected to drop sharply. When freed of the economic burden of large families, lower income parents could not only afford a better standard of living, they could also afford a better education for the children they did have so that the next generation could raise itself to a better socio-economic position.

Of course, education itself would be vastly improved if placed on the free market. At present, most students waste a considerable amount of each school day. This is chiefly due to two factors: first, "democratic" insistence on forcing everyone through the same educational mill regardless of ability or previous upbringing, and second, the rigidity of a socialized system which has no competition and can thus tolerate a large measure of stagnation. Free-market educational institutions in competition with each other would take quick advantage of every new advance in educational methods and materials and would undoubtedly do a far better job in a shorter time and for much less money. It is probable that this free-market application of new educational techniques would enable all but the slowest students to finish school anywhere from months to years earlier than they now do, providing a tremendous saving of the young person's time and his parents' money, as well as increasing his years of productivity (and everyone's standard of living).

A laissez-faire system of competing, free-market education would provide a tremendous variety of schools to meet the needs of people with various interests, aptitudes, beliefs, and life-styles. Devout christians could send their children to religious schools which held prayer before every class without infringing on the right of atheists to have their children educated by the use of reason exclusively. Black Panthers could send their children to all-black schools, white segregationists to all-white schools, and integrationists of all races could patronize integrated schools (*forced* integration is as bad as *forced* segregation). There would be schools for exceptionally bright youngsters, for those with special educational problems, and for those with great aptitudes in various fields (music, mathematics, writing, etc.). These various schools would charge different amounts of tuition and operate under varying conditions and educational methods. Some would be strict, some permissive. Some might have a 12-month school year, some a 6-month year. Virtually every kind of education which consumers wanted would be offered, and selection of a school would be strictly on the basis of individual free choice. No

A Free and Healthy Economy 47

longer would every child be forced through the same educational machine, a machine geared for the great "average" majority and, therefore, harmful to minorities of all kinds.

Although the schools in a free economy would be paid for by tuition rather than by the theft of taxation, it is not necessarily the case that parents would have to stand the entire expense of their children's education, especially in high school and college. Even today, scores of companies in search of well-trained and competent mathematicians, engineers, chemists, etc., offer generous, no-strings-attached scholarships to any talented student in hopes of luring him to work for them when he graduates. In the healthy economy of a totally free-market society, companies would be looking for even more employees (and, also, for independent sub-contractors) in an even greater variety of skilled fields. Not only would such companies put promising students through college, they might very well even pay their high school tuition. And many of them might also offer free high school curriculums to any ambitious student of average competence in return for his contractual guarantee to learn some skill useful to the company and work for them exclusively for a stated period of time.

Many firms are already manifesting a great and speedily growing interest in education, in spite of its rigidly socialized condition. They are particularly interested in research in better teaching methods, including the use of computers and other mechanical aids to improve the speed and quality of instruction. It is difficult to imagine the extent of the beneficial influence such businesses would have on the field of education if it were free of the rigor mortis of government control.

Of course, education doesn't necessarily have to take place in a classroom. One of the least expensive and most promising of educational tools is television. At present, most educational TV is undeniably poor in quality and interest level. This is largely due to lack of competition resulting from the stultifying regulations imposed by the Federal Communications Commission, which has virtual dictatorial control over who may enter the field and what kind of programs they may telecast. In a laissez-faire society, anyone who could find an unused channel could go into the business of telecasting, and he could air any type of material he wished. If his programs were offensive to his audience, he would, of course, soon go out of business for lack of viewers. Competition, as always, would impel toward excellence.

With television freed from governmental meddling, many groups would go into the business of educational TV. Educational broadcasters could offer their programs free and still make profits by charging for texts and tests (a charge which would be small, with student-viewers numbering in tens of thousands). Or, texts and tests could be furnished free, with support coming from commercials, just as it now does with entertainment TV. Sponsoring companies might advertise not only for customers but for employees with the knowledge and skills taught in their TV courses. This would have the happy effect of providing both a pool of potential employees for the company and readily accessible job opportunities for the student-viewers. Also, with stiff competition for student-viewers, educational broadcasters would develop the most efficient and "fun" ways of learning possible in order to capture and hold their audiences.

In spite of lower cost, more efficient and higher quality education, the role of industry in providing scholarships, and educational TV, it is probable that some children would get very little education, and a few might go through life as illiterates. These would be children who lacked either the capacity or the desire for learning, since children who had both ability and desire would tend to attract help even if their parents did neglect them. Before calling for a government to educate these unschooled and illiterate few, however, one should consider the shockingly high rate of illiterates *graduated* from *government* high schools. Sitting in a school room for a period of years is not equivalent to receiving an education. In fact, children who are forced to sit through years of schooling which they find painfully boring are far more likely to rebel against their imprisonment and "society" in general than to develop a love of knowledge. No one can be taught unless he has a genuine desire to learn, and forcing schooling on a child against his will is hardly likely to increase this desire.

Competing educational systems would offer the consumer a free choice in his purchase of education for himself and/or his children. This would end forever squabbles over curriculum (more athletics? more academics? Black Studies programs?), student body (segregated or integrated?—shall we bus to integrate?), control of education (should it be in the hands of parents, teachers, voters, the school board, or the colleges?), and all the other insoluble questions which plague government's coercive control of education. If each consumer were free to choose among competing schools the type of education he valued most, all these problems would be solved automatically to the satisfaction of everyone. Competition in education would protect students and parents from exploitation by a coercive governmental monopoly.

In a similar manner, competition would protect the consumer in every other field. If any firm tried to exploit its customers or employees, it would be signalling other firms to enter into competition

A Free and Healthy Economy

with it in order to reap some of the profits it was enjoying. But this competition would quickly bid prices down, quality up, or wages up, as the case might be, and eliminate the exploitation.

In a free market, consumers always have alternatives. Only force or fraud can compel a man to act against his judgment, but a firm which initiated force or used fraud in a free market would drive away its customers. Coercive monopolies are the product of government and can't exist without government support. In a laissez-faire society, the economy would be free of exploitation, both by government and by business seeking to establish and maintain market control by force or fraud.

It has been objected that a very large firm could afford to use force and fraud to at least a limited extent, because the breadth of its market would prevent the news of its aggressive actions from reaching enough of its customers and competitors to do it serious damage. This is to overlook the role of the news media in a laissez-faire society.

As a test, take the front page of any metropolitan daily and count the headlines which have nothing at all to do with any government—national, state, or local. Unless there has just been some natural disaster, you will probably find no more than two or three, sometimes none. Newsmen must write about something, since that's how they make their living. If there were no government, they would have to shift their emphasis to the doings of outstanding individuals, business, and industry. Not only inventions and medical and scientific discoveries would be news, so would any aggression or fraud, especially when committed by large and well-known companies. It's very hard to hide things from hotly competing newspapermen looking for a "scoop," not to mention the representatives of radio, television, movies, magazines, and the wire services. In a laissez-faire society, where there was no government to claim the lion's share of the spotlight, it would be considerably more difficult to keep any departure from integrity hidden.

Of course, stiff competition between businesses is the consumer's best guarantee of getting a good product at a reasonable price—dishonest competitors are swiftly "voted" out of business by consumers. But, in addition to competition, the market would evolve means of safeguarding the consumer which would be vastly superior to the contradictory, confusing, and harassing weight of governmental regulations with which the bureaucrats claim to protect us today. One such market protection would be consumer rating services which would test and rate various products according to safety, effectiveness, cost, etc. Since the whole existence of these rating services would depend on their being right in their product evaluations, they would be extremely thorough in their tests, scrupulously honest in their reports, and nearly impossible to bribe (which is not always true of government officials!).

Businesses whose products were potentially dangerous to consumers would be especially dependent on a good reputation. Drug manufacturers, for example, would know that if their products caused any illness or death through poor quality, insufficient research and preparation, or inadequate warnings on the labels they would lose customers by the thousands. The good reputation of a manufacturer's brand name would be its most precious asset, an asset which no firm would knowingly risk. Besides this, drug stores would strive for a reputation of stocking only products which were high quality, safe when properly used, and adequately labeled. In place of the present inflexible, cumbersome, and expensive prescription system, they might employ pharmacists for the sole purpose of advising customers who wanted to know which medicines to take (and not to take) and whether their ailments were serious enough to require the attention of a physician (a practice which would take a great load of minor complaints off the shoulders of overworked doctors and sharply reduce the cost of medical service).

A good reputation would also be important to doctors in the absence of government-required licensing. Of course, any man would be free to hang out a shingle and call himself a doctor, but a man whose "treatments" harmed his patients couldn't stay in business long. Besides, reputable physicians would probably form medical organizations which would only sanction competent doctors, thereby providing consumers with a guide. Insurance companies, who have a vested interest in keeping their policyholders alive and healthy, would provide another safeguard in the field of drugs and medical care. Insurance companies might well charge lower rates on life and health insurance to policyholders who contracted to use only those medicines and to patronize only those doctors sanctioned by a reputable medical association. This free-market system of consumer protection would end the doctor shortage and drastically reduce the cost of most medical care, since anyone could practice medicine in any area in which he was competent, regardless of the number of years he'd spend in college (or not spent in college, as the case might be). A brain surgeon might require 12 years of formal training, while a doctor who treated colds, flu, and ingrown toenails might need only 2—or none. The free-market system wouldn't commit the absurdity of requiring the same basic training for the colds-and-ingrown-toenails man as for the brain surgeon, thereby putting their fees on nearly the same level.

A Free and Healthy Economy

The efficiency of these free-market safeguards contrasts sharply with the way the Food and Drug Administration "protects" us. The FDA doesn't want anyone to be killed by *drugs* (that would look bad for the FDA's record). But they don't care how many people die of *diseases* because governmental restrictions prevented the development and sale of curative drugs . . . those deaths can't be blamed on the FDA, effectively (yet). Insurance companies, on the other hand, are deeply concerned with keeping their policyholders from dying for any reason at all. They would, therefore, not only discourage the use of harmful medications, but they would also encourage the discovery and development and sale of helpful ones. The free-market way of doing things is always superior to the only method government can use—coercion, as freedom is always superior to slavery.

When government sets out to protect the consumer, it does so by formulating a series of standards and attempting to enforce them. These standards must be artificial, since the decision as to how high to set them depends on nothing more than a bureaucrat's whim. But even if the standards fit the situation to begin with, they seldom stay appropriate for long. Conditions on the market change with research, the introduction of new products, and changes in consumer demand; but the bureaucrat's rules remain rigid and become outdated. For these reasons, governmental "consumer protection" can only result in the *prevention* of real consumer protection made available in a competitive, free market. It is an observable fact that government regulations reduce consumer safety by setting standards lower than the unhampered market would have set (or by enforcing standards which are inapplicable to the product). Many businessmen accept these low standards because doing so relieves them of further responsibility. Consumers accept them because they feel secure in the belief that a wise government is protecting them from the predations of greedy businessmen (which they learned in government schools). Actually, consumers are served well by the actions of profit-seeking businessmen; they are only taxed, regulated, and harrassed by power-seeking politicians.

The area in which the consumer is probably most in need of protection, and in which government most endangers him, is in maintaining the value of his money. Money is the lifeblood of any industrial economy—if the money loses its value, the entire economy must collapse.

Money is the commodity which, because of its high marketability, is used as a medium of exchange. In order to become money, a commodity must have high marketability—that is, people must be eager to accept it for its own value. This means that the money commodity must have a high value as a commodity, in addition to its exchange value, in order to become and remain money.

Over the centuries, two commodities have become prominent as money throughout the civilized world—gold and silver. They have high marketability because of their value for ornamental and industrial uses, and because of their relative rarity. They are homogeneous, divisible into equal units, non-spoilable, and fairly easy to transport. For these reasons they have gained a wider acceptance for exchange than any other commodities.

Money, then, is at present gold and silver. It is not, and cannot be, merely pieces of paper, because paper doesn't have enough value to be highly marketable. Pieces of paper can be money *substitutes* if, and only if, there is a stock of gold and/or silver for which they can be freely exchanged at any time.

Governments can't give any value to pieces of paper, and pieces of paper have no value except as they have a gold/silver backing and any holder of such paper notes may exchange them for gold and/or silver at any time. A government which uses paper for money without holding a freely accessible gold and/or silver reserve is forcing its economy to live on borrowed time. When some crisis causes its monetary fraud to become apparent, the value of its worthless paper money will sink to zero and the economy will collapse into ruin and starvation. This is what happened to Germany in 1923, when it took a basketful of paper Mark notes to buy a loaf of bread (which was one of the main factors in Hitler's rise to power). It is also what must happen to America if the politicians continue their present course.

In a laissez-faire society, only gold would be accepted as the standard of monetary value—there can be only one standard (and the free market *has* established gold as the commodity which is the standard of value). There would be no government to issue paper "fiat" notes, call them "money," and pass laws prohibiting people from using any other media of exchange. Since it is most convenient to use gold when it is minted into coins of a known weight and fineness, private enterprise minting companies would arise. They would mint coins, stamp them with their trademark, and guarantee their value. The companies whose value-guarantees were most reliable and whose minting services were most satisfactory would acquire a majority of the coin business. (Counterfeiting—which is a form of fraud—would be dealt with in the same manner as any other initiated aggressive action. See Chapters 9 and 10.)

Some critics of the free market have contended that private coinage would lead to a confusion of brands and values of coin, all exchanging at different ratios, making trade impossibly cumbersome.

A Free and Healthy Economy

But the market always moves toward the greatest consumer satisfaction. If consumers found the varying coin values cumbersome to deal with, they would soon stop accepting coins of "oddball" value, thus forcing merchants to standardize.

Governments have always made a practice of debasing their legally enforced media of exchange in order to divert extra wealth into the national treasury. In earlier times, the sovereign would call in all coins and clip their edges, keeping the gold thus obtained and returning the smaller coins to the people. In our modern and enlightened era, the same goal is accomplished through inflation, which enables the government to spend more "printing press money" and so debase the value of the currency already in the economy.

Because a government has a legal monopoly over the media of exchange in its country, it can make a practice of gradually reducing monetary value with very little to stop the process until the eventual and inevitable financial catastrophe. No free-market minting company could get away with such a fraud. If it issued devalued coins, people would simply refuse to accept them (Gresham's Law in reverse—good money drives out bad). Then the dishonest company would go broke . . . but it wouldn't take a whole nation of innocent people into ruin with it. The free market would, at last, give consumers protection in an area where they have never had it (because of governments) and desperately need it—the value of their money and, with it, the strength of their economy.

In addition to gold (and possibly silver) coin, money substitutes would be used in a free market because of their convenience, particularly for large transactions. These money substitutes would be in the form of bank notes, certifying that the bearer had on deposit in a certain bank a specific amount of gold. The banks would have to hold a 100% reserve of gold against these notes, because not to do so would be fraud and would cause them to lose their customers to banks with less risky policies. Since the banks would hold a 100% reserve of gold, these money substitutes would not inflate the currency as do unbacked government notes. Nor would there be any danger of runs on banks, leaving the banks insolvent and many of their customers ruined. Such runs are the product of fractional reserve banking, which exists because it is legally condoned and enforced by governments.

With competition to guarantee that only gold was used as a monetary standard of value and that all money substitutes had 100% gold backing, a laissez-faire society would be permanently safe from monetary crises. The free society's healthy economy would remain strong because its money would be of permanent value and, therefore, unassailable.

6

Property—The Great Problem Solver

Most social problems which perplex national leaders could be solved fairly simply by an increase in the amount and type of property owned. This would entail the equally important, general recognition that ownership is and must be total, rather than merely a governmental permission to possess and/or manage property so long as certain legal rules are complied with and "rent" in the form of property taxes is paid. When a man is required to "rent" his own property from the government by paying property taxes on it, he is being forbidden to fully exercise his right of ownership. Although he owns the property, he is forced into the position of a lessee, with the government the landlord. The proof of this is that if he fails to pay the taxes the government will take his property away from him (even though it is *his* property and not the government's), just as a landlord would kick out a tenant who failed to pay the rent. Similarly, if a man must comply with laws dictating the use or upkeep of his property (or any other rule except that of not using the property to initiate force or fraud against others), he is being forbidden to fully exercise his right of ownership. Because a man must use his time—which is part of his life—to acquire, utilize, and care for property, he has a right to own and control that property fully, just as he has a right to fully own and control his life (so long as he doesn't use it to coerce any other man). Any form of property tax or regulation denies the individual's right to fully control his own property and, therefore, his own life. For this reason, taxation and regulation of property is always wrong—taxation is theft and regulation by initiated force is slavery.

In a governmentally controlled society, the unrestricted enjoyment of property ownership is not permitted, since government has the power to tax, regulate, and sometimes even confiscate (as in eminent domain) just about anything it pleases. In addition, much potential property is not permitted to be owned. In a laissez-faire society, everything which was valued and rationally claimed would be owned, and this ownership would be total[1]

Property is anything which is owned. Ownership is the right to possess, use, and/or dispose of anything to which one has a moral claim. Property may be acquired by producing it, by exchange with others, as a gift, or by claiming an unowned value. The claiming of unowned values is the way in which all property originally came to be owned.

An unowned value cannot become one's property simply because one makes a verbal (or written) statement claiming it. If it could, you could say right now, "I claim the ocean bottoms of the entire earth and all the surface of the moon," and, provided you were the first to make the claim, they would be yours. Obviously, this would lead to a welter of contradictory and unenforceable claims.

In addition to making a verbal claim, something must be done to establish that claim as having a basis in reality. In the case of portable items, there is no problem. Anything which can be transported by either hand or machine can simply be moved by the new owner and placed within the confines of some other piece of his property—his suitcase, car, house, or land. The newly claimed item may also be marked in some way to furnish more evidence of ownership (the owner's name, initials, or some sort of serial number or symbol is frequently used).

Non-movable items, such as a fully grown tree, a dam, or a piece of land, present a different kind of situation. All non-movable items may be considered as land, since even if the item itself is not land it cannot be separated from the land on which it stands. Since a non-movable item can't be carried away, it must be marked as the new owner's property where it stands. Because a non-movable item always occupies some land space, the land, too, must be marked.

All land is contiguous to other land (including islands, as can be seen if one considers the fact that submerged land is ownable). This means that the most important things to mark are the boundaries. This may be done by fencing, by a series of signposts at intervals, or in any other way which leaves a clearly visible evidence of possession on the land itself. Obviously, the better job of marking one does, the less likely one is to have trouble from someone with a conflicting claim.

Conflicting claims would be settled by bringing them before private arbitration agencies for binding arbitration. Since neither disputant would be able to sell the land, have much chance of

---

[1] In the case of joint ownership, each owner would have total ownership of a part of the whole, and his part would be specified in the voluntary agreement with the other owner or owners.

renting it or even any security of possession so long as his claim was in dispute, both parties would be impelled to bring the matter to arbitration. The free-market arbitration agency, if it wanted to stay in business, would have to make as fair a decision as it possibly could. Both disputants would then be impelled to abide by the arbiter's decision, since a man who contracted to abide by the results of arbitration and then broke his contract would be announcing himself as unreliable, and no one would want to risk having any business dealings with him.[2]

The fact that conflicting claims could arise and that they would have to be settled before impartial arbiters provides the answer to the question, "How well does a piece of property have to be marked to establish a man's claim to it?" Obviously, if the new owner wants his property to be secure, it has to be bounded (in the case of land) and marked clearly enough to establish his claim in the face of all possible conflicting claims. Suppose an eager prospector claimed a square mile of land in hilly, heavily wooded territory and marked it by erecting a six-foot tall signpost at each of the four corners. Six months later, a student who wanted the privacy of a quiet retreat came and fenced in two acres, part of which lay within the prospector's claim. When the conflict was discovered and the matter brought to arbitration, the arbiters would very likely decide in favor of the student, even though his claim had been made later in time. It could reasonably be held that the student should not have been expected to know of the existence of the four signposts hidden in the woods and that, therefore, the prospector's "bounding" of his land had been insufficient to clearly establish his claim. Similarly, a man could land on a new planet, fence in a square mile, and then claim that, since the planet was a closed sphere, he owned all the territory *outside* the fence (that is, all the planet except the square mile enclosed by his fence). But he would find that no arbitration agency would decide in favor of his ridiculous claim if it were contested by a group of colonists who later landed on the other side of the planet (who could be expected to know nothing of the claim).

Different kinds of claims would have to be established by different kinds and degrees of bounding and marking, and each claim would be an individual case to be decided on its own merits. But the fact that all conflicting claims could be submitted to arbitration and that the integrity of the arbitration would be guaranteed by competition in a free market would insure the maximum justice humanly possible.

In a laissez-faire society, there would be no government to pre-

---

[2]The nature and function of arbitration agencies, as well as the market forces which would impel the disputants to bring their claims to arbitration and to abide by the decision of the arbiters, will be discussed fully in the next chapter.

Property—The Great Problem Solver

empt the field of registering deeds. Businesses in a free market would take over this function, since it is a salable service. These companies would keep records of titles and would probably offer the additional service of title insurance (a service already offered by specialized insurance companies today). Title insurance protects the insured against loss resulting from a defect in the title of the property he buys (as, for example, if the long-lost niece of a deceased former owner shows up and claims the property by inheritance). It would substantially reduce problems of conflicting claims, since title insurance companies would be unlikely to insure a title without first checking to make sure there was no conflict. In a free society, title insurance might also protect the insured against loss of his property due to aggression or fraud committed against him. In this case, the aggressor would be dealt with in the same manner as would any other aggressor (a subject which will be covered in Chapters 9 and 10).

There would probably be a plurality of companies competing in the field of title registration and insurance, so they would no doubt find it in their interest to maintain a computerized central listing of titles in the same way that other agencies now keep extensive files on the credit rating of consumers. In this way, they would be in the same relationship of cooperative competition as are present-day insurance companies.

Because they would have competition, title insurance companies would have to be extremely careful to maintain a good business reputation. No honest person would jeopardize the value of his property by registering it with a company which had a reputation for dishonest dealing. If he made use of a shady company, other individuals and firms would have doubts about the validity of his title and would be reluctant to buy his property or to loan money on it. In a totally free market, companies would usually act honestly because it would be in their interest to do so. (The question of dishonest companies will be dealt with in Chapter 11.)

An old and much respected theory holds that for a man to come into possession of a previously unowned value it is necessary for him to "mix his labor with the land" in order to make it his own.[3] But this theory runs into difficulties when one attempts to explain what is meant by "mixing labor with land." Just how much labor is required, and of what sort? If a man digs a large hole in his land and then fills it up again, can he be said to have mixed his labor with the land? Or is it necessary to effect a somewhat permanent change in the land? If so, how permanent? Would planting some tulip bulbs in a clearing do it? Perhaps long-living redwood trees would

---

[3] In this quote, "land" is used not in the common sense of real estate but in the economic sense of any nature-given original factor of production.

be more acceptable? Or is it necessary to effect some improvement in the economic value of the land? If so, how much and how soon? Would planting a small garden in the middle of a 500-acre plot be sufficient, or must the whole acreage be tilled (or put to some other economic use)? Would a man lose title to his land if he had to wait ten months for a railroad line to be built before he could improve the land? What if he had to wait ten years? And what of the naturalist who wanted to keep his land exactly as it was in its wild state in order to study its ecology?

Of course, making visible improvements in the land would certainly help to establish a man's title more firmly by offering further proofs of ownership. It is also true that very little of the potential economic value of most land could be actually realized without some improvements being made (even a scenic wilderness area must have roads or helicopter landing fields or something to make it accessible to tourists before any profits can be made from it). But mixing one's labor with the land is too ill-defined a concept and too arbitrary a requirement to serve as a *criterion* of ownership.

It has been objected that simply having to mark the boundaries of newly claimed property would permit a few ambitious people to acquire far more property than they could use. It is difficult to understand, however, what would be so objectionable about this situation. If the first comers were ambitious, quick and intelligent enough to acquire the property before anyone else, why should they be prevented from reaping the rewards of these virtues in order to hold the land open for someone else? And if a large chunk of land is acquired by a man who is too stupid or lazy to make a productive use of it, other men, operating within the framework of the free market, will eventually be able to bid it away from him and put it to work producing wealth. As long as the land is privately owned and the market is free, the land will come to be allocated to its most productive uses and its prices will be bid down to market level.

Intangible property may also be marked in various ways. For example, a man may claim a certain radio wave length by broadcasting his claim to ownership on that frequency (provided, of course, that no one else has beaten him to it). Ideas in the form of inventions could also be claimed by registering all details of the invention in a privately owned "data bank." Of course, the more specific an inventor was about the details of his invention, the thought processes he followed while working on it, and the ideas on which he built, the more firmly established his claim would be and the less would be the likelihood of someone else squeezing him out with a fake claim based on stolen data. The inventor, having registered his invention to establish his ownership of the idea(s), could then buy insurance (from either the data bank firm or an independent insurance company) against the theft and unauthorized commercial use of his invention by any other person. The insurance company would guarantee to stop the unauthorized commercial use of the invention and to fully compensate the inventor for any losses so incurred. Such insurance policies could be bought to cover varying periods of time, with the longer-term policies more expensive than the shorter-term ones. Policies covering an indefinitely long time-period ("from now on") probably wouldn't be economically feasible, but there might well be clauses allowing the inventor to re-insure his idea at the end of the life of his policy.

One of the most far-reaching differences in a free-market society would spring from the fact that anything which had the potential for being property would be owned. In our present society, there is an enormous amount of potential property which does not, in actual fact, belong to anyone. Such unowned potential property falls into two categories—1—things that remain unowned because the legal system does not recognize the possibility of their becoming property, and 2—"public property."

Today's legal system, having been developed in prescientific times, recognizes that a man can own a piece of land beside an ocean but does not recognize that he can just as well own a piece of land under that ocean. And yet, as companies drilling for off-shore oil have proved, there is no reason why a piece of land cannot be owned and used simply because it is covered by water. In a similar manner, lake bottoms, and, in fact, the lake itself, can be owned by one or by several individuals. Rivers are also potential property, as is the air space above and around your home, and, further up, the "corridors" of air space which airliners use in flying their regular routes.

Granted, new rules would have to be figured out governing the rights of, say, the owner of a section of river in relation to owners of portions of that same river upstream and downstream from him, but if a man can own something as nonmaterial as the copyright to a song, surely he can own a river! The problem is not that such things are by their nature unownable but that the legal system, trapped in its own archaic rigidity, prohibits them from being owned. In a free society, a man who could mine a section of ocean bottom could claim and use it without having to wait for a legislature to pass a law saying that it could be owned. This would remove a tremendous barrier to progress and to the production of wealth.

The other type of unowned potential property is what is usually known as "public property." The concept of "public property" has come down from the days when the king or local feudal noble owned the land and all those under his jurisdiction were merely allowed to hold pieces of it "in fief." Gradually, as feudalism and monarchy gave way to democracy, such royal property came to be thought of as belonging to the public as a whole and as being administered for the public by the government.

Ownership necessarily involves the right of use and disposal as the owner sees fit, barring coercion against others. Since the king was an individual, he could actually exercise control over royal properties, using them and disposing of them according to his desires. But "the public" is not an individual—it is merely the aggregate of all the individuals who happen to be living in a certain area at a certain time. As such, "the public" has no mind or will or desires of its own. It cannot make decisions, and so it cannot decide how to use or dispose of a piece of property. "Public property" is, in fact, a fiction.

Nor can the government morally claim to own "public property." Government does not produce anything. Whatever it has, it has as a result of expropriation. It is no more correct to call the expropriated wealth in government's possession its property than it is to say that a thief rightfully owns the loot he has stolen. But if "public property" doesn't belong to either the public or to the government, it doesn't actually belong to anyone, and it is in the same category as any other unowned values. Among the items in this classification are streets and highways, schools, libraries, all government buildings, and the millions of acres of government-owned lands which comprise the major portion of many Western States.[4]

In a laissez-faire society, all property formerly "belonging" to government would come to be owned by private individuals and would be put to productive use. The economic boom this would be can be glimpsed from the following illustration: recently, several companies have sought to develop low-cost and plentiful power sources by tapping the energy of hot, underground water (the same thing that causes geysers and hot springs). There are several promising sources of this geothermal power, but most are on government land and the entrepreneurs were stopped because there are no laws *permitting* them to carry on such activities on "public property"!

As the laissez-faire society matured, it would eventually reach a state in which all potential property was actually owned. In the process of claiming unowned potential property and government "property," the present poor and dispossessed elements of our population would have plenty of opportunities to "homestead" on rural

---

[4]The land area of the State of Nevada was 86.4% "owned" by the Federal Government (U. S. A.) in June, 1968, according to the *Statistical Abstract of the United States of 1969.*

lands and in urban buildings formerly "owned" by various branches of government. This would give them a proprietary interest in something for the first time and teach them, as nothing else can, to respect the products of their own labor and of the labor of others—which means, *to respect themselves and other men.*

This situation of total property ownership would automatically solve many of the problems plaguing our present society. For instance, shiftless elements of the population, who had acquired no property and were not willing to work in order to earn enough money to rent living quarters, would be literally pushed to the geographic edge of the society. One can't sleep on park benches if the private owner of the park doesn't permit bums on his property; one can't search the back alleys for garbage if he is trespassing on alleys belonging to a corporation; one can't even be a beachcomber if all the beaches are owned. With no public property and no public dole, such undesirables would quickly "shape up or ship out."

Total property ownership would also lower crime rates in the same manner. A private corporation which owned streets would make a point of keeping its streets free of drunks, hoodlums, and any other such annoying menaces, hiring private guards to do so if necessary. It might even advertise, "Thru-Way Corporation's streets are guaranteed safe at any hour of the day or night. Women may walk alone with perfect confidence on our thoroughfares." A criminal, forbidden to use any city street because all the street corporations knew of his bad reputation, would have a hard time even getting anywhere to commit a crime. On the other hand, the private street companies would have no interest in regulating the dress, "morals," habits, or life-style of the people who used their streets. For instance, they wouldn't want to drive away customers by arresting or badgering hippies, girls in see-thru blouses or topless bathing suits or any other non-aggressive deviation from the value-standards of the majority. All they would ask is that each customer pay his dime-a-day and refrain from initiating force, obstructing traffic, and driving away other customers. Other than this, his life-style and moral code would be of no interest to them; they would treat him courteously and solicit his business.

Another aspect of total property ownership is that it would make immigration laws unnecessary and meaningless. If all potential property were actually owned, any "immigrant" would have to have enough money to support himself, or a marketable skill so he could go right to work, or someone who would help him out until he got started. He couldn't just walk into the free area and wander around—he'd be trespassing. Those who were skilled and ambitious would come; those who were lazy wouldn't dare to. This is much more just and effective than the present "national quota" system.

The pollution problem would also be well on its way to being solved. If I own the air space around my home, you obviously don't have the right to pour pollutants into that air space any more than you have a right to throw garbage onto my lawn. Similarly, you have no right to dump sewage into my river unless we have a contract specifying that you may rent the use of my river for such purposes (and that contract would have to include the consent of all those individuals who owned sections of the river downstream from me, too). Since pollution is already a problem in many areas, it would have to be understood that anyone buying a piece of property, by his act of buying it, consented to the average pollution level at the time of the sale but had the right to see that others kept it free of any further pollution. Initially, this would mean that established companies could not increase the level of their pollution, nor could new companies begin polluting. But as pollution control methods and devices became common and relatively inexpensive, the established companies would seek to reduce and even to eliminate their pollution in order to keep from losing their employees to new industries operating in pollution-free areas. Pollution problems could not continue to exist in a competitive, laissez-faire, free-market environment— an environment which governments destroy.

Total property ownership, contrary to the current popular belief, is the only feasible way of conserving natural resources. The conservation of resources is a subject badly befogged by misconceptions and unclear thinking. For example, it is contended that the market wastes scarce resources, thus robbing future generations of their use. But by what criterion does the critic decide which employments of resources are permissible and which are merely waste? If it is wrong to use up resources to produce *some* things consumers value, how can it be right to use them to produce *any* such things? And if natural resources must be saved for future generations, how can they ever be used at all, since each future generation still has a theoretically infinite number of future generations coming after it, for which it must save? The only answer to the problem of scarce resources is to leave it up to free men trading in a free market. This will insure that resources are used in the most value-productive way possible and that they are used at the rate which consumers desire. Besides this, the technology stimulated by a free market continually uses natural resources to discover new natural resources. This means more than just the discovery of new deposits of previously valuable resources, such as vast new oilfields. It also includes the discovery of how to use previously valueless resources, often to replace a scarcer resource in some area of use, thereby conserving it. An example of this is the many new uses of glass and plastic, some of which can replace steel and other metals derived from scarce resources.

There is a curious misconception that to prevent the wholesale waste of natural resources it is necessary to remove control of them from the hands of "greedy capitalists" and give it to "public-spirited government officials." The ridiculous fallacy of this position becomes obvious when one considers the nature of the control exercised by a government official.

To the extent that he has control over a natural resource (or anything else), a government official has a quasi-ownership of it. But this quasi-ownership ends with the end of his term in office. If he is to reap any advantage from it, he must make hay while his political sun shines. Therefore, government officials will tend to hurriedly squeeze every advantage from anything they control, depleting it as rapidly as possible (or as much as they can get away with). Private owners, because they can hold their property as long as they please or sell it at any time for its market price, are usually very careful to conserve both its present and future value. Obviously, the best possible person to conserve scarce resources is the owner of those resources who has a selfish interest in protecting his investment. The worst guardian of scarce resources is a government official —he has no stake in protecting them but is likely to have a large interest in looting them.

Among the resources which would be conserved best under a system of total property ownership are wild-life and scenic recreation areas. Consumer demand for parks, campgrounds, wild-life sanctuaries, hunting grounds, natural scenery, etc., is evident from a study of recreational patterns. In a free-market society, just as much land would be set aside for these purposes as consumer demand warranted.

A system of total property ownership would be based on the moral requirement of man's life as a rational being,[5] as man's survival is sub-human to the extent that the right to own property (beginning with self-ownership) is not understood and respected. (As a matter of actual fact, life itself would not be possible if there were no right to own property.) A system of total property ownership in a free society—i.e., in a society in which the right to own property is

---

[5]That man is a rational being means, simply, that he is capable of rational thought and behavior; it does not mean that he will automatically think and behave rationally since, for this, he must make the choice to do so. Since man's consciousness is volitional, he is free to 1—not choose and to 2—choose not to think, as well as being free to choose to think. To survive, man *must* think; the choice to do so must be made by each person, individually and independently—by himself, alone. The choice to think or not can only be made by individuals—society does not have a brain to think with.

generally understood and respected—would produce a peaceful environment in which justice was the rule, not the exception (as it is today). An environment of justice is based on the moral principle of "value for value"—that no man may justifiably expect to receive values from others without giving values in exchange (and this includes spiritual values, such as love and admiration, as well as economic values). Some people express shock and even horror at the thought of having to make some sort of payment for every value they receive. They seem to prefer, for example, to pay for their use of roads via taxation (even though this method is demonstrably more expensive) in order to be able to pretend to themselves that they are actually getting the service free. Upon examination, such people usually prove to be suffering from a deficiency of self-esteem—lacking a sense of personal efficacy and worth, they feel a sneaky, unadmitted doubt about their ability to survive in a world where they will never be provided with the unearned. But their psychological problems do not alter the nature of reality. It still remains a fact that the only moral way for men to deal with one another is by giving value for value, and that the man who seeks the unearned is a parasite. The man of self-esteem realizes this and takes pride in his ability to pay for the values he receives.

From an examination of the areas covered in this and the preceding chapter, it is clear that a non-governmental, free-market society would, by its very nature, foster responsibility, honesty, and productivity in the individuals who lived in it. This would cause a substantial improvement in the moral tone of the culture as a whole and a sharp drop in the crime rate. Nevertheless, since human beings are creatures with a volitional consciousness and are thus free to act irrationally if they so choose, there can be no such thing as a Utopia. A free-market society would still have to have means for the arbitration of disputes, the protection and defense of life and property, and the rectification of injustice. In the absence of government, institutions to provide these services would arise naturally out of the market. The next few chapters will examine these institutions and their functioning in a free-market environment.

7
Arbitration of Disputes

Whenever men have dealings with one another, there is always a chance for disagreements and disputes to arise. Even when there has been no initiation of force, two persons can disagree over such matters as the terms and fulfillment of a contract or the true title to a piece of property. Whether one party to the dispute is trying to cheat the other(s) or whether both (or all) are completely honest and sincere in their contentions, the dispute may reach a point where it can't be settled without binding arbitration by a disinterested arbiter. If no mechanism for such arbitration existed within a society, disputes could only be resolved by violence in every situation in which at least one person abandoned reason—man's only satisfactory means of communication. Then, that society would disintegrate into strife, suspicion, and social and economic breakdown, as human relationships became too dangerous to tolerate on any but the most limited scale.

Advocates of "limited government" contend that government is necessary to maintain social order because disputes could never be satisfactorily settled without a single, final court of appeal for everyone and without the force of legal rules to compel disputants to submit to that court and to abide by its decision(s). They also seem to feel that government officials and judges are somehow more impartial than other men because they are set apart from ordinary market relations and, therefore, have no vested interests to interfere with their judgments.

It is interesting to note that the advocates of government see initiated force (the legal force of government) as the only solution to social disputes. According to them, if everyone in society were not *forced* to use the same court system, and particularly the same final court of appeal, disputes would be insoluble. Apparently it doesn't occur to them that disputing parties are capable of freely choosing their own arbiters, including the final arbiter, and that this final arbiter wouldn't need to be the same agency for all disputes which occur in the society. They have not realized that disputants would, in fact, be far better off if they could choose among competing arbitration agencies so that they could reap the benefits of competition and specialization. It should be obvious that a court system which has a monopoly guaranteed by the force of statutory law will not give as good quality service as will free-market arbitration agencies which must compete for their customers. Also, a multiplicity of agencies facilitates specialization, so that people with a dispute in some specialized field can hire arbitration by experts in that field . . . instead of being compelled to submit to the judgment of men who have little or no background in the matter.

But, the government advocates argue, there must be an agency of legal force to compel disputants (particularly those who are negligent or dishonest) to submit to arbitration and abide by the decision of the arbiter, or the whole arbitration process would be futile. It is true that the whole process would be meaningless if one or both disputants could avoid arbitration or ignore the decision of the arbiter. But it doesn't follow that an institution of initiated force is necessary to compel the disputants to treat the arbitration as binding. The principle of rational self-interest, on which the whole free-market system is built, would accomplish this end quite effectively. Men who contract to abide by the decision of a neutral arbiter and then break that contract are obviously unreliable and too risky to do business with. Honest men, acting in their rational self-interest, would check the records of those they did business with and would avoid having any dealings with such individuals. This kind of informal business boycott would be extremely effective in a governmentless society where a man could acquire nothing except what he could produce himself or get in trade with others.

Even in cases where the pressure of business ostracism was insufficient to insure compliance with arbiters' decisions, it doesn't follow that government would be necessary to bring the contract-breaker to justice. As will be shown in Chapters 9 and 10, free men, acting in a free market, are quite capable of dealing justly with those few who harm their fellowmen by any form of coercion, including contract-breaking. It's hardly necessary to institutionalize aggressive violence in order to deal with aggressive violence!

Perhaps the least tenable argument for government arbitration of disputes is the one which holds that governmental judges are more impartial because they operate outside the market and so have no vested interests. In the first place, it's impossible for anyone except a self-sufficient hermit to operate completely outside the market. The market is simply a system of trade, and even Federal judges trade with other men in order to improve their standard of living (if they didn't, we would have to pay them in consumable goods instead of money). In the second place, owing political allegiance to

Arbitration of Disputes

government is certainly no guarantee of impartiality! A governmental judge is always impelled to be partial . . . in favor of the government, from whom he gets his pay and his power! On the other hand, an arbiter who sells his services in a free market knows that he must be as scrupulously honest, fair, and impartial as possible or no pair of disputants will buy his services to arbitrate their dispute. A free-market arbiter depends for his livelihood on his skill and fairness at settling disputes. A governmental judge depends on political pull.

Excluding cases of initiated force and fraud (which will be dealt with in later chapters), there are two main categories of disputes between men—disputes which arise out of a contractual situation between the disputing parties (as disagreements over the meaning and application of the contract, or allegations of willful or negligent breach of contract) and disputes in which there was no contractual relationship between the disputants. Because of the importance of contractual relationships in a laissez-faire society, this type of dispute will be discussed first.

A free society, and particularly an industrialized one, *is* a contractual society. Contracts are such a basic part of all business dealings that even the smallest business would soon collapse if the integrity of its contracts were not protected. (Not only million dollar deals between industrial giants, but your job, the apartment you lease, and the car you buy on time represent contractual situations.) This creates a large market for the service of contract-protection, a market which is at present pre-empted by government. In a laissez-faire society, this market would be best served by professional arbitration agencies in conjunction with insurance companies.

In a free-market society, individuals or firms which had a contractual dispute which they found themselves unable to resolve would find it in their interest to take their problem before an arbitration agency for binding arbitration. In order to eliminate possible disputes over which arbitration agency to patronize, the contracting parties would usually designate an agency at the time the contract was written. This agency would judge in any dispute between them, and they would bind themselves contractually to abide by its decisions. If the disputing parties had lacked the foresight to choose an arbitration agency at the time their original contract was made, they would still be able to hire one when the dispute arose, provided they could agree on which agency to patronize. Obviously, any arbitration agency would insist that all parties involved consent to its arbitration so that none of them would have a basis for bringing any action against it later if dissatisfied with its decision(s).

It would be more economical and in most cases quite sufficient to have only one arbitration agency to hear the case. But if the parties felt that a further appeal might be necessary and were willing to risk the extra expense, they could provide for a succession of two or or even more arbitration agencies. The names of these agencies would be written into the contract, in order from the "first court of appeal" to the "last court of appeal." It would be neither necessary nor desirable to have one single, final court of appeal for every person in the society, as we have today in the United States Supreme Court. Such forced uniformity always promotes injustice. Since the arbitration agencies for any particular contract would be designated in that contract, every contracting party would choose his own arbitration agency or agencies (including the one to whom final appeal was to be made if more than one was wanted). Those who needed arbitration would thus be able to reap the benefits of specialization and competition among the various arbitration agencies. And, since companies must compete on the basis of lower prices and/or better service, competition among arbitration agencies would lead to scrupulously honest decisions reached at the greatest speed and lowest cost which were feasible (quite a contrast to the traditional governmental court system, where justice is often a matter of clever lawyers and lucky accident).

Arbitration agencies would employ professional arbiters, instead of using citizen-jurors as governmental courts do. A board of professional arbiters would have great advantages over the present citizen-jury system of "ignorance times twelve." Professional arbiters would be highly trained specialists who made a career of hearing disputes and settling them justly. They would be educated for their profession as rigorously as engineers or doctors, probably taking their basic training in such fields as logic, ethics, and psychology, and further specialization in any field likely to come under dispute. While professional arbiters would still make errors, they would make far fewer than do the amateur jurors and political judges of today. Not only would professional arbiters be far better qualified to hear, analyze, and evaluate evidence for the purpose of coming to an objective judgment than are our present citizen-jurors, they would also be much more difficult to bribe. A professional arbiter who tried to "throw" a case would be easily detected by his trained and experienced colleagues, and few men would be so foolish as to jeopardize a remunerative and highly respected career, even for a very large sum of money.

Justice, after all, is an economic good, just as are education and medical care. The ability to dispense justice depends on knowledge and on skill in assessing people and situations. This knowledge and

Arbitration of Disputes

skill must be acquired, just as medical knowledge must be acquired before medical advice can be dispensed. Some people are willing to expend the effort to get this knowledge and skill so that they can sell their services as professional arbiters. Other people need their services and are willing to buy them. Justice, like any other good or service, has economic value.

The reason for the superiority of professional arbiters over citizen-juries can be readily seen by an examination of the moral basis for each system. The citizen-juror's "service" is based on the concept of performing a duty to the state or to his fellow citizens—another variation of the irrational and immoral belief that the individual belongs to the collective. The professional arbiter, on the other hand, is a trader, selling his specialized services on the free market and profiting to the degree of his excellence.

Because arbitration agencies would be doing business in a free market, they would have to attract customers in order to make profits. This means that they would find it in their interest to treat all disputants who came to them with every courtesy and consideration possible. Instead of taking the authoritarian stand of a governmental judge and handing down arbitrary rulings with little or no regard for the interests and feelings of the disputants, they would make every effort to find a solution which was, as nearly as possible, satisfactory to both of the conflicting parties. If a disputant disagreed with the arbiters' proposed solution, they would first attempt to sell him on it by reasoning with him (which means that it would have to be a reasonable solution to begin with). Only as a last resort would they invoke the clause in the contract between disputants and arbitration agency which made the arbitration binding. Arbitration agencies, because they would obtain their customers by excellence of service rather than by coercion, would have to act like arbiters helping to settle a dispute . . . rather than like judges handing down a sentence.

Insurance companies, looking for new fields of business, would offer contract insurance, and most individuals and firms would probably take advantage of this service. (In fact, insuring the monetary value of contracts is common practice today. Nearly all instalment contracts carry insurance against the debtor's failure to pay because of death or some default.) This insurance would be sold to the contracting parties at the time the contract was ratified. Before an insurance company would indemnify its insured for loss in a case of broken contract, the matter would have to be submitted to arbitration as provided in the contract. For this reason there would be a close link between the business of contract insurance and the business of arbitration. Some arbitration agencies would probably develop as auxiliary functions of insurance companies, while others would arise as independent firms.

Suppose the inventor of a Handy-Dandy Kitchen Gadget entered into a contract with a small-time factory owner concerning the manufacture of the Kitchen Gadget, and they had the contract insured. Suppose that the factory owner then changed the design of the Kitchen Gadget and began making and selling it as his own invention, in order to avoid paying royalties to the inventor. After appealing to the manufacturer unsuccessfully, the inventor would take his complaint to the company insuring the contract. The insurance company would then arrange a hearing before the arbitration agency named in the contract as "first court of appeal." Here the dispute would be submitted to one or more professional arbiters for a judgment to resolve it. (The number and general composition of the arbiters, if more than one arbiter were called for, would have been specified in the original contract.)

If the decision reached by the professional arbiters was satisfactory to both the Kitchen Gadget inventor and the manufacturer, their ruling would be observed and the disputed matter would be settled. If the ruling were not satisfactory to either the inventor or the manufacturer and the dissatisfied party felt he had a chance of obtaining a reversal, he could appeal the decision to the next arbitration agency named in the contract. This agency would consent to hear the case if it felt the dissatisfied party had presented enough evidence to warrant a possible reversal. . . . And so on, up through the arbitration agency named as "final court of appeal."

When a contract is willfully or carelessly broken, the principle of justice involved is that the party who broke the contract owes all other contracted parties reparations in the amount of whatever his breach of contract has cost them (such amount to be determined by the arbitration agency previously specified by the parties to the contract) plus the cost of the arbitration proceedings.

If the arbiters of the final arbitration agency to whom appeal was made decided that the factory owner had, in fact, breached his contract with the inventor, they would set the reparations payment as close as humanly possible to the amount which the facts warranted —i.e., they would attempt to be as objective as possible. If the manufacturer were either unable or unwilling to make the payment, or to make it immediately, the insurance company would indemnify the inventor for the amount in question (within the terms of the policy). With the inventor paid according to the terms of the insurance policy, the insurance company would then have the right of subrogation— that is, the insurance company would have the right to collect the reparations in the inventor's place and the manufacturer would now owe the insurance company rather than the inventor (except for any valid claim for damages the inventor might have for an amount in excess of what the insurance company had paid him).

If the inventor didn't have insurance on his contract with the manufacturer, he would take much the same steps as those described above, with two exceptions. First, he, himself, would have to make all arrangements for a hearing before the arbitration agency and for the collection of the debt, and he would have to stand the cost of these services until the manufacturer paid him back. Second, he would not be immediately indemnified for his loss but would have to wait until the manufacturer could pay him, which might be a matter of months or even years if, for example, the manufacturer had gone broke because of his shady dealings and had to make payment on an instalment basis.

Because those who were guilty of breaches of contract would pay the major costs occasioned by their negligent or improper behavior, the insurance companies would not have to absorb large losses on contract insurance claims, as they do on fire or accident claims. With only minimal losses to spread among their policyholders, insurance companies could afford to charge very low premiums for contract insurance. Low cost, plus the great convenience afforded by contract insurance, would make such insurance standard for almost all important contracts.

Before examining what steps an insurance company (or the original offended party if the contract were uninsured) could morally and practically take in the collection of a debt, it is necessary to examine the concept of "debt" itself. A debt is a value owed by one individual to another individual, with consequent obligation to make payment. A condition of debt arises when:

1—an individual comes into possession of a value which rightfully belongs to another individual, either by voluntary agreement, as in a purchase made on credit, or by theft or fraud;

2—an individual destroys a value which rightfully belongs to another individual.

A debt is the result of an action willingly or negligently taken by the debtor. That is, even though he may not have purposed to assume a debt, he has willingly taken some action or failed to take some action which he should have taken (as in the case of what is now termed "criminal negligence") which has directly resulted in the loss of some value belonging to another individual. A debt does not arise from an unforeseeable or unpreventable circumstance, such as an accident or natural disaster. (In such cases, insurance companies would act just as they do now, indemnifying the insured and spreading the loss among all their policyholders.)

When a debt is owed, the debtor is in either actual or potential possession of a value (or of values) which is the rightful property of the creditor. That is, the debtor is in possession of either:
1—the original value-item(s), e.g., a refrigerator which he bought on time and for which he has defaulted on the payments, or
2—an amount of money equal in value to the original item if he has disposed of or destroyed that item, or
3—the ability to earn the money with which to make payment (or at least partial payment) for the item.

Since the debtor is in actual or potential possession of a value(s) which rightfully belongs to the creditor, the creditor has the right to repossess his property . . . because it is his property. And he has the right to repossess it by any means that will not take or destroy values which are the rightful property of the debtor. If the creditor, in the process of collecting his property, does deprive the debtor of values which rightfully belong to the debtor, the creditor may well find that he has reversed their roles, that he is now the one in debt.

To return to the insurance company and its collection of the debt owed by the manufacturer in the Handy-Dandy Kitchen Gadget case, the insurance company would have the right to repossess the amount of the debt, which was now its property due to the right of subrogation. It could do so by making arrangements with the manufacturer for repayment, either immediately or in instalments, as he was able to afford. If, however, the manufacturer refused to make payment, the insurance company would have the right to make whatever arrangements it could with other individuals or companies who had financial dealings with him, in order to expedite collection of the debt. For example, the insurance company might arrange with the manufacturer's bank to attach an appropriate amount of his bank account, provided the bank was willing to make such an arrangement. In the case of a man who was employed, the insurance company might arrange with his employer to deduct payment(s) for the debt from the man's wages, if the employer was willing. Practically speaking, most banks would no doubt have a policy of cooperating with insurance companies in such matters, since a policy of protecting bank accounts from just claims would tend to attract customers who were undependable, thus increasing the cost of banking and forcing the bank to raise its charges. The same would be true of employers, only more so. Most employers would hesitate to attract undependable labor by inserting a clause in their employment contracts guaranteeing protection from just claims against them.

Such drastic means of collection as these would rarely be necessary, however. In the great majority of cases, the debtor would make payment without direct, retaliatory action on the part of the

Arbitration of Disputes

insurance company, because if he failed to do so he would be inviting business ostracism. Obviously, a man who refused to pay his debts is a poor business risk, and insurance companies would undoubtedly cooperate in keeping central files listing all poor risks, just as credit associations do today. So if the manufacturer refused to pay his debts, he would find all insurance companies he wanted to deal with either rating his premiums up or refusing to do business with him altogether. In a free society, whose members depended on the insurance industry for protection of their values from all types of threat (fire, accident, aggressive violence, etc.) and where, furthermore, insurance companies were the force guaranteeing the integrity of contracts, how well could a man live if he couldn't get insurance (or couldn't get it at a rate he could afford)? If the insurance companies refused to do business with him, he would be unable to buy any protection for his values, nor would he be able to enter into any meaningful contract—he couldn't even buy a car on time. Furthermore, other businesses would find it in their interest to check the information in the insurance companies' central files, just as they check credit ratings today, and so the manufacturer's bad reputation would spread. If his default were serious enough, no one would want to risk doing business with him. He would be driven out of business, and then he might even find it difficult to get and keep a good job or to rent a decent apartment. Even the poorest and most irresponsible man would think twice before putting himself in such a position. Even the richest and most powerful man would find it destructive of his interests to so cut himself off from all business dealings. In a free society, men would soon discover that honesty with others is a selfish, moral necessity!

If, in the face of all this, the manufacturer still remained adamant in his refusal to pay the debt, the insurance company would have the right to treat him in the same manner as a man would be treated who had taken another man's property by aggressive force. That is, the insurance company would have the right to use retaliatory force against the manufacturer, since he would be in wrongful possession of property which actually belonged to the insurance company. But, since this problem falls into the area of aggression and the rectification of injustices, which is covered in subsequent chapters, the manufacturer's case will be dropped at this point.

The moral principle underlying the insurance company's actions to collect from the manufacturer is this: When a man is willfully or negligently responsible for the loss of value(s) belonging to another individual, no one should gain from the default or aggression, but the party responsible for the loss should bear the major burden of the loss, as it was the result of his own dishonest and irrational behavior.

Neither the inventor nor the insurance company should profit from the manufacturer's dishonesty, as this would be to encourage dishonesty. And neither *does* profit. While the inventor is not forced to bear the financial burden of the manufacturer's default, he does suffer some inconvenience and probably also the frustration of some of his plans. The insurance company loses to some degree because it indemnifies the inventor immediately but must usually wait some time and perhaps even go to the expense of exerting some force to collect from the manufacturer. This principle is the same one which causes present day insurance companies to write deductible clauses into their coverage of automobiles, in order that none of the parties involved will profit from irrationality and carelessness and so be tempted to make a practice of such actions.

Neither the inventor nor the insurance company was responsible for the manufacturer's default, however, so neither the inventor nor the insurance company should bear the burden of paying for it. Especially should the insurance company not be left holding the bag if it is at all possible to collect from the guilty party, as the insurance company will simply be forced to pass the loss on to its other policyholders who are innocent of the whole affair. The manufacturer is guilty of the default, and the manufacturer should pay for it—in accordance with the moral law that each man should reap the reward or suffer the consequence of his own actions. Actions *do* have consequences.

It will be argued by statists that the free-market system of contract insurance would leave helpless individuals at the mercy of the predatory greed of huge and unscrupulous insurance companies. Such an argument, however, only demonstrates the statists' ignorance of the functioning of the free market. Insurance companies would be forced to be scrupulously just in all their dealings by the same forces which keep all businesses in a free market honest—competition and the value of a good reputation. Any insurance company which failed to defend the just interests of its policyholders would soon lose those policyholders to other, more reputable firms. And any insurance company which defended the interests of its policyholders at the expense of doing injustice to non-policyholders with whom they had dealings would soon lose its policyholders. No one would want to risk dealing with the policyholders of such a company as long as they held that brand of insurance, thus forcing them to change companies. Business ostracism would work as well against dishonest insurance companies as it would against a dishonest individual, and plentiful competition, plus the alertness of news media looking for a scoop on business news, would keep shady dealers well weeded out.

Arbitration of Disputes

Disputes which did not involve a contractual situation (but which didn't arise out of the initiation of force or fraud) would be much rarer than contractual disputes in a laissez-faire society. Examples of such disputes would be conflict over a land boundary or the refusal of a patient to pay for emergency medical care administered while he was unconscious—on the grounds that he hadn't ordered that particular kind of care. Non-contractual disputes would usually not involve insurance, but they would be submitted to arbitration in much the same manner as would contractual disputes.

In a non-contractual dispute, as in a contractual one, both parties would have to agree on the arbitration agency they wanted to employ, and they would have to bind themselves, contractually with the agency, to abide by its decision. If the disputants couldn't settle the matter themselves, it is unlikely that either one would refuse to submit to arbitration because of the powerful market forces impelling toward dispute-settlement. Disputed goods, such as the land in the boundary conflict, are less useful to their owners because of the lack of clear title (for example, the land couldn't be sold until the dispute was settled). But, more important than the reduced usefulness of disputed goods, the reputation of a man who refused arbitration without good reasons would suffer. People would hesitate to risk doing business with him for fear that they, too, would be involved in a protracted dispute.

As in the case of contractual disputes, the threat of business ostracism would usually be enough pressure to get the dispute submitted to arbitration. But occasionally, the accused might want to refuse arbitration; and he could be guilty, or he could be innocent. If an accused man were innocent, he would be very foolish to refuse to submit evidence of his innocence to representatives of the arbitration agency and, if necessary, defend himself at an arbitration hearing. Only by showing that his accuser was wrong could he protect his good reputation and avoid being saddled with a debt he didn't deserve. Also, if he could prove that he had been falsely accused, he would stand a very good chance of collecting damages from his accuser. If, however, the accused man were guilty, he might refuse arbitration because he feared that the arbiters would rule against him. If the accused did refuse arbitration and the injured party had good grounds for his case, he could treat this recalcitrant disputant just as he would treat a man who had stolen something from him—he could demand repayment (for details of how he would go about this and how repayment would be made, see Chapters 9 and 10).

In the matter of arbitration, as in any other salable service, the free-market system of voluntary choice will always be superior to government's enforcement of standardized and arbitrary rules. When consumers are free to choose, they will naturally choose the companies which they believe will give them the best service and/or the lowest prices. The profit and loss signals which consumer-buying practices send businesses guide these businesses into providing the goods and services which satisfy customers most. Profit/loss is the "error signal" which guides businessmen in their decisions. It is a continuous signal and, with the accurate and sophisticated methods of modern accounting, a very sensitive one.

But government is an extra-market institution—its purpose is not to make profits but to gain power and exercise it. Government officials have no profit and loss data. Even if they wanted to satisfy their forced "customers," they have no reliable "error signal" to guide their decisions. Aside from sporadic mail from the small minority of his constituents who are politically conscious, the only "error signal" a politician gets is the outcome of his re-election bids. One small bit of data every two to six years! And even this tidbit is hardly a clear signal, since individual voters may have voted the way they did because of any one of a number of issues, or even because they liked the candidate's sexy appearance or fatherly image. Appointed bureaucrats and judges, of course, don't even get this one small and usually confusing data signal; they have to operate completely in the dark.

This means that even the best intentioned government officials can't possibly match the free market in generating consumer satisfaction in any area. Government doesn't have, and by its nature can't have, the only signal system—profit and loss—which can accurately tell an organization whether it is giving consumers what they want. Because he lacks the profit/loss signal, no government official—including a government judge—can tell whether he's pleasing the "customers" by preserving or increasing their values, or whether he's harming them by destroying their values.

The best conceivable government, staffed by the most conscientious politicians, couldn't possibly handle the job of arbitrating disputes (or any other task) as can private enterprise acting in a free market.

8
Protection of Life and Property

Because man has a right to life, he has a right to defend that life. Without the right to self-defense, the right to life is a meaningless phrase. If a man has a right to defend his life against aggression, he also has a right to defend all his possessions, because these possessions are the results of his investment of time and energy (in other words, his investment of parts of his life) and are, thus, extensions of that life.

Pacifists deny that man may morally use force to defend himself, objecting that the use of physical force against any human being is never justifiable under any circumstances. They contend that the man who uses force to defend himself sinks to the same level as his attacker. Having made this assertion, they offer no evidence based on fact to prove it but merely treat it as an arbitrary primary, a given standard by which everything else must be judged.

To say that *all* use of force is evil is to ignore the moral difference between murder and self-defense and to equate the actions of a crazed thrill-killer with those of a man defending the lives of himself and his family. Such an absurd view, though supposedly based on a moral principle, actually completely disregards the moral principle of justice. Justice requires that one evaluate others for what they are and treat each person as he objectively deserves. One who has an uncompromising regard for justice will grant his respect and admiration to men of virtue, and his contempt, condemnation, and rational opposition to men whose behavior is harmful to human existence. To object verbally while non-violently submitting to an aggression is the behavior of a hypocrite whose talk and actions are diametrically opposed. In fact, hypocrisy is the pacifist's only real protection against his "moral" code.

To ignore the principle of justice is to penalize the good and to reward the evil. Pacifism encourages every thug to continue his violent ways, even though the pacifist may devoutly wish he wouldn't (wishes don't create reality). Pacifistic behavior teaches the aggressor that crime does pay and encourages him to more and bigger aggressions. Such sanctioning of injustices is immoral, and because it is immoral it is also impractical. A "free society of pacifists" would be short-lived, if it could come into existence at all. Such a society of helpless sheep would unwittingly call every wolf in the world to come and dine at their expense. Justice is indispensable to the perpetuation of a free society.

Since pacifism's failure to actively oppose injustice is immoral, it follows that every man has not only the right but the moral obligation to defend his life and property against aggression whenever it is feasible for him to do so. This is a personal obligation, because only the individual himself can know just what he values, how much he values it, and what other values he is willing to part with in order to defend it.

The fact that self-defense is a personal responsibility doesn't mean that every man must turn his home into an armed fortress and wear a six-shooter whenever he steps outside. Taking care of one's health is a personal responsibility, too (certainly no one else is responsible for seeing that I remain healthy), but this does not mean that every individual must take an extensive course in medical school, build his own hospital and perform surgery on himself whenever he needs an operation. A man assumes his respositivities by either taking care of the matter himself or, if that is impossible or impractical, hiring someone else to do it for him. This means that a man's right and responsibility to defend himself and his other values can be exercised for him by a hired agent so long as he, himself, designates that agent. The agent may take any actions which the man himself would have the right to take but may not do anything which the man would not have the right to do (such as the initiation of force against someone else).

Several advocates of liberty have proposed that this agent should be (or even must be) a "voluntary" government. By this they mean that the individuals in a society, seeing that they needed an agency of self-defense, would band together and set up a government which would be limited to acting as an agent to defend them. Each would then agree to forgo using retaliatory force on his own behalf (except in emergency situations) and to let the government defend him and be the final arbiter in any disputes he might have. Such a "voluntary" government, acting as nothing more than an agent of individual self-defense, may sound good on the surface but on examination proves to be unworkable because government, even the most limited government, is a coercive monopoly. An institution cannot at the same time be both coercive and voluntary. Even if it could manage to support itself without taxation, and even if it did not force people to buy its services, it would still have to prohibit competition in its area or it would cease to exist as a government. This "voluntary" government would be in the same position as a grocer who said to the people in his town, "You may voluntarily buy your groceries from me; you are free not to buy your groceries from me; but you may not buy them from anyone else." Thus, a "voluntary" government would "defend" its citizens by forcing them (either openly or subtly) to forgo defending themselves and to buy their defense only from it . . . at which point the citizens might be badly in need of someone to defend them from their "defenders."

The right to self-defense and the responsibility to defend oneself go hand in hand. A man can enter into a voluntary transaction, hiring someone else to do the job for him, but he cannot cede the responsibility to a coercive monopoly and still be free to exercise the right. The man who "hires" a government to be his agent of self-defense will, by his very act of entering into a relationship with this coercive monopoly, make himself defenseless against his "defender." A "voluntary government, acting as an agent of self-defense," is a contradictory and meaningless concept.

Advocates of government have objected that self-defense could not be the object of a market transaction because "force is different from all other goods and services—it is by its very nature an extra-market phenomenon and can never be a part of the market." This claim is based on two factors—when force is used, 1—the exchange is not a willing one, and 2—there is no mutual benefit to those involved in the exchange.

The error in this assertion springs from a failure to distinguish between initiated force and retaliatory force. A market phenomenon is a willing exchange of goods and/or services which does not involve the use of coercion by the parties to the transaction against anyone. It is true that *initiated* force is not and can never be a market phenomenon because it acts to destroy the market. But, *retaliatory* force not only does not act to destroy the market, it restrains aggressors who would destroy it and/or exacts reparations from them.

When an individual uses retaliatory force on his own behalf, his action is, of course, not a market phenomenon, any more than it is a market phenomenon when he fixes his own car. But if he hires an agent to protect him (with the use of retaliatory force if necessary), this action *is* a market phenomenon, just as the hiring of a mechanic to fix his car is.

For example, suppose a hard-working, private enterprise coin minter believes that he may be attacked and his business robbed. The minter performs a market transaction—he hires a big, husky guard. The contract between the minter and the guard involves the willing exchange of the minter's money for the guard's services. The guard's services consist of protection and, if necessary, active defense of the minter's person and property; that is, the guard agrees to take whatever retaliatory action is feasible to protect and defend his new employer from possible harm whenever force may be initiated against him. The next night an armed burglar breaks into the mint and attacks the minter, who is working late. The guard successfully wards off the attack by the use of retaliatory force and captures the burglar. In doing so, the guard fulfills in this particular instance his contractual agreement with the minter. It is obvious that the retaliatory force used by the guard is *a part of a market phenomenon*, by virtue of his contract with the minter.

Those who claim that "force is not a market phenomenon" consider the "exchange" of force between the guard and the burglar in complete isolation from the other circumstances of the case (they are guilty of dropping the context). It is true that the "exchange" between the guard and the burglar is not a willing one and that there is no mutual benefit derived from it—in fact, it is not even an exchange in the market sense. The exchange which *is* a market phenomenon is the coin minter's money for the guard's services; this exchange is a willing one, there is mutual benefit to both parties to the transaction, and neither of them *initiates* the use of physical force against anyone. The relationship between the minter and the guard is clearly a market phenomenon—a willing exchange of values which does not involve the use of coercion by the parties to the transaction against anyone.

Though force per se is not a market phenomenon, the hiring of an agent for self-defense is. The claim that "force can never be a part of the market" is so unclear that it has no intelligible meaning.

In a laissez-faire society, there would be no governmental police forces, but this does not mean that people would be left without protection except for what they could furnish for themselves. The market always moves to fill customers' needs as entrepreneurs look for profitable innovations. This means that private enterprise defense agencies would arise, perhaps some of them out of the larger private detective agencies of today. These companies have already proved their ability to provide efficient and satisfactory service, both in protection of values and the detection of crooks.

Compared (or contrasted) with a governmental police force, how well would a private enterprise defense agency perform its functions? To answer this question, one must first determine what are the functions of a private defense agency and of a governmental police force.

The function of a private defense service company is to protect and defend the persons and property of its customers from initiated force or any substitute for initiated force. This is the service people are looking for when they patronize it, and, if the defense agency can't provide this service as well or better than its competitors, it will lose its customers and go out of business. A private defense service company, competing in an open market, couldn't use force to hold onto its customers—if it tried to compel people to deal with it, it would compel them to buy protection from its competitors and drive itself out of business. The only way a private defense service company can make money is by protecting its customers from aggression, and the profit motive guarantees that this will be its only function and that it will perform this function well.

But, what is the function of a governmental police force? In dictatorships, it is obvious that the police force exists to protect the government. What little protection (if it can be called that) the citizens are given from private thugs is only to keep the society on an even keel so the rulers won't be shaken out of their comfortable positions. And, of course, the citizens aren't protected from their government at all.

It is commonly held that in democratic countries the function of the police is to protect the citizens. The police, however, don't actually *protect* people (except high ranking government officials—e.g., the President)—they only apprehend and punish some of the criminals *after* an act of aggression has been committed. If you suspect that a thug is planning to rob your home, the police will tell you, "Sorry, but we can't do anything until a crime has been committed." Only after you've been robbed and beaten can you call on the police to take action. And then, if they catch the thug, they won't even make him pay your hospital bills . . . they'll just lock him up for a while in a "school for crime," where he'll learn to do the job of robbing you more successfully next time.

Still, it is held that the police do protect honest citizens in an indirect way, because their very presence discourages crime (although the rapidly rising crime figures are beginning to make people wonder about this, too). But this theory fails to take into account the fact that governmental prohibitions, enforced by the police, create black markets, and black markets foster large-scale, organized crime (see Chapter 11). A black market is nothing more than a normal area of trade which the government has forbidden (usually under the pretense of "taking care of the people," who are presumably too stupid to look after themselves). People who trade on a black market are simply doing what they should never have been forbidden to do in the first place—they are trading for goods and services which they believe will increase their happiness, and they aren't bothering to ask permission from the politicians and bureaucrats. But a black market, though there is nothing intrinsically wrong with the goods being traded, is a forbidden market, and this makes it risky. Because of the danger, peaceful individuals are driven out of this forbidden area of trade, and men of violence, who dare to take the risks for the sake of the high profits, are attracted to it. Black markets attract, create, and support criminals, and especially large criminal gangs. In fact, organized crime finds its main support in black markets such as gambling, prostitution, and drugs. By enforcing laws which forbid men to trade peacefully as they please, the police *create* a social environment which breeds crime. The small-time burglar who is frightened away by the police is far outweighed by the Mafia boss who makes millions off the black market in prostitution and gambling, which activities are fraught with violence because of government prohibitions.

Not only do governmental police make possible more crime than they discourage, they enforce a whole host of invasive laws designed to make everyone behave in a manner which the lawmakers considered morally proper. They see to it that you're not permitted to foul your mind with pornography (whatever that is—even the courts aren't too sure) or other people's minds by appearing in public too scantily clad. They try to prevent you from experiencing the imaginary dangers of marijuana (in the '20s they protected you from liquor, but that's not a no-no any more). They even have rules about marriage, divorce, and your sex life.

No, the police don't offer the citizen any protection from such invasions of privacy . . . they're too busy enforcing the invasive laws! Nor do they protect him from the many governmental violations of his rights—if you try to evade being enslaved by the draft, the police will help the army, not you. The police prevent the establishment of an effective, private enterprise defense system which could offer its customers real protection (including protection from governments). In fact, they often prevent you from protecting yourself, as in New York City, where women, even in the most crime-ridden areas, are forbidden to carry effective self-defense devices. Guns, switch-blade knives, tear gas sprayers, etc., are illegal. Of course, the criminals ignore these laws, but the peaceful citizens are effectively disarmed and left at the mercy of hoodlums.

In addition to failing to protect citizens from either private criminals or the government, making it almost impossible for the citizens to protect themselves, encouraging crime by creating black markets, and invading privacy with stupid and useless "moral" laws, the police compel citizens to pay taxes to support them! If a citizen requests to be relieved of police "protection" and protests by refusing to pay taxes for the upkeep of the government and its police, the police will initiate force by picking him up and the government will fine and/or imprison him (unless he attempts to defend himself against the police's initiated violence, in which case his survivors will be forced to bury him at their expense). With the entire weight of the law behind them, this gives the police the safest protection racket ever devised.

If the police in a democracy don't exist to protect the citizens, what *is* their function? It is essentially the same as that of the police in a dictatorship—to protect the government. Since in a democracy the current government is always the product of the established social order, the function of police in a democracy is to protect the government by protecting the established social order—the Establishment—whatever it may be. And the police usually perform this function very well.

The superiority of a private enterprise defense service company springs from the fact that its function—its *only* function—is to protect its customers from coercion and that it must perform this function with excellence or go out of business.

Since the main aim of defense service companies would be to protect their customers, their primary focus would be on preventing aggression. They would furnish guards for factories and stores, and men to "walk the beat" on the privately owned streets. They would install burglar alarms with a direct connection to their office in both businesses and private homes. They would maintain telephone switchboards and roving patrol cars and perhaps even helicopters to answer calls for help. They would advise customers who felt themselves to be in danger on the most efficient and safest protective devices to carry in their particular case (from tear gas pens to pistols) and would offer help in obtaining them. They would probably eventually offer any client a small, personal alarm device which could be carried about in a pocket and would sound an alarm at the defense service's offices when activated. Besides these more ordinary services, each company would strive to develop new protective devices that were better than anything its competitors had . . . which would lead to tremendous frustration for would-be crooks.

For a private enterprise defense agency, prevention of aggression would be a profitable business, whereas punishment of aggressors in jails, government-style, would be a losing proposition. (Who would pay for the convicts' food and other upkeep if the revenues couldn't be forced out of taxpayers?[1]) But in a governmental society, the police don't reap any extra profits from the prevention of crime. In fact, too much crime prevention would reduce the police department's business (since their business is to apprehend and punish criminals,

---
[1] The correctional institutions which would develop in a laissez-faire society will be examined in Chapter 10.

which requires a good supply of criminals). In spite of propaganda to the contrary, the police can hardly be expected to be too eager to get rid of the high crime rate and overflowing jails—after all, a lot of police jobs are at stake.

But, because no amount of protection, no matter how excellent, can prevent all aggression, the defense service companies would have to be prepared to deal with initiated force and fraud. So, they would maintain detective bureaus, excellent criminal laboratories, extensive files on all known aggressors, and they would keep staffs of experts in all fields of scientific crime detection. They would also have the men and equipment to apprehend dangerous aggressors, as well as secure facilities for holding and transporting them. They might also have a part in running the correctional institutions. All these services would not only be efficient and effective, in contrast to those forced on us by governmental police, they would be considerably less expensive, too. Companies competing in a free market would be forced to produce at the lowest feasible cost—i.e., they would keep their prices at market level—or their competitors would run them out of business. This is in sharp contrast to socialized institutions which have no competition. Also, private defense service companies would not have to waste their resources enforcing all those foolish and tyrannical laws designed to compel everyone to "live a decent and moral life" (as, for example, the laws against liquor, drugs, gambling, prostitution, and nudity), to "protect the public" (licensing and anti-trust laws), or to support the vast structure of bureaucracy itself (tax laws).

Private defense service employees would not have the legal immunity which so often protects governmental policemen. If they committed an aggressive act, they would have to pay for it, just the same as would any other individual. A defense service detective who beat a suspect up wouldn't be able to hide behind a government uniform or take refuge in a position of superior political power. Defense service companies would be no more immune from having to pay for acts of initiated force and fraud than would bakers or shotgun manufacturers. (For full proof of this statement, see Chapter 11.) Because of this, managers of defense service companies would quickly fire any employee who showed any tendency to initiate force against anyone, including prisoners. To keep such an employee would be too dangerously expensive for them. A job with a defense agency wouldn't be a position of power over others, as a police force job is, so it wouldn't attract the kind of people who enjoy wielding power over others, as a police job does. In fact, a defense agency would be the worst and most dangerous possible place for sadists!

Government police can afford to be brutal—they have immunity from prosecution in all but the most flagrant cases, and their "customers" can't desert them in favor of a competent protection and defense agency. But for a free-market defense service company to be guilty of brutality would be disastrous. Force—even retaliatory force —would always be used only as a last resort; it would never be used first, as it is by governmental police.

In addition to the defense agencies themselves, there is one type of business which has a particular, vested interest in seeing that values are protected and aggressive violence held to a minimum, and which would, in a laissez-faire society, have a natural connection to the business of defense. This is the insurance industry.

There are two main reasons for the insurance companies' interest in the business of defense: 1—acts of aggressive violence result in expenses for insurance companies, and 2—the more secure and peaceful the society, the more value-production there will be, and the more value-production there is, the more things there will be which require insurance coverage, which means more insurance sales and more profits (which is the primary business aim of insurance companies). Furthermore, the concern of the insurance companies for a secure and peaceful environment is economy-wide; that is, their interest extends as far as their market is or is likely to be.

In a laissez-faire society, insurance companies would sell policies covering the insured against loss resulting from any type of coercion. Such policies would be popular for the same reason that fire and auto insurance are—they would provide a means of avoiding the financial disaster resulting from unexpected crises. Since the insurance companies couldn't afford to insure poor risks at the same rates they charged their other customers, insurance policies would probably specify certain standard protective measures which the insured must take in order to buy the policy at the lowest rates—burglar alarms connected to the defense service company's office, for example. Policies would also state that the insured must buy his protection from a defense agency which met the standards of the insurance company, to avoid having him hire an inefficient or fly-by-night defense agency at a cheap price while counting on his insurance to make up for any loss which their ineffectiveness caused him.

A man who carried insurance against coercion could call on a defense company for help in any emergency covered by the policy, and his insurance would pay the bill. Even if a man had no coercion insurance and no contractual arrangement with any defense company, if he were attacked by a thug he would be helped by any nearby defense company agent and billed later. This is no more a problem than is emergency medical care. Accident victims are always rushed to a hospital and given emergency care, regardless of whether they are able to ask for help and to pay for it. Victims of hoodlum attack would be aided by defense companies in much the same manner, both because of a respect for human life and because it would be good publicity for the defense companies involved.

Because of the close connection between insurance and defense, some of the larger insurance companies would probably set up their own defense service agencies in order to offer their clients the convenience of buying all their protection needs in the same package. Other insurance companies would form close ties with one or more independent defense service agencies which they had found to be effective and reliable, and they would recommend these agencies to their insurance customers. This close affinity between insurance and defense would provide a very effective check on any defense agency which had an urge to overstep the bounds of respect for human rights and to use its force coercively—i.e., in a non-defensive manner. Coercive acts are destructive of values, and value-destruction is expensive for insurance companies. No insurance company would find it in its interests to stand idly by while some defense agency exercised aggression, even if the values destroyed were insured by a competing company—eventually the aggressors would get around to initiating force against their own insureds . . . with expensive results!

Insurance companies, *without any resort to physical force,* could be a very effective factor in bringing an unruly defense agency to its knees via boycott and business ostracism. In a laissez-faire, industrialized society, insurance is vitally important, especially to business and industry, which are the most important segment of the economy and the biggest customers for any service. It would be difficult, indeed, for any defense company to survive if the major insurance companies refused to sell insurance not only to it, but to anyone who dealt with it. Such a boycott would dry up the major part of the defense company's market in short order; and no business can survive for long without customers. There would be no way for a defense agency to break such a boycott by the use of force. Any threatening or aggressive actions toward the insurance companies involved would only spread the boycott as other businesses and individuals attempted to stay as far away from the coercive agency as possible. In a laissez-faire society, where individuals are always free to act in their own rational self-interest, the gun cannot win out over the mind.

Of course, insurance companies would be reluctant to undertake such a boycott because it would be troublesome and would be likely to lose them a few customers. This means they would not take such a course unless they could clearly show that the defense agency in question was really at fault; if they could not prove its guilt, the boycott might turn against them instead, and they would have sawed

Protection of Life and Property

off the limb they were sitting on. But where there was clear evidence of coercive intent, their fear of further aggressions would sooner or later overwhelm their caution and they would make an investigation, marshall their facts, and take a stand. The news media would be eager for the story, of course, and would be a great help in spreading the word.

The powerful insurance companies, with their vast and varied resources and their vested interest in seeing values protected and aggressive violence held to a minimum, would act as a natural check upon the defense service agencies. (Other such checks will be examined in Chapter 11.) This is an example of how the market, *when left unhampered,* constantly moves toward a situation of maximum order and productivity. The market has its own built-in balancing mechanism which automatically keeps it running smoothly with the best long-range results for every peaceful individual. This mechanism would work as well in the area of value protection as it does in any other market area . . . government is only so much sand in the gears.

9
Dealing With Coercion

Throughout history, the means of dealing with aggression (crime) has been punishment. Traditionally, it has been held that when a man commits a crime against society, the government, acting as the agent of society, must punish him. However, because punishment has not been based on the principle of righting the wrong but only of causing the criminal "to undergo pain, loss, or suffering," it has actually been revenge. This principle of vengeance is expressed by the old saying, "An eye for an eye, a tooth for a tooth," which means: "When you destroy a value of mine, I'll destroy a value of yours." Present day penology no longer makes such demands; instead of the eye or the tooth, it takes the criminal's life (via execution), or a part of his life (via imprisonment), and/or his possessions (via fines). As can be readily seen, the principle—vengeance—is the same, and it inevitably results in a compound loss of value, first the victim's, then the criminal's. Because destroying a value belonging to the criminal does nothing to compensate the innocent victim for his loss but only causes further destruction, the principle of vengeance ignores, and in fact opposes, justice.

When an aggressor causes the loss, damage, or destruction of an innocent man's values, justice demands that the aggressor pay for his crime, not by forfeiting a part of his life to "society," but *by repaying the victim* for his loss, plus all expenses directly occasioned by the aggression (such as the expense of apprehending the aggressor). By destroying the victim's values, the aggressor *has created a debt* which he owes to the victim and which the principle of justice demands must be paid. With the principle of justice in operation, there is only one loss of value; and, while this loss must initially be sustained by the victim, ultimately it is the aggressor—the one who caused the loss—who must pay for it.

There is a further fallacy in the belief that when a man commits a crime against society, the government, acting as the agent of society, must punish him. This fallacy is the assumption that society is a living entity and that, therefore, a crime *can be* committed against it. A society is no more than the sum of all the individual persons of which it is composed; it can have no existence apart from, or in contradistinction to, those individual persons. A crime is always committed against one or more persons; a crime cannot be committed against that amorphous non-entity known as "society." Even if some particular crime injured every member of a given society, the crime would still have been committed against individuals, not society, since it is only the individuals who are distinct, separate, independent, living entities. Since a crime can only be committed against individuals, a criminal cannot be rationally regarded as "owing a debt to society," nor can he "pay his debt to society:" the only debt he owes is to the injured individual(s).

Every dispute is between aggressor(s) and victim(s); neither society nor its members as a group have any direct interest in the matter. It is true that all honest members of a society have a general interest in seeing aggressors brought to justice in order to discourage further aggression. This interest, however, applies not to specific acts of aggression but to the total social structure which either encourages or discourages acts of aggression. An interest in maintaining a just social structure does not constitute a direct interest in the solution of any particular dispute involving aggression.

Because crimes cannot be committed against society, it is fallacious to regard government as an agent of society for the punishment of crime. Nor can government be considered to be the agent of the individual members of society, since these individuals have never signed a contract naming the government as their agent. There is, therefore, no valid reason for government officials to be designated the arbiters of disputes and rectifiers of injustice.

Granted, we are used to the governmental punishment-of-crime, so that to many people it seems "normal" and "reasonable," and any other means of dealing with aggression seems suspicious and strange; but an unbiased examination of the facts shows that this governmental system is actually traditional rather than rational.

Since neither "society" nor government can have any rational interest in bringing a specific aggressor to justice, who *is* interested? Obviously, the victim—and secondarily, those to whom the victim's welfare is a value, such as his family, friends, and business associates. According to the principle of justice, those who have suffered the loss from an aggresive act should be compensated (at the aggressor's expense), and, therefore, it is those who have suffered the loss who have an interest in seeing the aggressor brought to justice.

The steps which the victim may morally take to bring the aggressor to justice and exact reparations from him rest on the right to property, which, in turn, rests on the right to life. A man's property is *his* property, and this fact of ownership is not changed if the property comes into the possession of an aggressor by means of an act of force. The aggressor may be in possession of the property, but only the owner has a moral right to it. To illustrate: Suppose that as you come out of a building you see a stranger in the driver's seat of your car, preparing to drive it away. Would you have the moral right to push him out and thus regain possession of your car by force? Yes, since the thief's temporary possession does not alter the fact that it is your property. The thief used a substitute for initiated force when he attempted to steal your car, and you are morally justified in using retaliatory force to regain it.

Suppose that instead of catching the thief immediately you are forced to chase him and your car for two blocks and only catch up with him as he's stopped by a train. Do you still have the right to push him out and regain your car? Yes, since the passage of time does not erode your right to possess your property.

Suppose instead that the thief gets away, but that two months later you spot him downtown getting out of your car. You verify by serial number that it is, indeed, your car. Do you have the moral right to drive it away? Yes; again the passage of time makes no difference to your property rights.

Suppose that instead of yourself it is the detective you have hired to recover the car who spots the thief getting out of it. The detective, acting as your agent, has the right to repossess your car, just as you would.

You find that a front fender and headlight of your car are smashed in, due to the aggressor's careless driving. Repairs cost you $150. Do you have the right to collect this amount from the aggressor? Yes, you were the innocent victim of an act of aggression; it is the thief, not the victim, who is morally obligated to pay all costs occasioned by his aggression.

To summarize: the ownership of property is not changed if the property is stolen, nor is it eroded by the passage of time. The theft, damage, or destruction of another person's property constitutes an act of coercion, and the victim has a moral right to use retaliatory force to repossess his property. He also has a right to collect from the aggressor compensation for any costs occasioned by the aggression. If he wishes, the victim may hire an agent or agents to perform any of these actions in his place.

It should be noted that aggression often harms not only the victim but also those who are closely associated with him. For example, when a man is assaulted and seriously injured, his family may be caused expense, as well as anxiety. If he is a key man in his business, his employer or his partners and/or his company may suffer financial loss. All this destruction of value is a direct result of the irrational behavior of the aggressor and, since actions do have consequences, the aggressor has the responsibility of making reparations for these secondary losses, as well as for the primary loss suffered by the victim. There are practical limits to the amount of these secondary reparations. First, no one would bother to make such a claim unless the reparations he hoped to be paid were substantial enough to offset the expense, time, and inconvenience of making the claim. Second, the total amount of reparations which can be collected is limited by the aggressor's ability to pay, and first consideration goes to the victim. For the sake of simplicity, only the victim's loss will be dealt with here, but all the principles and considerations which apply to him apply as well to any others who have suffered a direct and serious loss as a result of the aggression.

In the process of collecting from the aggressor, the victim (or his agents) may not carelessly or viciously destroy values belonging to the aggressor or take more from him than the original property (or an equivalent value) plus costs occasioned by the aggression. If the victim does so, he puts himself in debt to the aggressor (unless, of course, the aggressor has made the destruction inevitable by refusing to give up the victim's property without a fight).

If the accused aggressor claims he is innocent or that the amount of reparations claimed by the victim is excessive, a situation of dispute exists between them which may require arbitration. The conditions of such arbitration, the forces impelling both parties to accept it as binding, and the market guarantees of its justice will now be examined.

In a laissez-faire society, insurance companies would sell policies covering the insured against loss of value by aggression (the cost of the policy based on the worth of the values covered and the amount of risk). Since aggressors would, in most instances, pay the major costs of their aggression, the insurance companies would lose only when the aggressor could not be identified and/or apprehended, when he died before making full reparations, or when the reparations were too great for him to be able to pay in his lifetime. Since the companies would recover most of their losses and since aggression would be much less common in a free-market society, costs of aggression insurance would be low, and almost all individuals could afford to be covered. For this reason, we shall deal primarily with the case of an insured individual who becomes the victim of aggression.

Upon suffering the aggression (assuming that immediate self-defense was either impossible or inappropriate), the victim would, as soon as possible, call his insurance company. The company would immediately send an investigator to determine the validity of his claim and the extent of the loss. When the amount was ascertained, the company would fully compensate the victim within the limits of the terms of the insurance policy. It would also act where feasible to minimize his inconvenience—e.g., lend him a car until his stolen one is recovered or replaced—in order to promote customer good will and increase sales (anyone ever heard of a government police department doing this?).

When the terms of the policy had been fulfilled, the insurance company, exercising its right of subrogation, would attempt to identify and apprehend the aggressor in order to recover its losses. At this point, the victim would be relieved of any further responsibilities in the case, except possibly appearing as a witness at any arbitration hearings.

If necessary, the insurance company would use detectives to apprehend the aggressor. Whether it used its own company detectives or hired an independent defense service would depend on which course was more feasible under the circumstances. Obviously, a competitive private enterprise defense agency, whether an auxiliary of a particular insurance company or an independent firm hired by several insurance companies (as are some claims adjusting companies today) would be far more efficient at the business of solving crimes and apprehending aggressors than are the present governmental police departments. In a free market, competition impels toward excellence!

Upon apprehending the aggressor, the insurance company's representatives would present him with a bill covering all damages and costs. Their first approach would be as peaceful as the situation permitted, since force is a nonproductive expenditure of energy and resources and is, therefore, avoided by the market whenever possible. First, the insurance company's representatives would attempt a voluntary settlement with the accused aggressor. If he was obviously guilty and the amount of reparations requested was just, it would be in his interest to agree to this settlement and avoid involving an arbitration agency, since the cost of any arbitration would be added on to his bill if he lost in his attempt to cheat justice.

If the accused aggressor claimed innocence or wished to contest the amount of the bill and he and the insurance company's representatives could come to no agreement, the matter would have to be submitted to binding arbitration, just as would a contractual dispute. Legislation forcing the parties to submit to binding arbitration would be unnecessary, since each party would find arbitration to be in his own self-interest. Nor would it be necessary to have legal protection for the rights of all involved, because the structure of the market situation would protect them. For example, the insurance

Dealing With Coercion

company would not dare to bring charges against a man unless it had very good evidence of his guilt, nor would it dare to ignore any request he made for arbitration. If the insurance company blundered in this manner, the accused, especially if he were innocent, could bring charges against the company, forcing it to drop its original charges and/or billing it for damages. Nor could it refuse to submit to arbitration on his charges against it, for it would do serious damage to its business reputation if it did; and in a free-market context, in which economic success is dependent on individual or corporate reputation, no company can afford to build a reputation of carelessness, unreliability, and unfairness.

It is worthy of note here that the notion of always presuming a man innocent until he is proved guilty by a jury trial can be irrational and sometimes downright ridiculous. For instance, when a man commits a political assassination in plain sight of several million television viewers, many of whom can positively identify him from the films of the incident, and is arrested on the spot with the gun still in his hand, it is foolish to attempt to ignore the facts and pretend he is innocent until a jury can rule on the matter. Though the burden of proof always rests on the accuser and the accused must always be given the benefit of the doubt, a man should be presumed neither innocent nor guilty until there is sufficient evidence to make a clear decision, and when the evidence is in he should be presumed to be whatever the facts indicate he is. An arbiter's decision is necessary only when the evidence is unclear and/or there is a dispute which cannot be resolved without the help of an unbiased third party.

The accused aggressor would desire arbitration if he wanted to prove his innocence or felt that he was being overcharged for his aggression, since without arbitration the charges against him would stand as made and he would have to pay the bill. By means of arbitration, he could prove his innocence and thus avoid paying reparations or if guilty he would have some say about the amount of reparations. If innocent, he would be especially eager for arbitration, not only to confirm his good reputation, but to collect damages from the insurance company for the trouble it had caused him (and thereby rectify the injustice against him).

A further guarantee against the possibility of an innocent man being railroaded is that every individual connected with his case would be fully responsible for his own actions, and none could hide behind legal immunity as do governmental police and jailers. If you knew that a prisoner put into your custody to work off his debt could, *if innocent*, demand and get reparations from *you* for holding him against his will, you would be very reluctant to accept any prisoners without being fully satisfied as to their guilt.

Thus, the unhampered market would, in this area as in any other, set up a situation in which irrationality and injustice were automatically discouraged and penalized without any resort to statutory law and government.

The insurance company and the accused aggressor, as disputing parties, would mutually choose an arbitration agency (or agencies, in case they wished to provide for an appeal) and contractually bind themselves to abide by its decision. In the event they were unable to agree on a single arbitration agency, each could designate his own agency preference and the two agencies would hear the case jointly, with the prior provision that if they disagreed on the decision they would submit the case to a third agency previously selected by both for final arbitration. Such a course might be more expensive.

The insurance company could order its defense agency to incarcerate the accused aggressor before and during arbitration (which would probably be only a matter of a few days, since the market is always more efficient than the bumbling government), but in doing so they would have to take two factors into consideration. First, if the accused were shown to be innocent, the insurance company and defense agency would owe him reparations for holding him against his will. Even if he were judged guilty, they would be responsible to make reparations if they had treated him with force in excess of what the situation warranted; not being government agents, they would have no legal immunity from the consequences of their actions. Second, holding a man is expensive—it requires room, board, and guards. For these reasons, the defense company would put the accused aggressor under no more restraint than was deemed necessary to keep him from running off and hiding.

It would be the job of the arbitration agency to ascertain the guilt or innocence of the accused and to determine the amount of reparations due. In settling the reparations payment, the arbiters would operate according to the principle that justice in a case of aggression consists of requiring the aggressor to compensate the victim for his loss *insofar as is humanly possible*. Since each case of aggression is unique—involving different people, actions, and circumstances, reparations payments would be based on the circumstances of each case, rather than on statutory law and legal precedent. Although cases of aggression vary widely, there are several expense factors which, in varying combinations, determine the amount of loss and, thus, the size of the reparations.

A basic expense factor is the cost of any property stolen, damaged, or destroyed. The aggressor would be required to return any stolen property still in his possession. If he had destroyed a replaceable item, such as a television set, he would have to pay the victim an amount of money equal to its value so that the victim could replace it. If the aggressor had destroyed an item which couldn't be replaced but which had a market value (for example, a famous art work like the Mona Lisa), he would still have to pay its market value, even though another one couldn't be bought. The principle here is that, even though the value can never be replaced, the victim should at least be left no worse off financially than if he had sold it instead of losing it to a thief. Justice requires the aggressor to compensate the victim *insofar as is humanly possible*, and replacing an irreplaceable value is impossible.

In addition to the basic expense of stolen and destroyed property, an act of aggression may cause several additional costs, for which the aggressor would be responsible to pay. An aggressor who stole a salesman's car might cause the salesman to lose quite a bit of business—an additional financial cost. A rapist who attacked and beat a woman would be responsible not only for paying medical bills for all injuries he had caused her and reparations for time she might lose from work, but he would also owe his victim compensation for her pain and suffering, both mental and physical. Besides all debts owed to the primary victim, the aggressor might also owe secondary reparations to others who had suffered indirectly because of his actions (for example, the victim's family). In addition to these expenses, occasioned by the aggression itself, the aggressor would also be responsible for any reasonable costs involved in apprehending him and for the cost of arbitration (which would probably be paid by the loser in any case).

Since the arbitration agency's service would be the rendering of *just* decisions, and since justice is the basis on which they would compete in the market, the arbiters would make every attempt to fix reparations at a fair level, in accordance with market values. For instance, if the defense company had run up an excessively high bill in apprehending the aggressor, the arbiters would refuse to charge the aggressor for the excessive expense. Thus, the defense company would be forced to pay for its own poor business practices instead of "passing the buck" to someone else.

In case the reparations amounted to more than the aggressor could possibly earn in his lifetime (for example, an unskilled laborer who set a million dollar fire), the insurance company and any other claimants would negotiate a settlement for whatever amount he could reasonably be expected to pay over time. This would be done because it would be no profit to them to set the reparations higher than the aggressor could ever hope to pay and thus discourage him from working to discharge his obligation. It is worth noting here that quite a large percentage of a worker's pay can be taken for a long period of time without totally removing his incentive to live and work—at present the average American pays out well over a third of his income in taxes and expects to do so for the rest of his life, yet those who go on the government "welfare" dole are still in the minority.

Many values which can be destroyed or damaged by aggression are not only irreplaceable, they are also non-exchangeable—that is, they can't be exchanged in the market, so no monetary value can be placed on them. Examples of non-exchangeable values are life, a hand or eye, the life of a loved one, the safety of a kidnapped child, etc. When confronted with the problem of fixing the amount of reparations for a non-exchangeable value, many people immediately ask, "But how can you set a price on a human life?" The answer is that when an arbitration agency sets the reparations for a loss of life it isn't trying to put a monetary price on that life, any more than is an insurance company when it sells a $20,000 life insurance policy. It is merely trying to compensate the victim (or his survivors) to the fullest extent possible under the circumstances.

The problem in fixing reparations for loss of life or limb is that the loss occured in one kind of value (non-exchangeable) and repayment must be made in another kind (money). These two kinds of values are incommensurable—neither can be measured in terms of the other. The value which has been destroyed not only can't be replaced with a similar value, it can't even be replaced with an equivalent sum of money, since there is no way to determine what *is* equivalent. And yet, monetary payment is the practical way to make reparations.

It is useful to remember here that justice consists of requiring the aggressor to compensate his victims for their losses *insofar as is humanly possible*, since no one can be expected to do the impossible. Even a destroyed item which has a market value can't always be replaced (e.g., the Mona Lisa). To demand that justice require the impossible is to make justice impossible. To reject the reparations system because it can't always replace the destroyed value with an equivalent value is like rejecting medicine because the patient can't always be restored to as good a state of health as he enjoyed before his illness. Justice, like medicine, must be contextual—it must not demand what is impossible in any given context. The question, then, is not how arbiters can set a price on life and limb; it is, rather, "How can they see that the victim is fairly compensated, insofar as is humanly possible, without doing injustice to the aggressor by requiring overcompensation?"

In attempting to reach a fair compensation figure, the arbitration agency would act, not as a judge handing down a sentence, but as a mediator resolving a conflict which the disputants can't settle themselves. The highest possible limit on the amount of reparations is, obviously, the aggressor's ability to pay, short of killing his incentive to live and earn. The lowest limit is the total amount of economic loss suffered (with no compensation for such non-exchangeables as anxiety, discomfort, and inconvenience). The reparations payment must be set somewhere in the broad range between these two extremes. The function of the arbitration agency would be to aid the disputants in reaching a reasonable figure between these extremes, not to achieve the impossible task of determining the monetary value of a non-exchangeable.

Although the limits within which the reparations payment for a non-exchangeable would be set are very broad, the arbitration agency could not capriciously set the amount of reparations at any figure it pleased. An arbitration agency would be a private business competing in a free market, and the action of the market itself would provide guidelines and controls regarding the "price" of aggression, just as it does with any other price. Any free-market business, including an arbitration agency, can survive and prosper only as customers choose to patronize it instead of its competitors. An arbitration agency must be chosen by both (or all) disputants in a case, which means that its record of settling previous disputes of a similar nature must be more satisfactory, to both complainant and defendant, than the records of its competitors. Any arbitration agency which consistently set reparations too high or too low in the opinion of the majority of its customers and potential customers would lose business rapidly. It would have to either adjust its payments to fit consumer demand . . . or go out of business. In this way, arbitration agencies whose levels of reparation displeased consumers would be weeded out (as would any other business which failed to satisfy customers). Arbitration agencies which wanted to stay in business would adjust reparation levels to meet consumer demand. In a relatively short time, reparations payments for various non-exchangeable losses would become pretty well standardized, just as are charges for various kinds and amounts of insurance protection.

The manner in which the amount of reparations for a non-exchangeable value would be set by the action of the free market is very similar to the way in which the market sets any price. No good or service has an intrinsic monetary value built into it by the nature of things. A commodity has a particular monetary value because that amount of money is what buyers are willing to give for it and sellers are willing to take for it. "Value" means *value to the people who trade that commodity in the market.* All the traders determine what the price will be. In a similar way, the people who bought the services of arbitration agencies would determine the levels of reparations payments—the levels they considered just and fair compensation for various kinds of losses. It is impossible for us to foresee, in advance of the actual market situation, just where these levels would be set. But we can see, from a knowledge of how a free market operates, that the market would determine them in accordance with consumer desires.

Each reparation claim would be a complex combination of compensations for losses of various kinds of exchangeable and non-exchangeable values. For example, if a hoodlum beat a man and stole $100 from him, the aggressor would be required not only to return the $100 but also to pay the victim's medical bills, his lost earnings, compensation for pain and suffering, and reparations for any permanent injuries sustained. If the victim were a key man in his business, the aggressor would also have to pay the business for the loss of his services. Each reparation claim is also a highly individual matter, because the destruction of the same thing may be a much greater loss to one man than to another. While the loss of a finger is tragic for anyone, it is a much more stunning blow to a professional concert pianist than to an accountant. Because of the complexity and individuality of reparations claims, only a system of competing free-market arbitration agencies can satisfactorily solve the problem of what constitutes just payment for losses caused by aggression.

Murder poses a special problem in that it constitutes an act of aggression which, by its very nature, renders the victim incapable of ever collecting the debt owed by the aggressor. Nevertheless, the aggressor did create a debt, and the death of the creditor (victim) does not cancel this debt or excuse him from making payment. This point can be easily seen by supposing that the aggressor did not kill, but only critically injured the victim, in which case the aggressor would owe reparations for injuries sustained, time lost from work, physical disability, etc. But if the victim then died from his injuries before the debt could be paid, the debtor obviously would not be thereby released from his obligation.

In this connection, it is useful to recall what a debt actually is. A debt is property which morally belongs to one person but which is in the actual or potential possession of another. Since the debt occasioned by the attack on the victim would have been his property had he survived that attack, his death places it, together with the rest of his property, in his estate to become the property of his heirs.

In addition to the primary debt owed to the estate of the victim, the aggressor also owes debts to all those whom the victim's death has caused a direct and major loss of value (such as his family), even though such people may also be his heirs. (Not to pay reparations to heirs simply because they will also inherit the reparations which would have been paid the victim had he survived, would be like refusing to pay them because they would inherit any other part of the victim's property.)

But suppose an aggressor murdered a grouchy old itinerant fruit picker who had neither family, friends, nor aggression insurance. Would the aggressor "get off scott free" just because his victim was of value to no one but himself and left no heirs to his property? No, the aggressor would still owe a debt to the fruit picker's estate, just as he would if there were an heir. The difference is that, without an heir, the estate (including the debt occasioned by the aggression) becomes unowned potential property. In our society, such unowned potential property is immediately expropriated by the government, as is much other unowned wealth. Such a practice can be justified only if one assumes that the government (or "the public") is the original and true owner of all property, and that individuals are merely permitted to hold property by the grace and at the pleasure of the government. In a free-market society, unowned wealth would belong to whatever person first went to the trouble of taking possession of it. In regard to the debt owed by an aggressor to the estate of his victim, this would mean that anyone who wished to go to the trouble and expense of finding the aggressor and, if necessary, proving him guilty before professional arbiters, would certainly deserve to collect the debt. This function could be performed by an individual, by an agency specially constituted for this purpose (though it seems unlikely that there would be enough situations of this nature to support such an agency), or by a defense agency or an insurance company. Insurance companies would be most likely to take care of this kind of aggression in order to deter violence and gain customer good will.

Before taking up the means by which an aggressor would be forced to pay reparations (if force were necessary), the position of an uninsured victim of aggression will be examined briefly. Whenever a demand for a service exists, the market moves to fill it. For this reason, a man who was uninsured would also have access to defense services and arbitration agencies. But, although he would have a similar recourse to justice, the uninsured man would find that his lack of foresight had put him at a disadvantage in several ways.

The uninsured victim would not receive immediate compensation but would have to wait until the aggressor paid reparations (which might involve a span of years if the aggressor didn't have the money to discharge the debt immediately and had to pay it off in instalments). Similarly, he would run the risk of being forced to forgo all or most of his compensation if the aggressor were not caught, died before being able to complete payment, or had incurred a debt too large to pay during his life. Also, the uninsured victim would have to bear all costs of apprehending the aggressor and, if necessary, of arbitration, until the aggressor was able to pay them back.

In addition to these monetary disadvantages, he would be put to extra inconvenience. If he wished to collect reparations, he would have to detect and apprehend the aggressor himself or (more likely) hire a defence agency to do it for him. He would also have to make his own arrangements for arbitration. Taking everything into consideration, a man would find aggression insurance well worth the expense, and there is little doubt that most people would have it.

10
Rectification of Injustice

Since aggression would be dealt with by forcing the aggressor to repay his victim for the damage caused (whenever the use of force was required), rather than by destroying values belonging to the aggressor, the free market would evolve a reparations-payment system vastly superior to and different from the present governmental prisons.

If the aggressor had the money to make his entire reparations payment immediately or could sell enough property to raise the money, he would do so and be free to go his way with no more than a heavy financial loss. Situations of this kind, however, would probably be very rare, because aggression is expensive. Even a small theft or destruction can quickly pile up a fairly large debt when related expenses, secondary payments to others who suffered because of the victim's loss, cost of defense and arbitration, etc., are taken into account. In a totally free society, men tend to be financially successful according to their merit. Few successful men would desire to commit aggression. Few unsuccessful men could afford to make immediate payment for it.

Assuming the aggressor could not make immediate payment of his entire debt, the method used to collect it would depend on the amount involved, the nature of the aggression, the aggressor's past record and present attitude, and any other pertinent variables. Several approaches suggest themselves.

If the aggression were not of a violent nature and the aggressor had a record of trustworthiness, it might be sufficient to leave him free and arrange a regular schedule of payments, just as would be done for any ordinary debt. If the aggressor could not be trusted to make regular payments, a voluntary arrangement could be made between the insurance company, the aggressor, and his employer, whereby the employer would be compensated for deducting the reparations payment from the aggressor's earnings each pay period.

If the aggressor were unable to find or hold a job because employers were unwilling to risk hiring him, he might have to seek employment from a company which made a practice of accepting untrustworthy workers at lower than market wages. (In an economy of full employment, some companies would be motivated to adopt such a practice in order to reach new sources of labor. Although the price of their product would remain close to that of their competitors, as prices are determined by supply and demand, the wages they paid would necessarily be lower to compensate for the extra risk involved in hiring employees of dubious character.)

If the facts indicated that the aggressor was of an untrustworthy and/or violent nature, he would have to work off his debt while under some degree of confinement. The confinement would be provided by rectification companies—firms specializing in this field, who would maintain debtors workhouses (use of the term "prison" is avoided here because of the connotations of value-destruction attached to it). The labor of the men confined would be furnished to any companies seeking assured sources of labor, either by locating the debtors workhouses adjacent to their plants or by transporting the debtors to work each day. The debtors would work on jobs for wages, just as would ordinary employees, but the largest part of their earnings would be used to make reparations payments, with most of the rest going for their room and board, maintenance of the premises, guards, etc. To insure against refusal to work, the reparations payment would be deducted from each pay before room and board costs, so that if a man refused to work he would not eat, or at most would eat only a very minimal diet.

There would be varying degrees of confinement to fit various cases. Many debtors workhouses might provide a very minimum amount of security, such as do a few present-day prison farms where inmates are told, "There are no fences to keep you here; however, if you run away, when you are caught you will not be allowed to come back here but will be sent to a regular prison instead." Such workhouses would give the debtor a weekly allowance out of his pay, with opportunities to buy small luxuries or, perhaps, to rent a better room. Weekend passes to visit family and friends, and even more extended vacations, might be arranged for those who had proved themselves sufficiently trustworthy.

Other workhouses would provide facilities of greater security, ranging up to a maximum security for individuals who had proved themselves extremely violent and dangerous. A man whose actions had forced his confinement in such a workhouse would find himself at a disadvantage in several ways. He would find he had less liberty, less luxuries, limited job opportunities, and a longer period of confinement because, with more of his earnings spent on guards and security facilities, it would take him longer to pay off his debt.

Since there will be cases of mental imbalance even in the most rational of cultures, it is probably that there will be an occasional individual who will refuse to work and to rehabilitate himself, regardless of the penalties and incentives built into the system. Such an individual would be acting in a self-destructive manner and could properly be classified as insane. Obviously, neither the rectification company, the defense service that brought him to justice, nor the insurance company or other creditor has any obligation to go to the expense of supporting him (as victims are forced through taxation to do today). Nor would they wish to turn him loose to cause further destruction. And if they allowed him to die, they would cut off all hope of recouping the financial loss he had caused. What, then, could they do?

One solution that suggests itself is to sell his services as a subject of study by medical and psychiatric doctors who are doing research on the causes and cures of insanity. This should provide enough money to pay for his upkeep, while at the same time advancing psychological knowledge and ultimately offering hope of help for this aggressor and his fellow sufferers. If such an arrangement were made, it would be in the interests of all concerned to see that the aggressor received no ill treatment. In a rational culture, severe mental illness would be much rarer than it is in ours, and the medical-psychiatric team would not wish to damage such a valuable specimen. The rectification company in charge of the aggressor would be even more eager to protect him from harm, since no arbitration agency could afford the reputation of sending aggressors to a debtors workhouse where there was ill treatment of the inmates.

This free-market system of debtors workhouses would have numerous practical advantages over the Dark Ages barbarity of the present governmental prison system. These advantages are a necessary consequence of the fact that the system would be run for profit—from the standpoint of both the insurance companies and the rectification companies operating the workhouses. In a laissez-faire economy, it is impossible to make consistent profits over a long-range period unless one acts with maximum rationality, which means: with maximum honesty and fairness.

A practical example of this principle can be seen in the results of the insurance company's desire to recoup its loss quickly. Because it would be in the insurance company's interest to have the aggressor's reparations instalments as large as possible, it would have him confined to no greater degree than his own actions made necessary, since closer confinement means greater expense, which means less money left for reparations payments. Thus, it would be the aggressor himself who would determine, by his character and his past and present behavior, the amount of freedom he would lose while repaying his debt and, to a certain degree, the length of time it would take him to pay it. Furthermore, at any time during his confinement, should the aggressor-debtor show himself to be a good enough risk, the insurance company would find it in their interest to gradually decrease his confinement—an excellent incentive to rational behavior.

Because both the insurance companies and the rectification companies would want to run their businesses profitably, it would be in their interest to have debtors be as productive as possible. In an industrialized society, a laborer's productivity depends not on his muscles but on his mind, his skills. So the debtor would be allowed to work in an area as close to the field of his aptitudes as possible and encouraged to develop further productive skills by on-the-job training, night school courses, etc. All this would help prepare him for a productive and honest life once his debt was paid. Thus, the application of free-market principles to the problem of aggression provides a built-in rehabilitation system. This is in sharp contrast to government-run prisons, which are little more than "schools for crime," where young first offenders are caged with hardened criminals and there is no incentive or opportunity for rehabilitation.

A system of monetary repayment for acts of aggression would remove a great deal of the "profit" incentive for aggressors. A thief would know that if he were caught he would have to part with all his loot (and probably quite a bit of his own money, too). He could never just stash the booty, wait out a five year prison term, and come out a rich man.

The insurance company's desire for speedy repayment would be the aggressor-debtor's best guarantee against mistreatment. Earning power depends on productivity, and productivity depends on the use of the mind. But a man who is physically mistreated or mentally abused will be unwilling and even unable to use his mind effectively. A mistreated man is good for little more than brute physical labor—a situation of prohibitively low productivity.

Another strong guarantee of good treatment for the aggressor-debtor is that, in a laissez-faire society, every man would be fully responsible for his own actions. No guard in a debtors workhouse could beat a debtor and get away with it. The mistreated debtor could complain to a defense service agent or to the insurance company to whom he was making reparations. If he could prove his assertion of mistreatment, the guilty guard would soon find himself paying a debt to his former prisoner. Furthermore, the guard's employers would never dare to support their guard if the debtor had a good case, because if they knowingly permitted the guard's sadism the debtor could bring charges against them, too.

A guard in a government prison can treat the prisoners as less than animals and never be brought to account for it, because he is protected by his status as part of the policing arm of the government. But a guard in a debtors workhouse couldn't hide behind the skirts of the rectification company which employed him, the way the prison guard hides behind the skirts of the government. The debtors workhouse guard would be recognized as an individual, responsible for his own actions. If he mistreated a debtor in his custody, he would be held personally responsible, and he couldn't wriggle out of it by putting the blame on "the system."

A free-market system of dealing with aggression would operate with a maximum of justice precisely because it was based on the principle of self-interest. The entirety of a man's self-interest consists of rational thought and action and the rewards of such behavior; the irrational is never in man's self-interest. As long as a man is behaving rationally, he cannot intentionally harm any other noncoercive person. One of the reasons for the success of a laissez-faire society is that the free-market system impels men to act in their own rational self-interest to the extent that they wish to successfully paricipate in it. It thus rewards honesty and justice and penalizes dishonesty and the initiation of force. This principle would work just as well if the market were free to deal with the problem of aggression as it does when the market deals with the supply of food or the building of computers.

There have been several questions and objections raised concerning the proposal that payment for aggression be made in monetary terms. For instance, it has been objected that a thief could "get off the hook" simply by voluntarily returning the stolen item. But this is to overlook two important facts—additional expenses and loss of reputation. First, as long as the thief held the item in his possession he would be causing its owner inconvenience and expense, plus the ever-mounting cost involved in the owner's attempt to recover the item, all of which would be part of the debt created by the thief's act of aggression. In aggressive acts of any seriousness at all, it would be almost impossible for the aggressor to return the stolen item quickly enough to avoid incurring additional costs. For example, suppose a man stole $20,000 at gunpoint from a bank, but, regretting his action a few minutes later, came back and returned the money. Could he get by without paying any further reparations? No, because his irrational actions interrupted the bank's business and may have caused a financial loss, for which he is directly responsible. In order to get the money, he had to threaten force against the teller and possibly other bank employees and customers, so he would owe them **reparations** for endangering their lives and safety. Also, as soon as he left the bank, the teller undoubtedly tripped an alarm, summoning the bank's defense agency, so the aggressor is responsible for paying the cost of the defense agency's coming to answer the call, plus any other related expenses.

But the second factor, loss of reputation, would be even more damaging to the aggressor. Just as specialized companies would keep central files, listing poor contractual risks, they would also list aggressors so that anyone wishing to do business with a man could first check his record. Insurance companies in particular would make use of this service. So our bank robber would find insurance companies listing him as a very poor risk and other firms reluctant to enter into contracts with him. Thus, if a man were foolish enough to engage in such a whim-motivated action as this bank robbery, he would find that he had caused himself considerable expense and loss of valuable reputation but had gained absolutely nothing.

In a similar vein, it has been objected that a very rich man could afford to commit any number of coercive acts, since all he would lose would be a little of his vast fortune. It is a bit difficult to imagine such a mentally ill person being able to continue existing uncured and unchallenged in a predominantly rational culture, but, assuming that he did, he would immediately find that money was hardly the only loss his actions cost him. As soon as his career of aggression was recognized for what it was, no honest man would take the chance of having anything to do with him. The only individuals who would not avoid him like The Plague would be those who felt they were tougher or craftier than he, and their only purpose in risking an association with him would be to part him from as large a share of his money as possible. Furthermore, he would run an immense risk of being killed by some victim acting in self-defense. Considering his reputation for aggression, a man would probably be justified in shooting him for any threatening gesture. So, in spite of his ability to pay, his life would be miserable and precarious, and his fortune would probably dwindle rapidly.

Again, it has been said that if a man confined himself to thefts so petty that the recoverable amount would be smaller than the cost of recovering it, thus making prosecution of the case economically unfeasible, he could get away with a career of aggression (of sorts). But such a "bubblegum thief" would lose much more than he could possibly gain, because he would lose his good reputation as his acts of aggression were discovered and recorded.

In each of these incidents, it is obvious that the aggressor's loss of reputation would be at least as damaging as his financial loss and that his lost reputation could not be regained unless he made reparations for his aggressive act and showed a determination to behave more reasonably in the future. He might shrug off the financial loss, but the loss of a good reputation would force him to live a substandard life, cut off from insurance protection, credit, reputable business dealings, and the friendship of all honest persons.

All the foregoing objections to a monetary payment assume that it would not be sufficiently costly to deter aggression, or, in other words, that it is severity of punishment which deters aggression. The untruth of this assumption should be evident from an examination of such historical eras as Elizabethan England, in which punishments of extreme severity prevailed, including physical mutilation and hanging for petty theft. Yet in spite of the great loss of value imposed on criminals, crime rates were very high. The reason for this is that it is not severity, but justice, which deters aggression. To punish the aggressor with more severity than his actions warrant—that is, to impose on him a greater loss of value than that which is necessary for him to make reasonable reparations to the victim—is to commit an injustice against him. Injustice cannot be a deterrent to injustice. The aggressor who is treated with such excessive severity feels, quite rightly, that he has been victimized. Seeing little or no justice in his punishment, he feels a vast resentment, and often forms a resolve to "get even with society" as soon as possible. Thus, in dealing with aggression, excessive severity, as much as excessive laxity, can provoke further aggressive acts. The only valid answer to injustice, is justice! Justice cannot be served by excessive severity or by taking revenge against the aggressor, or by pacifism, but only by requiring the aggressor to pay the debt which he has created by his coercive action.

Dealing with a man justly helps him to improve himself and his life by inducing him to act in his own self-interest. In the case of an aggressor, justice induces him to want to, and be able to, live a productive, honest, non-coercive life, both while he is paying the debt he owes to his victim, and afterwards. Justice helps a man get on the right track by sending him the right signals. It penalizes him for his misdeeds—but only as much as he actually deserves. It also rewards him when he does the right thing. Injustice sends out incorrect signals which lead men astray. The injustice of letting an aggressor get away without paying for his aggressions teaches him to believe that "crime pays," which induces him to commit more and bigger crimes. The injustice of punishing an aggressor by making him pay more than he really owes the victim teaches the aggressor that he can't expect justice from others, so there's little point in his trying to treat them justly. He concludes that this is a dog-eat-dog world and that his best course is to "do it unto others before they do it unto him." Only justice sends the aggressor the right signals, so only justice can be a satisfactory deterrent to aggression.

It may be objected that some men will attempt to take advantage of a free-market system of dealing with aggression. This is true, as it is true of any other social system. But the big advantage of any action of the free market is that errors and injustices are self-correcting. Because competition creates a need for excellence on the part of each business, a free-market institution must correct its errors in order to survive. Government, on the other hand, survives not by excellence but by coercion; so an error or flaw in a governmental institution can (and usually will) perpetuate itself almost indefinitely, with its errors usually being "corrected" by further errors. Private enterprise must, therefore, always be superior to government in any field, including that of dealing with aggressors.

11
Warring Defense Agencies and Organized Crime

Some opponents of a laissez-faire society have contended that, because a governmentless society would have no single, society-wide institution able to legitimately wield superior force to prevent aggression, a state of gang warfare between defense agencies would arise. Then (as they argue), brute force, rather than justice, would prevail and society would collapse in internecine conflict. This contention assumes that private defense service entrepreneurs would find it to their advantage, at least in some circumstances, to use coercive, rather than market, means to achieve their ends. There is a further, unstated assumption that governmental officials would not only prevent coercion but would themselves consistently refrain from initiating force (or that the force they initiated would be somehow preferable to the chaos it is feared would result from an unhampered market).

The second of these assumptions is obviously groundless, since (as was shown in Chapter 4) government is a coercive monopoly which must initiate force in order to survive, and which cannot be kept limited. But what of the first assumption? Would a free market system of value-protection lead to gang warfare between the competing defense companies?

The "gang warfare" objection has been raised in regard to theories advocating a system of competing governments. When applied to any type of governments, the objection is a valid one. A government, being a coercive monopoly, is always in the position of initiating force simply by the fact of its existence, so it is not surprising that conflicts between governments frequently take the form of war. Since a government is a coercive *monopoly,* the notion of more than one government occupying the same area at the same time is ridiculous. But a laissez-faire society would involve, not governments, but private businesses operating in a free market.

All actions have specific consequences, and the nature of these consequences is determined by the nature of the action and by the context in which it takes place. What would be the consequences for a free-market defense company which committed an act of aggression in a laissez-faire society?

Suppose, for example, that the Old Reliable Defense Company, acting on behalf of a client who had been robbed of his wallet, sent its agents to break into and search every house in the client's neighborhood. Suppose further that the agents shot the first man who offered resistance, taking his resistance as proof of guilt.

The most immediate consequence of the aggression is that the defense company either does or does not realize its objective (in this case, the return of the wallet, together with damages), depending on the circumstances and the amount of counter-force it meets with. But this is only the first of several important consequences springing directly from the aggression.

Not only has Old Reliable's action put it in the precarious position of being a target of retaliatory force, it has also made the company the subject of severe business ostracism. All honest and productive individuals and businesses will immediately dissociate themselves from Old Reliable, because they will fear that any disagreement which may arise in their business dealings with it may turn its aggressive force against them. Further, they will realize that, even if they manage to remain on good terms with Old Reliable, they are in danger of becoming accidental casualties when retaliatory force is exercised by some indignant victim of Old Reliable's aggressions.

But there is an even stronger reason which will persuade Old Reliable's customers and business associates to quickly sever all relations with it. In a laissez-faire society, as has been pointed out, a good reputation is the most valuable asset any business or individual can have. In a free society, a man with a bad reputation would have a hard time getting customers, business associates, or credit and insurance at rates he could afford. Knowing this, no one would wish to risk his personal reputation or the business reputation of his firm by having any dealings with a known aggressor.

Insurance companies, a very important sector of any totally free economy, would have a special incentive to dissociate themselves from any aggressor and, in addition, to bring all their considerable business influence to bear against him. *Aggressive violence causes value loss,* and the insurance industry would suffer the major cost in most such value losses. An unrestrained aggressor is a walking liability, and no insurance company, however remotely removed from his original aggression, would wish to sustain the risk that he might aggress against one of its own clients next. Besides, aggressors and those who associate with them are more likely to be involved in situations of violence and are, thus, bad insurance risks. An insurance company would probably refuse coverage to such people out of a foresighted desire to minimize any future losses which their aggressions might cause. But even if the company were not motivated by such foresight, it would still be forced to rate their premiums up drastically or cancel their coverage altogether in order to avoid carrying the extra risk involved in their inclination to violence. In a competitive economy, no insurance company could afford to continue covering aggressors and those who had dealings with aggressors and simply pass the cost on to its honest customers; it would soon lose these customers to more reputable firms which could afford to charge less for their insurance coverage.

What would loss of insurance coverage mean in a free economy? Even if the Old Reliable Defense Company (or any other business or individual) could generate enough force to protect itself against any aggressive or retaliatory force brought against it by any factor or combination of factors, it would still have to go completely without several economic necessities. It could not purchase insurance protection against auto accidents, natural disasters, or contractual disputes. It would have no protection against damage suits resulting from accidents occurring on its property. It is very possible that Old Reliable would even have to do without the services of a fire extinguishing company, since such companies are natural outgrowths of the fire insurance business.

In addition to the terrific penalties imposed by the business ostracism which would naturally follow its aggressive act, Old Reliable would have trouble with its employees. Government employees are legally protected from suffering any personal consequences as a result of all but the most blatant of the aggressive acts which they perpetrate "in the line of duty." Such functionaries as police officials, judges, and Internal Revenue and narcotics agents can initiate force with immunity simply by taking protection under such cliches as "I don't write the law; I just enforce it," or "That's a matter for a jury to decide," or "This statute was passed by the duly elected representatives of the people." But employees of a free-market defense company would have no such legal immunity from retaliatory force; they would have to assume responsibility for their own actions. If a defense service agent carried out an order which involved the intentional initiation of force, both the agent and the entrepreneur or manager who gave him the order, as well as any other employees knowledgeably involved, would be liable for any damages caused. Since he could not take refuge in "the system," no honest defense service employee would carry out an order which involved the *initiation* of force (nor would an honest employer give such an order or sanction such action on the part of his employee). Thus, if Old Reliable managed to keep any employees at all, or to hire any new ones to replace those who had left, it would have to settle for people who were either terribly stupid or desperate enough to believe they had nothing to lose by being associated with aggression—in other words, simpletons and hoodlums.

In a laissez-faire society, a defense company which committed aggression, unless it acted speedily to rectify the injustices, would be left with no customers, associates, or employees except for undesirables. This raises the question of whether the criminal element in a laissez-faire society would, or even could, support their own "Mafia" defense company for the purpose of defending them against the retaliatory force of their victims.

Only a man who was willing to be openly identified as an aggressor would buy the services of such a "Mafia" defense agency, since the nature of the activities and clients of such a defense agency could not be kept hidden. This open aggressor would have to support himself entirely by aggression, because no honest man would take the chance of having business dealings with him. Furthermore, he would have to be existing very well financially, since the cost of protecting a man continually involved in acts of violence would be extremely high.

It is reasonable to conclude, therefore, that the only clients of such a "Mafia" defense company would be highly successful, big time, open aggressors. Since an aggressor could hardly hope to obtain that much money all by himself, the existence of such men presupposes the existence of a fairly extensive, well organized network of lesser hoodlums working for the "big operators." In other words, organized criminal gangs would be required to provide sufficient support for a "Mafia" defense company.

Although such an organized criminal gang may enter into many fields, organized crime finds its basic support in black market activities. A black market is any area of the market which is legally prohibited. If left unprohibited, it would be an area of trade involving peaceful, willing exchanges between sellers and buyers. But when government initiates force by forbidding this area of trade to honest men, it throws it open to men who are willing to take the risk of violating bureaucratic dictates and the statutory laws of the politicians. The violence and fraud associated with any black market do not spring from the nature of the good or service being sold; they are a direct result of the fact that entrepreneurs have been legally forbidden to deal in this area of the market, leaving it open to men who dare to ignore prohibitions and who are willing to resort to violence in order to do business without getting caught. Unless prohibited, every market activity is operated on the basis of willing exchange, without the initiation of force, because this is the only way a business can be operated successfully, as *force is a nonproductive expenditure of energy.*

An excellent example of a black market occurred during the Prohibition era of the 1920s. When government prohibited the manufacture and sale of liquor, an area of the market was arbitrarily closed to anyone who wished to remain law-abiding. Since there was still a market demand for liquor, hosts of criminals were attracted and created to fill the vacuum. Numerous gangs, including the Mafia, were founded and/or grew into organizations of immense power on the basis of the black market afforded by the Prohibition Amendment of the U. S. Constitution. Many of these organized criminal gangs are still with us; although they lost a great deal of their base with the repeal of Prohibition, they were able to survive by shifting the major part of their activities to other governmentally forbidden areas, such as gambling and prostitution. (It is interesting to note that the two organizations which fought hardest against the repeal of Prohibition were the Women's Christian Temperance Union and the Mafia!)

There is a compelling reason why organized crime must base its support in black market activities. Wealth does not exist in nature but must be created. The only means of creating wealth is value-production and free exchange—the manufacture and trade of some desired good or service. One may obtain wealth directly, by productive work, or one may obtain it indirectly, by looting it from a producer, but the wealth must be created by production in the first place in order to exist at all. The looter is a parasite who will not create his own wealth and its consequent power but is dependent on some producer to furnish it. This means that looting cannot be a profitable business in the long run (to the extent that producers are not disarmed by a false ideology—such as pacifism—or by being legally prohibited from acting in their own defense). *Producers* are the ones who hold the source of wealth and power, and in any long-range contest between looters and non-disarmed producers the weight of wealth and power must be on the side of the producers.

This is the reason that an organized hoodlum gang cannot support its large size and relatively complex structure by acts of aggression alone; the risk inevitably outweighs the profit (and this would be particularly true in a society where value-protection was a service sold in a competitive, free market). Such a gang can only support itself by obtaining its wealth directly, through production and trade in some black market. Thus, *organized* crime depends for its existence on black markets . . . *which are the result of government prohibitions.* Without *government-caused* black markets, criminals would have to operate singly or in small groups because they would have no area of production and trade to furnish support for large and complex organizations. So it is clear that the criminal element in a laissez-faire society couldn't possibly support a "Mafia" defense company.

It is also worth noting that much of the success of organized crime in our present society is due to the alliances which crime bosses are able to make with government officials on nearly all levels. From the $50 pay-off to the local cop, clear up to the $10,000 contribution to the senator's campaign fund, organized crime regularly protects itself by buying off governmental opposition. In a laissez-faire society, aggressors would not only be scattered, weak, and unorganized, they would find it next to impossible to buy off free-market protection and arbitration agencies. The customers of a defense company don't have to keep patronizing it if they find out that some of its employees have been accepting payoffs from aggressors. They are free to do what citizens can never do—find some other agency to protect them. A free-market agency, unlike a government, couldn't afford to have underworld connections, even with the small and unimportant "underworld" of a free society. When the news media revealed its shady dealings, its customers would all desert it, and the aggressors wouldn't be able to keep it in business . . . for the simple reason that the criminal element in a laissez-faire society would be too small and weak to support a "Mafia" defense company.

But even though a "Mafia" defense company could not exist in a free-market society, wouldn't it be possible for some respectable defense agency to attain a position of monopoly and then begin exercising its powers in a tyrannical manner? Of course there is some possibility that any social structure can be subverted—anything which some men can build, other men can find a way to destroy. What obstacles would a would-be tyrant (or group of tyrants) have to overcome in order to gain control of a free society?

First, the would-be tyrant would have to gain control of the defense company he intended to use, and it would have to be one which controlled a fairly strong army or had the means to build one. Even if he inherited the business lock, stock, and bankroll, he would still not control it in the same way that a government controls its bureaucrats and armies, because he would have no way of guaranteeing his employees immunity from retaliation if they committed coercive acts for him. Nor would he be able to hold his employees (as a government can with its conscript soldiers) if they objected to his orders or feared to carry them out.

But if this would-be tyrant were clever and subtle enough either to gain the loyalty of his employees or to keep them from realizing what he was about, he would still have only begun his task. In order to have sufficient power to carry out his schemes, he would have to gain monopoly or near-monopoly status. He could only do this by becoming the most efficient and excellent entrepreneur in his field; and he would have to continue this excellence, even after he had gained monopoly status, to prevent other large businesses from diversifying into his field to reap the benefits of higher profit margins. This means that our would-be tyrant couldn't charge his customers high prices in order to amass a fortune to buy weapons and hire soldiers to further his schemes of conquest.

In fact, the would-be tyrant's customers would probably be more of an obstacle to his ambitions than his employees would. He couldn't extract taxes from them, as a government does, and, at least until he reached the stage of full power, he couldn't even force them to buy his service and support his company at all. A market relationship is a free relationship, and if a customer doesn't like a company's service or mistrusts its goals, he is free to take his business elsewhere, or to start his own competitive company, or to do without the service altogether and just provide for himself. Furthermore, customers aren't imbued with the citizens' spirit of patriotic fervor and obedience and are, thus, much harder to lure into foolish collectivistic endeavors (such as "national unity"). Free men aren't in the habit of leaping like fools and sheep to "defend the Flag" or to "sacrifice for the Cause." In these vitally important respects, the free-market system differs fundamentally and completely from a government system of any sort.

The would-be tyrant might try to build his forces in complete secrecy until he was ready to make his coup, but he would find this far from easy. Imagine amassing the cash to buy guns, tanks, airplanes, ships, missiles, and all the other paraphernalia of modern warfare. Imagine finding such items and making deals to purchase them or have them manufactured. Imagine hiring and equipping a large force of soldiers and training them for months. Then imagine doing all this in complete secrecy while alert members of the news media were continually nosing around for a big story! If you can imagine such a thing, your ability at fantasizing is remarkable, indeed.

The fear of a tyrant is a very real one, and, in the light of history, it is well justified. But, as can be seen from the foregoing examination, it applies to a governmentally run society rather than to a free society. *The objection that a tyrant might take over is actually a devastating argument against government.*

12
Legislation and Objective Law

It has been objected by advocates of government that a laissez-faire society, since it would have no legislative mechanism, would lack the objective laws necessary to maintain social order and justice. This is to assume that objective law is the product of the deliberations of some legislative body, and this assumption, in turn, springs from a confusion about the meaning and nature of law.

The adjective "objective" refers to that which has an actual existence in reality. When used to refer to the content of one's mind, it means ideas which are in accordance with the facts of reality. Mental objectivity cannot be "apart from the human mind," but it is the product of perceiving the facts of reality, integrating them in a noncontradictory manner into one's consciousness, and, thereby, reaching correct conclusions. The truth to be noted here is that the mind does not create reality; the function of human consciousness is to perceive reality—reality is the object, not the subject, of the reasoning process. (As students of philosophy will recognize, this paragraph notes the distinction between metaphysical objectivity and epistemological objectivity.)

Objective laws, then, are rules, or principles, which are expressions of the nature of reality; they are not the expressions of the subjective whims and prejudices of some person or group of people or of the culture as a whole. An objective law is reality-centered. It springs from the nature of the entities and processes to which it relates and can never conflict with that nature. For this reason, an objective law always "works," while a law based on subjective whim, not firmly tied to reality, contradicts the nature of that to which it relates and so leads to confusion and destruction.

Because it is reality-centered, an objective law is always understandable to a man using his reason—that is, it always makes sense. It is also moral when regarding a principle of human behavior, because it operates in accordance with the nature of man and so acts to further his life, his welfare, and his interests as a rational being. With regard to human behavior, objective law, because it springs from the nature of reality—from things as they really are—must be practical, rational, and moral.

It is true that objective laws governing the nature of human relationships are necessary for the maintenance of societal order, but to conclude from this that statutory laws formulated by some legislative body are necessary for societal order is to be guilty of a non sequitur. In order to understand the nature of this non sequitur, it is necessary to examine two kinds of law—statutory law and natural law.

A natural law is a causal attribute which governs an entity's actions, which attribute is inherent in that entity's specific nature (the adjective "natural" means "of or pertaining to the nature of"—to what a thing is in reality). Since it is inherent in the nature of the entity to which it relates, natural law is always objective. It cannot help being reality-centered, because it is inherently inseparable from the nature of a real thing. This means that it's practical—it must always "work," because it relates to things as they really are (it could hardly relate to things as they really aren't). Natural law can't be repealed, nor does it have any loopholes. A man who "breaks" a natural law does so at his own peril. Immediately or eventually, it will break him.

A familiar example of natural law is the law of gravity. It is the nature of the earth to attract other bodies to itself, so when you drop something, it falls. This law is objective, universal, and inescapable. You may fly an airplane by making use of the natural laws of aerodynamics, but you have not thereby contradicted or repealed the law of gravity—the earth is still pulling downward on your plane, as you will discover if your engine fails.

Natural law applies to man as well as to his environment, because man is also an entity with a specific nature. Some actions are possible to man, and some are not. He can walk and run, but he can't turn into a pine tree. Since he is a being with a specific nature, man requires a specific course of action for his survival and well-being. He must eat or he will starve. His body requires certain substances to remain healthy—vitamin C to prevent scurvy, for example. If he wants to know something, he must use his senses and his mind to learn it. If he wants the great survival-values of friendship, trade, division of labor and sharing of knowledge, he must seek and merit human companionship.

While it is generally recognized that man's physical and even his mental nature are subject to the rule of natural law, it is just as generally assumed that the area of morality, and specifically moral human relationships, is completely outside the scope of natural law. This assumption is held tacitly, rather than being identified and defended, simply because it *can't* be rationally defended. It is completely foolish to assert that man is a being with a specific nature and therefore subject to the rule of principles derived from that nature in all areas . . . *except* when he deals with other men. Do men cease to have a specific nature when they come into relationship with other men? Of course not!

Natural law *does* apply to human relationships, and it is just as objective, universal, and inescapable in this area as in any other. The proof of this is that actions have consequences . . . in the area of human interaction as surely as in the area of human medicine. A man who swallows poison will become ill (even if he has complete confidence that the poison is nothing more than vitamin pills). A man who aggresses against others will be distrusted, avoided, and probably made to repay his victims (if some government doesn't interfere). A man who cheats his customers will be driven out of business by his more reputable competitors. The consequences of "breaking" natural law cannot be avoided. No matter how cleverly a man schemes, he will suffer if he insists on acting in a manner which contradicts the nature of human existence. The consequences may not be immediate, and they may not be readily apparent, but they are inescapable.

The free market is a product of the working of natural law in the area of human relationships, specifically economic relationships. Because man's survival and well-being are not given to him, but must be achieved, men act to maximize their welfare (if they didn't they couldn't keep on living). To maximize their welfare, they trade with other men, and when they trade, each man tries to get the best possible "deal." Buyers bid against each other and push prices up. Sellers bid against each other and push prices down. At the point where the two forces meet, the market price is set, and everyone who wants to trade at that price can do so without creating surpluses or shortages. Thus, the law of supply and demand, and all other market laws, are really natural laws, directly derived from the nature and needs of that specific entity, man. The fact that market laws are natural laws explains why the free market works so well without any outside regulation. Natural law is always practical—it always "works."

Government is an artificial construct which, because of what it is, is in opposition to natural law. There is nothing in the nature of man which demands that he be governed by other men (if there were, then we would have to find someone to govern the governors, for they, too, would be men with a need to be governed). In fact, the nature of man is such that, in order to survive and be happy, he must be able to make his own decisions and control his own life . . . a right which is unavoidably violated by governments. The ruinous consequences of government's inescapable opposition to natural law are written in blood and human degradation across the pages of all man's history.

Legislation and Objective Law

The operations of natural law in human relationships are much less apparent in a governmental society than in a laissez-faire society, because government, in an effort to get something for nothing, tries to dissolve or ignore the laws of cause and effect and so obscures the consequences of many actions (particularly bad ones). Politicians want power which they have no right to and plaudits which they have not earned, so they promise money which isn't theirs and favors they have no business granting. For instance, they promise to raise the wages of labor (a thing which only an increase in production can do, since the money for wages can't come out of nothing). When they pass a minimum wage statute, they seem to have bypassed natural-economic law, but actually they've only obscured it. Employers are forced to compensate for the wage increases to some of their employees by laying off others, which creates a class of jobless, hopeless poor. Wage rates go up for some at the expense of falling to zero for others. Natural law can't be legislated out of existence, no matter how hard the politicians try, because it is inherent in the nature of things. Natural law is just as operative in a governmental society as it would be in a laissez-faire one; it is simply harder to trace because of the complicated meddlings of the bureaucrats.

The tacit assumption that natural law does not apply to human relationships has led men to the belief that society must have a system of statutory laws to "fill the gap" and maintain social order. At the very least, it is believed that statutory law is necessary to codify natural law so that it will be objective, of universal application, and easily understood by all.

Statutory law is a code of rules established and enforced by governmental authority. Any particular statutory law may be based on an objective principle, or it may be based on a principle which is contrary to the nature of reality. It may even be a range-of-the-moment measure with no basis in any sort of principle at all (such laws are characteristic of governments when they feel themselves to be in crisis situations). There is nothing which can be built into the nature of a government which will guarantee that all, or even a majority, of the laws it passes will be based on objective principles—in fact, history shows that the reverse is usually the case; most laws are based on the subjective whim of some politician.

Statutory laws which are not based on objective principles are immoral and inescapably harmful; anything which is in opposition to reality—to things as they really are—can't work. Laws which are based on objective principles are merely a legal restatement of natural law, and are thus unnecessary. A man can identify a natural law, and he can even write it down in a textbook for other men to understand, but he cannot "pass" it because it already exists—inescapably. Once the natural law has been identified and understood, nothing more can be added by restating it in legal form and "making it compulsory." It already is compulsory, by its very nature.

A statutory law, even one based on an objective principle, must be written *before* the occurrence of the crimes which it is designed to inhibit or punish. Since every crime is committed by a different individual in a different set of circumstances, the law cannot possibly be made to fit all cases (except, perhaps, by making it so flexible as to nullify it altogether). This means that, although the *principle* behind the law was objective (reality-centered), the *application* of the law to specific circumstances cannot be objective. An objective principle is firm and unchanging because it is rooted in the nature of things, but the application of this unchanging principle must vary to fit the circumstances of various cases. Unless the application fits the case, it is non-objective and, therefore, unjust.

No matter how learned a body of legislators or how long and assiduously they debate, they can never reach the state of omniscience necessary to predict and allow for every circumstance of every individual case which will ever come within the jurisdiction of their law. In fact, by the very act of writing down the provisions of the law and making them binding on everyone in an equal manner regardless of individual variations, legislators freeze the application of their law so that it cannot be objective. Thus, no statutory law, even if based on objective principle, can be objective in its application.

Legislators are aware of the necessity of making laws flexible to fit a range of cases, and they do their best to solve this problem. They try to foresee and provide for as many situations as possible as they write each law, and they usually stipulate flexible punishments (a prison sentence of from two to ten years, for instance) which leaves the final decision up to the judge of each case. This sincere attempt, however, has the inevitable effect of making the law voluminous, complex, unwieldy, and difficult to interpret or even read. Legislation becomes bogged down in reams of words and men are often convicted or released on the basis of nothing more than the technical interpretation of an obscure wording in some statute. In an effort to be sufficiently flexible and yet totally precise, legislators often write laws of such appalling and complicated intricacy that even lawyers (who prosper in direct proportion to the size and complexity of the legal system) are confused. There are tens of thousands of complicated statutes, each in legal terms so specialized that it might as well be in a foreign language, and yet the puzzled citizen is curtly told that ignorance of the law is no excuse!

The attempt to make legislation flexible enough to fit individual cases also nullifies the universality of the law. A judge who has the

Legislation and Objective Law 121

option of giving a sentence which may be anywhere from two to ten years has nothing to guide him in his choice except his own private beliefs. Some judges are habitually lenient, and some habitually harsh, so that the fate of the accused usually depends as much on the personality and mood of his judge as on the actual circumstances of the case. Changing from a system of punishment in the form of prison sentences to a system of justice in the form of reparations payments to the victims would do nothing to solve this problem as long as the legal-judicial mechanism remained a function of government rather than of the free market. Free-market arbiters are guided in their choices by the desires of consumers, with profit and loss as a built-in "correction mechanism." But government judges have no signals to guide their decisions. Even if they wanted to please their "customers," they would have no signals to tell them how to do so. A government judge, faced with a flexible penalty, can have nothing to guide him but his own opinions and whims.

Natural law, as applied to human relationships in a free-market context, is objective in both its principles and its application. While the principles of natural law are unchanging, the application of these principles always fits each case, because the natural law involved in any case is derived from the nature of each individual and the unique situation in that particular case. When an aggression is committed, it results in a loss to the victim. This loss is specific and individual for each case. The victim lost a sum of money, or his car, or a leg, and reparations payments are based on the worth of that specific value. In setting the worth of losses (particularly non-exchangeable ones) the arbiters are governed by the value-structure of the consumers who purchase their service, and they have profit and loss signals to guide them. Each case is decided on its own merits. The aggressor's fate is determined on the basis of his own past and present actions—it isn't arbitrarily decided by a group of elected strangers acting without any knowledge of the particular case (and even before it happened).

Natural law, as applied by the free market, is also very short, simple, and easily understood. There is only one basic rule of just human relationships: No man or group of men may attempt to deprive a man of a value by the initiation of physical force, the threat of force, or any substitute for force (such as fraud). All other rules, such as prohibitions against murder, kidnapping, theft, counterfeiting, etc., are merely obvious derivatives of this one basic natural law. A man who wants to know whether he is acting properly toward his fellow man doesn't need a library of legal tomes and a university education. All he needs to do is ask himself one simple question, "Am I causing anyone a loss of value by an act of coercion?" As long as he can honestly answer no to that one question, he need fear no law or retaliatory force.

This basic natural law of human relationships is already tacitly understood by almost everyone throughout the world. It finds common expression in such terms as, "It's always wrong to start the fight." It is the widespread and almost automatic compliance with this natural law by the majority of people which accounts for the fact that human relationships have not completely disintegrated into bloody chaos in spite of the constant push of governments in this direction. Most people live with their neighbors quite peacefully on the basis of this natural law, and they very rarely call on a policeman or judge to take care of their disagreements. And they do so, for the most part, without even consciously identifying the natural law which guides their actions.

The assumption that statutory law is necessary to a society involves the more basic assumption that a legislative body has the moral right to pass laws which are binding on the rest of the population. Advocates of democracy claim that the fact that legislators are elected by the people gives them the right to "represent the people" in matters of legislation. But "the people" is a collectivistic concept; there is no such entity as "the people" which lives, breathes, has interests, opinions and goals. There are only individuals. Do legislators, then, have a moral right to represent the individuals "under their jurisdiction?"

In a democracy, the function of the legislature is, theoretically, to discover what is in "the public interest" and to pass legislation governing people accordingly. But just as there is no such entity as "the people," there is no such thing as "the public interest." There are only the multitude of individual interests of all the great variety of people who are subject to the government. So when legislators pass a law "in the public interest," they are actually favoring the interests of some of their citizens while sacrificing the interests of others. Since legislators, being elected officials, need money and votes, they usually favor the interests of those with political pull and sacrifice the interests of those without it. Also, since government's only source of gain is its productive citizens (the non-productive ones have nothing for government to take), the competent are usually sacrificed in favor of the incompetent, including the politicians.

This type of injustice is inescapably built into the structure of government. A government is a coercive monopoly which forces everyone in its geographical area to deal with it. As such, it must prevent its citizens from freely choosing between competing sellers the services which suit them best. Every citizen is forced to accept gov-

Legislation and Objective Law 123

ernment services and live by government standards, regardless of whether they are in his interest or not.

No matter how "democratic" and "limited" a government is, it cannot actually represent the interests of each one of the multitude of diverse individuals who are its citizens. But these individual interests are the only interests which really exist, because there is no such entity as "the public" and, therefore, no such thing as "the public interest." Since government can't represent the interests of each of its citizens, it must exist by sacrificing the interests of some to the alleged interests of others; and sacrifice always decreases the total store of value.

In a free market, there is no such thing as a coercive monopoly. Every man is free to pursue his own interests as long as he accords the same right to everyone else, and no one's interests are sacrificed to "the public good" or "the will of the majority." In a laissez-faire society, a man who wants to buy a good or service may patronize any business whose merchandise or service pleases him. If he prefers Brand X, he is not forced to buy Brand Y because 51% of his fellow consumers prefer Y and the system allegedly can't be run without unanimity.

But even if they could avoid sacrificing the interests of citizens, elected legislators still wouldn't be justified in making laws which were binding on anyone other than themselves. Opinions, even majority opinions, don't create truth—truth is true, regardless of what anyone thinks about it. Fifty million Frenchmen *can* be wrong, and frequently are. So, if the majority of voters are completely wrong in their support of a candidate, or the majority of legislators are terribly mistaken in their judgment of a law, their majority opinion doesn't change the fact that they are wrong. It is sheer superstition to believe that if enough people (or, perhaps, enough learned and influential people) think a thing is so, this will make it so. A law may be passed by a majority of legislators who were elected by a majority of citizens, and yet it may very well be immoral and destructive despite the majority's collective delusions to the contrary. And no group of people, even if they are in the majority, have the right to force an immoral and destructive law on anyone.

Some advocates of "limited government" have attempted to get around this problem by stipulating that the government must be limited to a very strict constitution to keep it confined to its "proper" functions and prevent it from passing immoral and destructive laws. But this is to ignore the fact that those who write the constitution and those who enforce it must be elected by majority vote (or else appointed by those who are elected). A constitution is only as good as the men who write and enforce it, and if majority opinion can't create truth in matters of legislation, it can't create truth in matters of constitutional formulation and interpretation, either. If it is wrong to employ the mass opinion-mongering method of voting to determine the policies of a government, it is even more wrong to use it to determine the form and structure of that government.

Besides, the idea of a written constitution as a social contract between the people and their government is a myth. A contract is only binding on those who sign it, which means that a contract between the people and the government would have to be signed by every citizen in order to be binding on "the people." The Constitution of the United States wasn't even signed by the citizens who were alive at the time it was written, let alone by all the millions born later who are supposedly bound by it.[1] If one were to institute a constitution and have it signed by every individual who wished to be bound by it, one would also have to admit the right of those who did not agree to refuse to sign and even to make their own arrangements for their protection, in which case one would have, not a government, but a business in competition with other businesses in a free market.

Government laws and constitutions can never be either right or practical. Statutory law, which is supposed to codify natural law in order to make it objective, of universal application, and easily understood, does just the opposite of all three. Natural law is objective in both its principles and its application because it is reality-centered and derived from the nature of the entities involved in each case. Statutory law, even when based on objective principles, cannot possibly be objective in its application because it can't vary with varying cases. Natural law is universally applicable because it is part of the very nature of things, and nothing can be separated from its own nature. Statutory law cannot be universally and equally applicable because if written inflexibly it won't fit individual cases, and if written flexibly it leaves judges with nothing to guide their decisions. The natural law of human relationships is easily understood and can be stated in one brief sentence. Statutory law is a writhing mass of impenetrable complexity, and it cannot avoid being so because it must attempt to fit a multitude of varying circumstances which haven't even happened yet.

Because the free market is a product of the working of natural law, it facilitates the application of natural law to any field in which it is involved. The rules which would govern the businesses of protecting values, arbitrating disputes, and rectifying injustice are merely outgrowths of general economic law, which is an outgrowth of natural

---

[1]For an excellent development of the invalidity of the U. S. Constitution, see *NO TREASON: The Constitution of No Authority*, by Lysander Spooner. Available from Rampart College, 104 West Fourth St., Santa Ana, Calif. 92701.

Legislation and Objective Law 125

law. The same economic rules which would guarantee consumers in a free market the best possible products, service, and prices in their grocery stores and which would protect them from dishonest and unscrupulous drug manufacturers, would work in the areas of protection, arbitration, and rectification. Natural law doesn't give up in puzzled helplessness just because some particular area has always been controlled by political bureaucrats.

Free men, acting in a free market, would manage their affairs in accordance with natural law. The market is, itself, a product of natural law and, therefore, acts to penalize those who "break" that law. Statutory law is a clumsy, anachronistic, and unjust hindrance and is no more necessary to regulate the affairs of men than are kings and tribal witch doctors.

13
Foreign Aggression

Many people ask, "But how in the world could a laissez-faire society deal with aggression by foreign nations, since it would have no government to protect it?" Behind this question are two unrealized assumptions: first, that government is some sort of extra-societal entity with resources of its own—resources which can only be tapped for defense by the action of government—and, second, that government does, in fact, defend its citizens.

In reality, government must draw all its resources from the society over which it rules. When a governmentally controlled society takes defensive action against an aggression by a foreign power, where does it get the resources necessary to take that action? The men who fight are private individuals, usually conscripted into government service. The armaments are produced by private individuals working at their jobs. The money to pay for these armaments and the pittance doled out to the conscripts, as well as the money to pay the salaries of that small minority comprising the other members of the armed forces, is confiscated from private individuals by means of taxation. Government's only contribution is to organize the whole effort by the use of force—the force of the draft, taxation, and other, more minor coercions, such as rationing, wage and price ceilings, travel restrictions, etc. So, to maintain that government is necessary to defend a society from foreign aggression is to maintain that it is necessary to use domestic aggression against the citizens in order to protect them from foreign aggression.

In spite of the obvious immorality of *forcing* men to protect themselves against force, some people still maintain that a coerced defense is more efficient than a willing one and is, therefore, permissible or even necessary in an emergency situation such as war. A brief examination will show the fallacy of this variation of the moral/practical dichotomy. The success of any endeavor, including war, depends on the amount of thought and effort put into it by those involved. Under the pressure of force, a man may be induced to put forth a great deal of effort and even a little thought, but his reluctant, fear-driven exertions can't compare in efficiency and productivity with the ambitious and tireless efforts of a free man striving to accomplish something he really wants to get done. The man who works enthusiastically not only works more efficiently, he also uses his mind to discover new and better ways of reaching the goal, and such innovation is the key to success.

Furthermore, a system of force is always wasteful of resources, because the more unwilling is the victim of the force, the more energy must be diverted to keeping him in line and the less is left to accomplish the task. Men who are forced to do what they don't want to (or not to do what they do want to) are amazingly good at devising devious and complicated ways to cheat on the system which enslaves them. This is why even the most totalitarian of governments find that they cannot wage war without huge propaganda efforts aimed at convincing their own people of the justice and necessity of the war.

Freedom is not only as moral as governmental slavery is immoral, it is as practical as government is impractical. It is foolish to suppose that men would not organize to defend themselves, and do so very effectively, if they were not forced to. Men are not so blind that they can't grasp the value of freedom, nor so indifferent to life that they will not defend their values. Nor are they so stupid that they need politicians, bureaucrats, and Pentagon generals to tell them how to organize and what to do. The freer people are, the more efficiently they will perform. This being true, a free-market system of defense against foreign aggression can be expected to be very effective, in contrast to a governmental system of comparable size, resources, and maturity.

The belief that society couldn't be defended without a government also assumes that government does, indeed, protect the society over which it rules. But when it is realized that government really has nothing except what it takes by force from its citizens, it becomes obvious that the government can't possibly protect the people, because it doesn't have the resources to do so. In fact, government, without the citizens on whom it parasitizes, couldn't even protect itself! Throughout history, people have been talked into submitting to the tyrannies of their governments because, they were told, their government was vitally necessary to protect them from the even more terrible depredations of other governments. The governments, having put over this bit of propaganda, then proceeded to cajole and coerce their citizens into *protecting them!* Governments never defend their citizens; they can't. What they do is make the citizens defend them, usually after their stupid and imperialistic policies have aggravated or threatened another government to the point of armed conflict. Governmental protection against foreign aggression is a myth (but a myth which, sad to say, most people actually believe in).

Government can't defend its citizens, and it is foolish and sacrificial for the citizens to defend a coercive monopoly which not only enslaves them but makes a practice of provoking conflicts with other coercive monopolies—i.e., with other governments. *In the matter of foreign aggression, government is far more of a liability than an asset,* and people would be much better off with a free-market system of defense.

The free-market means of defense against foreign aggression would differ in scope and intensity, but not in principle from the free-market means of defense against domestic aggression (such as a gang of local hoodlums). In either case, the principle involved is that each man has both the liberty and the responsibility to defend his own values to the extent *he* considers it to be in his own self-interest. Morally, no man may be prevented from defending himself and his values, nor may he be forced to defend them if he doesn't want to do so. If some of the people in an area feel that one of their neighbors is not "carrying his fair share of the defense burden," they are free to use rational persuasion to attempt to convince him that it would be in his interest to assume his own responsibility of self-defense. They may not, however, extort his compliance by any use or threat of force . . . even if they are clearly in the majority. Nor would it be practical for them to do so. A man who is coerced into defending his neighbors against a foreign aggressor may decide to spend part of his efforts on defending himself against his coercive neighbors instead.

In a laissez-faire society, defense against foreign aggression would be offered for sale on the free market, just as would any other type of defense. Because of the close natural connection between insurance companies and defense agencies, it would probably be most feasible to sell defense against foreign aggression in the form of insurance policies. That is, insurance companies would sell policies agreeing to protect their insureds against foreign aggression and to indemnify them for losses resulting from such aggression (the contract to be void, of course, if the insured provoked the conflict by his own aggressive actions). The insurance companies would see to it that whatever defenses were necessary to prevent the losses were provided, and they would make sure that a very efficient job of defense was done, since any losses would cost them large sums of money.[1]

---

[1]This is similar to the relationship which would prevail in a laissez-faire society between fire insurance and fire extinguishing companies. Insurance companies would sell fire insurance and would then either maintain their own facilities to put out fires or buy the services of independent fire extinguishing companies for their insureds (and anyone else who wanted to pay a fee for the services when used). Because the various insurance companies would find it convenient to have contractual agreements to buy each other's fire extinguishing services when more feasible than using their own, it would not be necessary to have a fire station for each insurance company in every area.

Critics have questioned whether insurance companies could afford to pay off all the claims caused by the widespread destruction of a modern war, should their defenses be overpowered. If the war were lost, of course, neither the insurance company personnel, nor their insureds, nor anyone else would be in a position to carry on normal financial dealings. If it were won, the insurance companies would have to either pay off or go out of business. In determining whether an insurance company would be financially able to pay, there are two important considerations—the extent and intensity of the damage, and the extent of the insurance company's assets.

The amount of damage is impossible to predict in advance of the actual situation, but there is no reason to assume that it would necessarily be so severe as to include the total destruction of all major cities. Governments usually launch wars of destruction only against areas which, because of the actions of their own governments, pose a threat to the attacker. A laissez-faire society, having no government to make imperialistic threats, would be unlikely to become the object of a war of destruction. A foreign government might decide to enrich itself by annexing the free territory, but it would attempt to do so by a war of conquest rather than by a war of destruction. Wars of conquest are much less devastating and call for the restrained use of conventional weapons rather than the use of nuclear weapons. The simple reason for this is that the conqueror stands to reap a great deal less profit from rubble and corpses than he does from factories and slaves.

Another reason to assume that a war against a laissez-faire society would not be totally destructive of that society is that effective defenses against modern warfare undoubtedly can be devised. The fact that governments have not yet devised such defenses only proves that governments are both profoundly inefficient and more interested in imperialistic power grabs than in defending their citizens. Given the efficiency of the free market and the incentive of the profit motive (because people would be willing to pay for effective defense "hardware" if they were allowed to buy it), innovators would doubtless come up with many defensive devices far superior to the military war machine now imposed upon us.

The second consideration in determining insurance companies' ability to pay claims arising from foreign aggression is the extent of their assets. Even in our society, where they are hamstrung by governmental regulations, insurance companies manage to hold vast and varied assets, spread over wide financial and geographic areas. They also make a practice of dividing large risks among various companies so that a sudden, extensive amount of destruction can be paid for without bankrupting any of them. This is the reason that insurance companies can pay out the millions of dollars in claims which arise from major hurricanes, tornadoes, earthquakes, etc., and can do so again and again without being driven out of business. In a laissez-faire society, insurance companies should be even better based financially than they are in our governmentally crippled economy. This means that an attacker would have to succeed in wiping out a large portion of the assets of the whole society in order to put the insurance companies out of business. But there is no reason to assume that a foreign government would attack the whole free area at once (since, without a government, it wouldn't be a single political entity) or that it would succeed in destroying most of it if it did. Although there is no absolute guarantee that insurance companies would be financially able to pay off the claims arising from an attack by a foreign power, the chances that they would are very good.

The actual defense of a laissez-faire society would be furnished by defense companies (both independent ones and those which were subsidiaries of insurance companies). These defenses would consist of whatever military personnel and materiel were necessary to defeat the forces of any nation threatening (or potentially threatening) the insureds. Such defenses would vary in size and type according to the threat posed, and they could include anything from spies and foot soldiers to radar networks and defensive missiles.

Since the development and maintenance of modern weaponry is quite expensive, all but the largest insurance companies would probably pool their efforts and resources under competitive pressure to provide the best possible protection at the lowest cost. For the same reasons of efficiency, they would tend to purchase all their foreign-aggression defense needs from a few outstanding companies which could cooperate closely with each other. Competition between the defense companies to get such profitable business would foster the development of the most powerful and efficient defense system rationally warranted. Technological innovations which are at present unforeseeable would constantly upgrade its safety and effectiveness. No governmental system, with its miles of red tape and built-in politicking, pork-barreling, wirepulling, and power-grabbing could even remotely approximate the potency and efficiency naturally generated by the free-market forces (which are always moving to meet demand).

Those who doubt that "the private sector" of the economy could sustain the expense of a free enterprise defense system would do well to consider two facts. First, "the public sector" gets its money from the same source as does "the private sector"—the wealth produced by individuals. The difference is that "the public sector" takes this wealth by force (which is legal robbery)—but it does not thereby have access to a larger pool of resources. On the contrary, by draining the economy by taxation and hobbling it with restrictions, the government actually diminishes the total supply of available resources. Second, government, because of what it is, makes defense far more expensive than it ought to be. The gross inefficiency and waste common to a coercive monopoly, which gathers its revenues by force and fears no competition, skyrocket costs. Furthermore, the insatiable desire of politicians and bureaucrats to exercise power in every remote corner of the world multiplies expensive armies, whose main effect is to commit aggressions and provoke wars. The question is not whether "the private sector" can afford the cost of defending individuals but how much longer individuals can afford the fearsome and dangerous cost of coerced governmental "defense" (which is, in reality, defense of the government, for the government . . . *by* the citizens).

A major portion of the cost of defense against foreign aggression in a laissez-faire society would be borne originally by business and industry, as owners of industrial plants obviously have a much greater investment to defend than do owners of little houses in suburbia. If there were any real threat of aggression by a foreign power, businessmen would all be strongly motivated to buy insurance against that aggression, for the same reason that they buy fire insurance, even though they could save money in the short run by not doing so. An interesting result of this fact is that the cost of defense would ultimately tend to be spread among the whole population, since defense costs, along with overhead and other such costs, would have to be included in the prices paid for goods by consumers. So, the concern that "free riders" might get along without paying for their own defense by parasitically depending on the defenses paid for by their neighbors is groundless. It is based on a misconception of how the free-market system would operate.

The role of business and industry as major consumers of foreign-aggression insurance would operate to unify the free area in the face of any aggression. An auto plant in Michigan, for example, might well have a vital source of raw materials in Montana, a parts plant in Ontario, a branch plant in California, warehouses in Texas, and outlets all over North America. Every one of these facilities is important to some degree to the management of that Michigan factory, so it will want to have them defended, each to the extent of its importance. Add to this the concern of the owners and managers of these facilities for their own businesses and for all the other businesses on which they, in turn, depend, and a vast, multiple network of interlocking defense systems emerges. The involvement of the insurance companies, with their diversified financial holdings and their far-flung markets would immeasurably strengthen this defensive network. Such a multiple network of interlocking defense systems is a far cry from the common but erroneous picture of small cities, businesses, and individuals, unprotected by a government, falling one by one before an advancing enemy horde.

Note, however, that such a defense network would not obligate any individual to contribute money or effort to any defensive action in which his values were not threatened. Under the present governmental system of collectivistic defense within arbitrary boundaries, a Californian would be forced to sacrifice his values and possibly his life in order to defend the State of Maine, even though he had no interest at all in the matter. At the same time, a man a few miles away in Quebec, because he was on the other side of a particular river, would have to sit idly by unless his own government decided to take some action. This is because governmental defense, like any other governmental action, is and must be collectivistic in nature. With a free-market defense system, each man acts to defend his own values to the extent he wishes to have them defended, regardless of what piece of real estate he happens to be occupying. No man is forced to sacrifice for the defense of the collective system of a coercive gang called government.

A free-market defense system would also make it very difficult for an attacker to obtain a surrender. Just as a laissez-faire society would have no government to start a war, it would have no government to capitulate. The defenders would fight as long, and only as long, as they believed was in their self-interest. Even the insurance companies and defense agencies couldn't negotiate a surrender, because their agreements could bind no one but the persons who actually signed them. It is interesting to speculate on what an aggressive foreign nation would do if confronted with such a situation.

In a free-market defense system, the size of the armies and the expenditures for armaments would be automatically regulated according to the need for them. Consumers, kept informed of the world situation by the news media and by insurance advertising, would buy more insurance when aggression threatened, and less when the tensions eased. This would be particularly true of the big businesses and industries constituting the largest single insurance customers. They would be very foresighted in their purchase of foreign-aggression insurance, just as they must be foresighted in all their other dealings. Furthermore, competition would force defense costs to be held down, so that all armaments would have to be either engaged in necessary defensive uses or disposed of, as idle armaments would not be worth their keep. No army could

Foreign Aggression

grow beyond what the market would support; and the market would never support an army larger than was actually necessary for defense, because force is a non-productive expenditure of energy.

This automatic responsiveness of arms to world situation, with a built-in arms limitation, would offer several important advantages. First, it would avoid the economic drain of maintaining standing armies larger than necessary, yet still allow for quick increase in arms when needed. Second, it would put an end to the dangerous irritations and provocations to foreign nations which are always incident to maintaining large, imperialistic armies around the world and, thus, would remove a major source of hostility and tension. Third, it would prevent all the various meddlings, aggressions, and "brushfire wars" which result from trying to play "world policeman" and regulate the affairs of everyone on the globe. And fourth, it would guarantee that an overgrown military machine could never be seized by a would-be dictator and used against the people of the laissez-faire society themselves (a guarantee which no constitution can possibly make).

A free-market defense system would also permanently end the danger that some careless or power-mad politician might "push the button" and bring down on the hapless citizens all the retaliatory violence of "the other side." A free-market business wouldn't gain power by "pushing the button;" it would lose a tremendous amount of assets. Consequently, any military action by the free-market protection agencies would be strictly defensive, and undertaken only when all other means of meeting the threat had failed.

And, along with all its other advantages, a free-market defense system would put a permanent end to the blood-spattered immorality of the draft. The professional, voluntary defense forces of the market would be far superior to governmental conscript forces. Conscript armies are terribly expensive to maintain because of the constant need for training new conscripts to fill the places of that great and sensible majority who leave as soon as their term is up. Furthermore, conscripts are notably ineffective and unwilling fighters as compared with volunteers, for obvious reasons. Once again, it is the moral approach which is practical.

Many prophets of doom have cried that there can be no defense against modern missile warfare. In fact, the danger of such a war is one of the chief arguments advanced in favor of a strong government. It is said that only by maintaining a strong government can we hope to deter an enemy attack or successfully meet it when it comes. And, since hundreds of missiles are already aimed at various parts of the globe and don't seem likely to be dismantled in the foreseeable future, we are told that we had better plan on keeping that government strong for a long time to come and not dream of experimenting with radical ways to improve our society, such as freedom.

Since life doesn't give any automatic guarantees of safety and success, it is true that even a strong free-market defense system might be overpowered by an all-out atomic-biological-chemical attack, should such an attack be launched. But so might a governmental "defense" system, so this statement doesn't really say anything about the relative merits of free-market defense vs. governmental "defense."

An examination of governmental "defense" shows that it depends on the use of initiated force against its own citizens and on much propaganda about government-fabricated foreign "dangers," and it requires citizens to sacrifice themselves for whatever government officials deem to be the good of the "public." The free market permits each man to defend his own values, uses no initiated force against and requires no sacrifice from customers, and penalizes those who refuse to live non-coercive lives. Governmental "defense" is unavoidably wasteful and a drain on the resources of the society. It is also ineffective in protecting the citizen against modern warfare and is likely to stay that way, because without competition and the profit motive it lacks sufficient incentive to innovate effectively. In the free market, competition forces businesses to cut costs and eliminate waste, and it also brings about continual improvements in effectiveness through technological innovation as businesses struggle to "keep ahead of the competition."

But worse than its waste and ineffectiveness, governmental "defence" is actually little more than an excuse for imperialism. The more government "defends" its citizens, the more it provokes tensions and wars, as unnecessary armies wallow carelessly about in distant lands and government functionaries, from the highest to the lowest, throw their weight around in endless, provocating power grabs. The war machine established by government is dangerous to both foreigners and its own citizens, and this machine can operate indefinitely without any effective check other than the attack of a foreign nation. If such a war machine is unopposed by the armies of other nations, it is almost inevitably used to promote rampant imperialism. But if it is opposed by a war machine of equal strength and deadliness, then a balance of terror ensues, with the constant threat of a holocaust. Businesses in a free market can't spare the cash for such perilous follies, because they gain customers by offering values to free men rather than by threatening force against disarmed subjects.

Governments don't really defend their citizen-subjects at all. Instead, they provoke wars, and then they force the citizens to sacrifice their money, their freedom, and often their lives to defend the government. Such "defense" is worse than no defense at all!

Foreign Aggression 135

It is true that the missiles, the deadly chemicals, and the plagues of modern warfare constitute a very real threat. But these implements of mass destruction were ordered to be constructed by governments, and these same governments are continually bringing new and more deadly weapons into existence. To say that we must have a government to protect us as long as these products of government are around is like saying that a man should keep his cancerous tumor until sometime in the future when he gets better, because it would be too dangerous to remove it now!

If collectivism has proved itself inefficient, wasteful, and dangerous in such areas as transportation and medicine, surely the worst place of all to have it is in the vital area of defense against foreign aggression. Wars and many other, less destructive kinds of human conflicts are the natural consequence of institutionalizing man-made violence in the form of governments!

14
The Abolition of War

A few hundred years ago, the devastation of periodic plagues and famines was unthinkingly accepted as a normal and inescapable part of human existence—they were held to be either visitations from an indignant God or nature's means of wiping out "excess population." Today, in spite of the volumes of frantically hopeful talk about peace, many people accept the necessity of wars in the same unthinking manner; or at least they feel that wars will be necessary for the rest of the foreseeable future. Are wars an unavoidable part of human society? And if not, why have all the years of negotiations, the reams of theories, the solemn treaties and unions of nations, and the flood of hopes and pious prayers failed to bring peace? After all the talking, planning and effort, why *is* our world filled with more brutal and dangerous strife than ever?

War is a species of violence, and the most basic cause of violence is the belief that it is right or practical or necessary for human beings to initiate force against one another—that coercion is permissible or even unavoidable in human relationships. To the extent that men believe in the practicality and desirability of initiating force against other men, they will be beset by conflicts.

But war is a very special kind of violence—it is "open, armed conflict between countries or factions within the same country" (Webster), which means an organized use of force on the largest scale possible and devastation of a breadth and thoroughness which cannot be matched by any other man-made catastrophe. Such carefully organized, massive, and deliberately destructive conflict cannot be accounted for simply by men's belief in the permissibility of initiating force against other men. There must be some further factor in human beliefs and institutions which causes millions of people to put such effort into the destruction and subjugation of other millions.

In searching for the cause of war, men have put the blame on everything from a supposed natural human depravity to the "dialectical necessities of history." The most popular current scapegoat is Big Business. We hear of war profiteers, economic imperialism, and

The Abolition of War

the military-industrial complex, and we are told that businessmen need wars of conquest to gain markets.

It is perfectly true that there is a fascistic alliance between government and many businesses in our present society and that this league results in the military-industrial-university complex which firmly supports the government and its imperialistic policies. The question is, what is the cause of this unholy alliance? Is it a perversion of normally peaceful and non-aggressive government by greedy businessmen, or is it a perversion of business by government?

The military-industrial complex came about as a result of government's power to use stick-and-carrot methods to rule business (which was just one part of the politicians' efforts to rule everyone). For a stick, the politicians use anti-trust laws, interstate commerce laws, pure food and drug laws, licensing laws, and a whole host of other prohibitions and regulatory legislation. Many years ago, the government succeeded in making regulatory legislation so complex, contradictory, vague, and all-encompassing that the bureaucrats could fine and imprison any businessman and destroy his business, regardless of what he did or how hard he tried to obey the law. This legal chicanery gives the bureaucrats life-and-death control over the whole business community, a control which they can and do exercise on any whim, and against which their victims have very little defense.

For a carrot, the politicians hold out large and lucrative governmental contracts. By crippling the economy with regulations and bleeding it by taxation, the government has drastically cut the number of large and profitable contracts available from the private sector, which forces many businessmen to get such contracts from the government or do without them. To stay in business, businessmen must make profits, and many of them have simply accepted government contracts, either without bothering to delve into the ethical questions or with the comforting thought that they were being patriotic. Government's stick-and-carrot control of business has been going on for so long that most businessmen accept it as normal and necessary (just as most people accept taxes as normal and necessary).

During the last hundred years or so, many businessmen have shortsightedly aided the growth of such fascism. Big industrialists who saw government intervention as a quick and easy way to eliminate threatening competition and gain unearned advantages, were often in the forefront of the forces demanding regulation and control of the market. Government, after all, is an instrument of force. It can be used by anyone who can gain temporary control of it to extort advantages from his fellowmen. Businessmen have made use of this instrument of force—so have labor leaders, social planners, racists, pious religionists, and many other societal forces. As long as such an organized institution of force exists, individuals and pressure groups will use it—if not to gain an unfair advantage, then to protect themselves from other advantage-seekers.

The present fascistic alliance between government and business, which definitely is aggressive and imperialistic, is a forced alliance—forced by government and by those who use government's power to extort advantages from legally disarmed victims. But if they were separated, which partner in this would be the aggressively malicious and imperialistic one? Is business or government the basic cause of aggressions?

Business, when separated from government, is not only non-imperialistic—it is strongly and uncompromisingly anti-coercive. Men who trade have nothing to gain and everything to lose from destruction. Wars of conquest do not gain markets for business. The most significant effect of war on markets is to damage and destroy them by killing and impoverishing multitudes of people and disrupting the economic life of entire areas. Private enterprise wins markets by the excellence of its products in competitive trading; it has nothing to gain from imperialism.

Nor does business as a whole gain from war profiteering. Wars are expensive, and the burden of supporting wars falls heavily on business, both directly and by taking spending money out of the pocket of the consumer. The vast amount of money poured out to support a war is permanently gone without bringing any economic return. After you have exploded a hundred thousand dollars worth of bombs, you have nothing to show for it except a hundred thousand dollars worth of bomb craters and rubble. Thus the gains made by munitions makers and government suppliers are more than swallowed up by the losses suffered by business as a whole. Those few who do make huge fortunes from war do so not because they are businessmen operating in a free market, but because they have political pull. And their profiteering from war harms all producers (as well as the consuming public) by hurting the economy as a whole.

Business is a natural opponent of war because businessmen are traders, and you can't trade amid falling bombs. An industrialist can gain nothing from the ruins and poverty which are the chief results of war. Furthermore, businessmen are a society's producers, and it is always the producers who must foot the bills.

It is not business which gains from war, but government. Successful wars leave governments with more power (over both their own citizens and those of the conquered nations), more money (in the form of plunder, tribute, and taxes), and more territory. The more totalitarian a government, the more booty it attempts to squeeze from its wars, but all governments, even relatively limited ones, gain large amounts of power and plunder from successful warfare. Besides this, war is often ideologically useful to unite the populace behind the government in the face of a "common enemy." People can be made to sacrifice more, with less resistance, if they believe they are in danger of being overrun by the terrible Russians (or the Red Chinese, or Krauts, or Japs, or "common enemies" ad infinauseum!).

Wars are initiated and carried on by governments. Governments, not private individuals, provoke massive conflicts by arms buildups and imperialistic territorial grabs. *It is rulers*, not businessmen and citizens, who declare wars, draft soldiers, and levy taxes to support them. There is no societal organization capable of waging a war of aggression except government. If there were no governments, there would still be individual aggressors and possibly even small gangs, but *there could be no war*.

It is not surprising that governments are the source of war when one considers the nature of government. A government is a coercive *monopoly*—an organization which must initiate force against its own citizens in order to exist at all. An institution built on organized force will necessarily commit aggressions and provoke conflicts. All wars are, in the final analysis, political wars. The are fought over the question of who is to rule.

So, to abolish war, it is not necessary to attempt the impossible task of changing man's nature so that he can't choose to initiate force against others—it is merely necessary to abolish governments. This doesn't mean that the establishment of one or even several laissez-faire areas will immediately end warfare, because as long as there is one viable and potent government left, the threat of war will remain and the free areas will need to keep up their guard. But if a laissez-faire society were to become a reality throughout the civilized world, war would cease to exist. Is there any practical hope of such a government-free, war-free situation coming into existence throughout the world after the establishment of one free area? To answer this question, it will be necessary to examine the effects which a laissez-faire society would have on the rest of the world.

A laissez-faire society could not have "foreign relations" with the nations of the world in the same sense that a government does, because each inhabitant would be a sovereign individual speaking only for himself and not for a collective aggregate of his fellows. Yet in spite of this, a laissez-faire society would have a profound and inescapable effect on the rest of the world as a result of its mere existence.

A laissez-faire society would, by virtue of its freedom, be superior to any governmental society in three key economic areas—scientific research, industrial development, and its monetary system. It is obvious that the more men are free to pursue any non-coercive interest, to realize the rewards of their research, and to fully own any property thus earned, the more intelligent effort they will put into research and the more discoveries will be made. And since the market rewards only productive research, a free society avoids the tremendous waste of effort and resources inherent in government-sponsored research programs. Similarly, freedom provides the greatest incentive to industrial development, as any governmental interference at all constitutes a distortion of the market. As to the monetary system, government currencies are seldom out of trouble for long, and the more closely they are controlled, the deeper and more perplexing become their problems. It is no exaggeration to say that, in a modern industrial society, a banking firm operating on the free market and issuing money in competition with other such firms would not dare to experiment with the sort of absurd and disastrous fiscal policies in which governments continually engage. Any free-market firm which issued a currency as undependable as that issued by most governments would speedily be run out of business by its more financially sound competitors.

In short, free men can and will build a stronger economy than men who are taxed, harassed, regulated, legislated, bound—that is, held in some degree of slavery by governments. This principle can be seen in operation even today in the contrast in economic strengths between the totalitarian, governmentally controlled Communist bloc nations and the less enslaved nations of the West. Soviet propaganda and the adulations of statist-minded Westerners to the contrary notwithstanding, the Soviet economy is continually beset with gross mismanagement, critical shortages, poor quality products, agricultural crises, severe unemployment, and general confusion. Russia's "rapid economic growth" is nothing but a myth.[1] In fact, it is extremely doubtful that the Communist tyranny could have survived at all without substantial aid from governments of the West, especially the U.S.A.[2]

The American economy, although crippled by government interferences and bilked of billions of dollars for "foreign aid," still manages to far surpass the stumbling economy of the Soviet Union, even though the Soviets have obtained from conquered European countries and American Governmental aid entire factories, hordes

---

[1]For verification, see *WORKERS' PARADISE LOST*, by Eugene Lyons.
[2]For documentation of this incredible aid, see *ROOSEVELT'S ROAD TO RUSSIA*, by George N. Crocker.

of technicians, streams of strategic goods, and shiploads of foodstuffs. A comparison of the American and Soviet economies gives a hint of the vast superiority which a laissez-faire economy would enjoy over any unfree economy. And military strength is necessarily based on economic strength.

Because of its economic strength, a laissez-faire society would exercise a profound effect on the nations of the world even though it would have no government to formulate and carry out a foreign policy. First, the existence of a free area would cause the rest of the world to experience a brain drain of such tremendous proportions as to make the brain drain which currently worries the British look laughable by comparison. As the economy of the laissez-faire society expanded almost explosively in response to freedom, it would produce a great demand for men of intelligence and ability, and it would be able to offer such men more—in terms of money, ideal working conditions, opportunity to associate with other men of ability, and (most important) freedom—than would any governmentally controlled society. Producers in every nation would want to move to the laissez-faire society. Many might decide to move not only themselves but their entire businesses to the free area. They would see that, by escaping taxation and regulation, they could make greater profits even if they had to pay additional shipping costs and higher wages. Such an influx of business would cause a high demand for competent labor in the free area, which would raise wages. It would also tend to make the nations which lost producers and businesses economically dependent on the laissez-faire society for necessary goods and services and, therefore, reluctant to attack it.

Governments wouldn't be able to offer the men of ability in their countries enough to keep them from flocking by the thousands to the exciting opportunities in the laissez-faire society. If they wanted to hold such men, the governments would have to hold them by force, as the iron curtain countries do now, and the experience of these iron curtain countries has shown that men of ability do not function well under constraint. A brain drain of this magnitude would constitute a crippling hemophilia for the nations of the world, and the only response the governments could make to it would be to institute restrictive measures—a move toward tyranny which would also be crippling—or to disband (which is unlikely, considering the nature of politics).

But a brain drain is not the only hemophilia which the governments of the world would experience as their citizens became aware of the opportunities in the free area—there would also be a capital drain. Investors always try to place their capital in areas of maximum profit and minimum risk (that is, minimum future uncertainty), and one of the greatest sources of future uncertainty is the power of bureaucrats to issue directives and regulations on any whim. This means that businesses in a laissez-faire society would be tops on the list of attractive investments for investors all over the world. Like the brain drain, the capital drain would strengthen the free area at the expense of the nations; and again, the only response their governments could make would be further restrictive legislation—which would further weaken their economies—or to disband.

The existence of a laissez-faire society would also have a profound effect on governmental monetary systems. Governments commonly sap the strength of their currencies by engaging in inflationary practices. (They do this because inflation is a sort of sneaky tax which allows the government to spend more money than it takes in, by putting extra currency into the economy, thus stealing a little of the real or supposed value of every unit of currency already there.) As tax burdens become more oppressive, few governments can resist the temptation to circumvent citizen protest by resorting to inflation. They then protect their shaky currencies from devaluation, as long as possible, by international agreements which fix the relative value of currencies and obligate nations to come to each other's aid in financial crises. In a sense, the main protection which an inflated currency has is the fact that all the other major currencies of the world are inflated, too. But the currencies of a laissez-faire society, being subject to the rules of the market, could not be inflated (inflated currencies would be driven off a free market by sound ones). Holders of capital naturally want to hold it in the form of the most sound money available, so they would move to sell government currencies and buy free-market money. This move itself would further weaken unsound governmental economies, as it would cause a de facto devaluation of their currencies. It might well precipitate a series of near-fatal financial crises among the nations. Thus, a government would have to choose between maintaining a sound currency (necessitating a strict limitation of government functions) or attempting to hedge its currency about with a wall of restrictive legislation which would paralyze its economy and, at best, would do little more than postpone its collapse.

These examples show how a sizable laissez-faire society, simply by existing, would amplify stresses within the nations and compel them to move rapidly toward either complete freedom or tyranny. The laissez-faire society wouldn't create these stresses; its presence would merely aggravate tensions created long ago by the irrational and coercive policies of governments. These stresses would destroy the precarious equilibrium of all the nations at the same time.

In every nation, there is some degree of conflict between citizens and government. In nations with relatively limited governments, this conflict may be only minor; but in totalitarian countries it can amount to a latent civil war between the ruled and the rulers.[3] To the extent people realize that freedom is practical but that it is being denied to them, this conflict is intensified. It is also intensified by the government's addition of new restrictive measures, especially if the measures are passed suddenly without much prior propaganda to prepare the citizenry. The existence of a successful laissez-faire society would both demonstrate the practicality of freedom and force governments to take sudden new restrictive measures, thus further amplifying their internal stresses by setting the people consciously against their governments.

By demonstrating that government is not only unnecessary but positively detrimental, a successful laissez-faire society would strip all governments of their mystical sanctity in the eyes of their citizens. The reason the institution of government has persisted into modern times is that people submit to its depredations, and they submit because they believe that without a government there would be chaos. This nearly universal belief in the necessity of government is tyranny's strongest defense. Once the idea of the nature of full liberty has been let loose in the world and its practicality demonstrated, governments will lose the respect of their citizens and will be able to evoke no more allegiance from them than they could obtain by force. It is ideas, after all, which determine how human beings will shape their lives and societies.

But government officials don't give up their power and patronage easily, even when there is a great popular demand for a reduction in government. In some countries, the idea of freedom might be strong enough and government weak enough for popular opinion to force a series of cutbacks in government size and power until the government was a figurehead and finally non-existent. It is probable, however, that the majority of governments would fight back by becoming more restrictive and tyrannical; and this is particularly true of countries well along on the road of government control. So most of the non-free world would degenerate into various combinations and degrees of tyranny, revolt, and social chaos.

Popular misconception to the contrary notwithstanding, the degree of a government's tyranny is the degree of its vulnerability, particularly in the sphere of economics. Totalitarian governments, in spite of their outward appearance of unconquerably massive solidarity, are inwardly rotten with ineptitude, waste, corruption, fear, and unbe-

---

[3] See Eugene Lyons' *WORKERS' PARADISE LOST*, page 105.

lievable mismanagement. This is, and must be, so . . . because of the very nature of government control.

Government control is control by force, since coercion is the source of government power (the source of market power is excellence of product and performance). The more totalitarian a country, the more its citizens must be motivated, not by the incentive of expected rewards (the profit motive), but by fear. Without freedom to enjoy the rewards of his productivity, a man has no incentive to produce except his fear of a government gun. But a threat will evoke only that minimum performance necessary to avoid the threatened harm, and that only insofar as the threatener is constantly watching.

Even more crippling is the fact that threats don't produce innovative ideas. A man's mind can only belong to him; he is the one person who can order that mind to produce ideas. Fear is paralyzing; if a threat is strong enough to motivate a man to try to produce an innovative idea, it will usually generate too much fear for him to think clearly. This is why dictatorships find it necessary to permit their scientists and other intellectuals a special privileged status with extra liberties and incentives. They must do this, even though it is extremely dangerous to a tyranny to harbor intellectuals who are free to think and express even mild condemnation of their rulers. Any dictatorship must walk a constant tightrope between giving its intellectuals too much freedom so that they become rebellious, and giving them too little so that they stop producing ideas. And what is true of intellectuals is true to a lesser degree of all the millions of ordinary, hard-working individuals whose little ideas of "how to do it better" contribute so much to economic advancement.

In addition to the initiative-smothering effects of replacing freedom with fear, the inevitable governmental rules and regulations enmesh and strangle the economy. When free from interference, the market is always in motion toward equilibrium—that is, toward a condition which eliminates shortages and surpluses and minimizes economic waste. To the degree the market is interfered with by governmental controls, it can no longer respond to economic reality and becomes distorted. Then shortages, surpluses, delays, waste, queues, ration books, high prices, and shoddy merchandise become the order of the day.

Nor is central planning the answer to such problems. The assumption that someone, or even a group of someones, could regulate an economy is absurdly naive. The biggest computer ever built couldn't begin to handle the volume of data which is automatically dealt with by individual choices made in the market every day.

Furthermore, this data is based on millions of individual value-choices all made from separate, individual frames of reference, so the items cannot possibly be measured and compared as required by a computer. "Central planning" only distorts the market by forcing it into configurations it would not normally assume and preventing it from being self-correcting. There is no way for a planned economy to work. The more completely it is planned, the more distorted and inflexible it will be, and the weaker will be the nation.

Tyranny is, by its very nature, counterproductive and full of internal stresses. The Soviet Union, for example, has derived its strength almost entirely from the massive amounts of aid furnished it by the relatively less enslaved countries of the West, particularly the United States of America. Without this aid provided by taxes confiscated from producers in less tyrannical nations, the Soviet dictatorship would have collapsed long ago.[4]

Tyranny *by itself* is impotent because looters don't produce and producers can't produce unless they're free to do so. The belief that totalitarian nations are naturally stronger than freer ones is an outgrowth of the moral/practical dichotomy. If that which is moral were, because of its morality, unavoidably impractical, then the good would necessarily be helpless and disarmed, since the evil would have all the practicality on its side.

Those who persist, in spite of all evidence to the contrary, in believing that totalitarianism makes a nation strong are revealing a sneaky admiration for dictatorship. Such an admiration springs from a psychological dependency which cannot conceive of having to be free and thrown on one's own uncertain resources. The psychologically dependent man longs either to be led and directed in order to escape the responsibility of decision-making, or to dictate to others in order to convince himself of an efficacy he doesn't possess.

Because tyranny is necessarily weak and vulnerable, the stresses created within the governmentally controlled nations by the existence of a laissez-faire society would force them to move toward either complete liberty or toward impotence and chaos. At the same time, the dazzling idea that real freedom is both possible and practical would create a surging groundswell of popular demand for this freedom in nations throughout the world. Governments would lose support as their citizens lost their irrational patriotism. Thus, the laissez-faire society, by its mere existence, would weaken its enemies and promote the rise of freedom outside its boundaries, causing the dismantling of governments and the rise of new free areas.

But the laissez-faire society would spread liberty throughout the

---

[4]This claim is adequately borne out by Werner Keller's excellent book, *EAST MINUS WEST EQUALS ZERO*.

rest of the world, not only in a passive way via the conditions caused by its existence, but actively—by trade relationships. Free individuals trading with natives of foreign countries would be under no obligation to recognize the validity of their governments, any more than they would be to recognize the validity of other kinds of hoodlum gangs. Because they would see governments for what they really were, they would be psychologically free to defend themselves against these governments. They would obey the trade restrictions of foreign states only insofar as it was in their interest to do so and would ignore and disobey them whenever it proved advantageous. They would have no compunctions about seeing governments topple, since an end of governments always means an increase in liberty and prosperity.

When free individuals entered into business in territories still under the control of governments, they would want their foreign holdings protected, just as were the rest of their properties. Insurance and defense companies, ever on the lookout for new sales opportunities, would offer this protection (at rates and with stipulations commensurate with the amount of danger involved in each separate nation, of course). Protection and defense services could apply simply to the depredations of private criminals. Or, if the government were not particularly strong, they could also safeguard the protected company from the threat of nationalization, and even from taxation and regulation.

Picture a small South American dictatorship, weakened by economic stresses and a popular demand for more freedom, resulting from the existence of a laissez-faire society nearby. What would the dictator of such a country do if faced by a large and powerful insurance company and its defense service (or even a coalition of such companies) demanding that he remove all taxes, trade restrictions, and other economic aggressions from, say, a mining firm protected by the insurance company? If the dictator refuses the demand, he faces an armed confrontation which will surely oust him from his comfortable position of rule. His own people are restless and ready to revolt at any excuse. Other nations have their hands full with similar problems and are not eager to invite more trouble by supporting his little dictatorship. Besides this, the insurance company, which doesn't recognize the validity of governments, has declared that in the event of aggression against its insured it will demand reparations payments, *not from the country as a whole,* but from every individual directly responsible for directing and carrying out the aggression. The dictator hesitates to take such an awful chance, and he knows that his officers and soldiers will be very reluctant to carry out his order. Even worse, he can't arouse the populace

The Abolition of War

against the insurance company by urging them to defend themselves —the insurance company poses no threat to them.

A dictator in such a precarious position would be strongly tempted to give in to the insurance company's demands in order to salvage what he could (as the managers of the insurance company were sure he would before they undertook the contract with the mining firm). But even giving in will not save the dictator's government for long As soon as the insurance company can enforce non-interference with the mining company, it has created an enclave of free territory within the dictatorship. When it becomes evident that the insurance company can make good its offer of protection from the government, numerous businesses and individuals, both those from the laissez-faire society and citizens of the dictatorship, will rush to buy similar protection (a lucrative spurt of sales foreseen by the insurance company when it took its original action). At this point, it is only a matter of time until the government crumbles from lack of money and support, and the whole country becomes a free area.

In this manner, the original laissez-faire society, as soon as its insurance companies and defense agencies became strong enough, would generate new laissez-faire societies in locations all over the world. These new free areas, as free trade made them economically stronger, would give liberty a tremendously broadened base from which to operate and would help prevent the possibility that freedom could be wiped out by a successful sneak attack against the original laissez-faire society. As the world-wide, interconnected free market thus formed became stronger and the governments of the world became more tyrannical and chaotic, it would be possible for insurance companies and defense agencies to create free enclaves within more and more nations, a sales opportunity which they would be quick to take advantage of.

It is obvious that, while a laissez-faire society might be vulnerable in its infancy, it would rapidly gain strength as it matured. At the same time, the nations of the world would become weaker and more chaotic, opening the way for the establishment of free enclaves which would destroy governments and form a world-wide free market. In the final maturity of this free market, there would be no more governments left, and so . . . no more wars. The only way this condition of world-wide peace and freedom could be lost is if a large number of people reverted to the "give us a leader" superstition and demanded a return of governments all over the world. There are strong safeguards against this disaster, however. Not only would it be hard to get such a movement going all over an enlightened world, but capable individuals tend not to want a leader, and incapable ones tend to be uninfluential in the just environment of a laissez-faire society.

The length of a laissez-faire society's possibly vulnerable infancy and the possibility and severity of any wars during this period depend on variable factors beyond our present foresight. For instance, the size and location of the original free area would have a great deal of influence on its strength and its consequent safety and rate of spread. A large, well industrialized country with adequate natural resources is obviously preferable, while a small island would run the risk of being overrun before is got well started.

Another important variable is the amount of economic deterioration present in the world as a whole at the time the laissez-faire society is established. Governmental fiscal policies are leading the world down on one-way street to economic disaster. It would be ideal to have the governments as economically weak as possible, but at the same time if the laissez-faire society arises in a time and place of financial ruin, much valuable energy will have to be expended just to bring fiscal order and sanity out of the resulting social disorder.

Probably the most important variables are involved in the extent to which the idea of the nature and practicality of liberty is spread. If an overwhelming majority of the people in the free area are firmly convinced of the personal benefits of liberty, they will obviously be a force to be reckoned with. In addition, the spread of the idea throughout the major nations would go far toward undermining their strength. It is useful to remember that ideas know no boundaries.

Since the governments of the world are largely controlled by men who have a profound disrespect for the importance and efficacy of ideas, it is somewhat questionable whether they would be able to recognize the threat which the idea of liberty poses to them in time to avert it. To men who live on the basis of range-of-the-moment pragmatism, ideas can be almost invisible. Furthermore, the leaders of the world are paralyzed by their cynical allegiance to the wornout and bloodstained philosophy of statism, which has long ago proved its inability to effect any human happiness. They have no idealistic fervor to spur them on and excite their followers, but only a tired and frightened clinging to a familiar status quo. The wave of progress has already passed them by.

Since life offers no automatic guarantees of safety and success, there is no guarantee that a laissez-faire society would survive and prosper. But freedom is stronger than slavery, and a good idea, once spread, is impossible to stamp out. *The idea of liberty* is the innoculation which can kill parasitical governments and prevent the disease of war.

PART III

HOW DO WE GET THERE?

"If the revolution comes by violence, and in advance of light, the old struggle will have to be begun again."—Benjamin R. Tucker

15

From Government to Laissez Faire

The prospect of real freedom in a laissez-faire society is a dazzling one, but how can such a society ever be brought about? Through the decades, government has silently grown and spread, thrusting insidious, intertwining tentacles into nearly every area of our lives. Our society is now so thoroughly penetrated by government bureaucracy and our economy so entangled in government controls that dissolution of the State would cause major and painful temporary dislocations. The problems of adjusting to a laissez-faire society are somewhat like those facing an alcoholic or heroin addict who is thinking of kicking the habit, and the difficulties and discomforts involved may make some people decide that we'd be better off just staying as we are.

It is naive, however, to assume that we *can* "just stay as we are." America, and most of the rest of the world, is caught in a wave of economic decay and social upheaval which nothing can stop. After decades of governmental "fine tuning," our economy is now so distorted and crippled that we have a tremendous and ever growing class of hopeless and desperate poor. These poor and dispossessed feel a very well-justified (if usually misdirected) resentment which they express in demonstrations and riots. Governmental attempts to aid them, even if such attempts could be free of bureaucratic pork-barreling and pocket-lining, merely make the situation worse. After all, government can only get its "aid" money by bleeding it from our already sick economy, thereby weakening the economy still further and creating more poor to be aided. As the poor see their lives becoming increasingly miserable in spite of all the political promises of help, their resentment must grow more violent.

Meanwhile, the bureaucrats' attempts to save an economy dying of governmental controls by imposing more and more controls are pushing us swiftly down the path of financial ruin. If they aren't stopped in their frantic efforts to cure our collectivist poisoning by forcing us to swallow more collectivism, they will sooner or later push us over the brink into total economic collapse—the kind of collapse where government money loses all its value and people starve to death in the streets.

The choice is not laissez-faire vs. the status quo, because we cannot possibly keep the status quo anyway. Tremendous socio-economic forces, set in motion long ago by governmental plundering and power-grabbing, are sweeping the present order out from under our feet. We can only choose whether we will allow ourselves to be pushed into economic chaos and political tyranny or whether we will resist the bureaucratic tyrants and looters and work to set up a free society where each man can live his own life and "do his own thing." Whichever we choose, the road ahead will probably be rough; but the important question is, "What kind of society do we want to arrive at in the end?"

How soon a laissez-faire society can be established and exactly what conditions may accompany a transition from government to freedom are impossible to predict because of two important variables —the rapidity with which the idea of freedom can be spread and how much longer our economy can withstand the effects of governmental meddling.

The economies of all the major nations are in various states of disintegration. For decades, governments have been inflating their currencies in order to siphon more money into the government treasuries than they could get by taxation alone. But the extra paper money pumped into the economy by inflation distorts the economy by causing malinvestments. This is the "boom" part of the dreaded business cycle. Governments don't mind a boom at all, since inflation enables them to collect more revenue without antagonizing the taxpayer (the bureaucrats can always lay the blame on "the wage-price spiral" or "Big Business" or "greedy unions"). But as soon as the effects of an inflationary input wear off, people see the error of the malinvestments and abandon them and the "boom" is replaced by a "bust." The only way a government can avoid the painful readjustment of a "bust" is to continually increase inflation, which continually decreases the value of each monetary unit in the economy. When the value of the paper dollar falls below the value of the gold dollar, the people are forbidden to own gold and the government sets an artificial "price on gold," which eventually leads to recurring gold crises. When the value of the paper dollar falls below the value of the silver in four quarters, people hoard the quarters and the government has to put out low-value cupro-nickel coins to alleviate the "coin shortage."

In this way the value of your money is gradually eroded until all you have in your pocket is unbacked paper and low-value cupro-nickel. (Although the dollar is nominally backed by gold, this does us no good, since the Government forbids us to own that gold!) The economy continues to operate on this fake money simply because people are used to believing that it has real value. But, as the government is forced to inflate more and more to avoid an ever more severe depression, hyper-inflation sets in and the value of the monetary unit falls with increasing speed. The resulting soaring prices force people to recognize the shrinking value of the money. Then there is a mad scramble to spend money quickly before it loses any more of its value. People rush to buy durable goods of any kind as storers-of-value in the place of the nearly worthless money. These frantic attempts to get rid of money and hold onto goods quickly reduce the trading value of the dollar to zero, and the economy is left without any medium of exchange and must fall back on barter. Since barter is completely insufficient to support an industrialized economy (how would General Motors pay its employees on a barter basis? how would your grocer pay the wholesaler from whom he buys the food?), there is mass unemployment, destitution and starvation.

So the bureaucrats' attempt to avoid the depression caused by their inflationary policies only succeed in making the depression far more severe when it does come. If they resort to hyper-inflation, the ensuing depression will involve the complete collapse of the monetary structure of the country, as in Germany after World War I. Germany was able to recover from its monetary collapse fairly quickly because many of the other nations still had fairly sound currencies to which Germans could turn for media of exchange. The collapse toward which we are slipping will be much harder to recover from. Most of the currencies of the world have no more actual value behind them than does America's, and furthermore, the major currencies are all tied to each other and to the dollar, so that if the dollar goes, they all go. Such a world-wide monetary collapse would leave us without any medium of exchange except for the gold and silver which a few far-sighted individuals have horded, and even this might have to be exchanged on a black market basis due to governmental prohibitions. Before this gold and silver could become sufficiently spread through the economies of the world to lift them from barter back to a monetary basis, millions may have starved to death. Governments can't create money out of paper, ink, and promises. Once they destroy their currencies, they can only wait for the processes of the market to re-establish a medium of exchange.

Since the state of our economy depends largely on the whims of bureaucrats and politicians, it is impossible to predict whether our currency will continue to function for several more months or for several years before going into hyper-inflation and final collapse. Similarly, it is impossible to say whether the collapse will happen rather suddenly, as in 1929-32, or whether it will come as a long-drawn-out series of fiscal crises, each worse than the last. The only thing we can say with certainty is that a day of reckoning must come for the badly inflated dollar and for all the other shaky currencies of the world, and that governments will inevitably pursue policies designed to put off that day of reckoning, thereby making it far more disastrous when it does come.

In making the transition from government control to a laissez-faire society, then, our first concern should be to minimize the effects of the inevitable economic breakdown caused by the politicians' fiscal meddlings. There are several measures which would greatly help, all of which involve abolishing existing laws and regulations—that is, they involve a return to freedom of the market.

First and foremost, the economy should be provided with media of exchange to replace the dying dollar. Since gold and silver have proved themselves through centuries of trading to be the most acceptable monetary media, this means that we must get as much gold and silver into the hands of as many private individuals as quickly as possible. All restrictions on the ownership and importation of gold in any form whatever should be gotten rid of as soon as possible, and Americans should be encouraged to exchange their dollars for all the gold and silver left in the Treasury at whatever price ratio the free market sets. All the many restrictions on gold mining should be dispensed with so that the demand for hard money could be partially met with newly mined gold.

Along with getting monetary metals into the hands of private individuals, there should be an end to all laws preventing private coinage of money. Businessmen should be as free to manufacture coins for exchange as they are to manufacture vacuum cleaners. In both cases, the processes of the free market will encourage those with the best products and eliminate the frauds.

The monopoly of the Federal Reserve System on banking should be broken so that entrepreneurs could set up completely private banks regulated by nothing but the processes of the market. It is through the mechanism of the Federal Reserve that the Government inflates the currency, and special privilege laws permitting banks to hold only fractional reserves against their demand deposits add to the problem. Private coinage and private banking will put a permanent end to inflation, depression, and monetary crises.

Critics will object that without the restrictions preventing private individuals from owning gold and coining their own money, nearly everyone would rush to exchange their paper dollars for gold and silver coins and certificates backed by such coins. This would precipitate a crisis for governmental money and a severe de facto devaluation of the dollar. And the critics are right—this *is* what would happen. But an economic crisis will come anyhow; the politicians have already made it inevitable. The crisis will be far less severe, and recovery far more rapid, if it comes as a result of people deserting the dollar for a truly valuable medium of exchange than if the dollar collapses from hyper-inflation, leaving them no money commodity at all. By forcing us to use an inflated and increasingly devalued currency, the bureaucrats are denying us our only chance to rescue our economy and our own private savings from the government-created fiscal chaos. The dollar can't be saved—it's already dying of governmental interference. Let's not let the bureaucrats kill the whole economy along with it in the name of trying to save their decaying, totalitarian monetary system.

The preceding discussion has assumed that the transition to a laissez-faire society can be gotten well underway before the economy collapses. If the economy collapses first, all of the above measures will still apply in order to facilitate recovery, but, of course, the recovery will be much more difficult and slower.

In making the transition to a laissez-faire society, many governmental institutions which have been an integral part of society for years or decades or centuries will have to be abolished. Taxes present the least problem—obviously, they should be abolished immediately. Taxation is theft, and there is never any justification for continuing theft. The abolition of all taxes would stimulate an immediate and rapid spurt of growth throughout the whole economy as money formerly drained into bureaucratic boondoggles and political pocketbooks became available for productive use. Imagine what it would do for your own personal prosperity to have your real income almost doubled overnight (taxes, including all hidden taxes, take over one-third of the average man's income). This same prosperity would be felt by the whole economy. As each productive man's real income shot upward, there would be a sharp increase in both consumption and investment. The consumption would mean a greater demand for all products and services, and the investment would provide the capital structure necessary to meet that demand. New products would be marketed, new jobs created, and the general standard of living would rise. (It is true that government both spends and invests tax revenues, but it always allocates these revenues differently from the way their rightful owners would have allocated them, thus distorting the market. Also, government investments are notably wasteful and counterproductive. For example, the U. S. Government once formed an Abaca Production and Sales bureau to take over the growing of hemp in four Central American countries, on the theory that hemp, which is used for the manufacture of rope, was vitally strategic. But this government-produced hemp was of such inferior quality that it couldn't be sold, even to the Government's own rope factory. To get out of its embarrassment, Abaca Production and Sales sold the worthless hemp to another Government agency, the Strategic Stockpile. The hemp was then stored, at taxpayers' expense, in specially built warehouses. Each year the previour year's crop was shoveled out and destroyed to make room to store the new crop. Total loss to the taxpayers averaged $3 million a year.[1]

Government employees would have to find jobs in private enterprise if they wanted to work. There are two major kinds of governmental employees—those whose services would be in demand in the free market (teachers, librarians, secretaries, firemen, etc.) and those who perform no useful function but simply keep the governmental machinery running (lawmakers, tax collectors, bureaucratic record keepers and paper shufflers, executives in the military-industrial complex, the President and the Vice President, etc.). The first kind would probably find only minor difficulties in adjusting to a free society. A forest ranger in Yellowstone National Park might find his job almost unchanged, as the Park was taken over by a private corporation to be run for profit. Those lawyers and judges whose minds were young and flexible enough to adjust to freedom instead of statutory law could sell their services to free enterprise arbitration agencies. On the other hand, men who had spent their lives as tax collectors for the Internal Revenue Service or as Federal narcotics agents would find no demand for their "services" and would have to change careers in order to survive—perhaps even to that of garbage collector or janitor (honorable work, for a change). In a sense, this would be a partial penalty for having been willing to make a career of ruling over others.

Switching to a laissez-faire society would certainly require large adjustments in the lives of many people. It's amazing, though, how swiftly and efficiently adjustments can be made in a free-market situation. When some men want to sell their services, other men want to buy services to manufacture a product, and still other men want to buy the product, nothing can stop them from getting together in a mutually beneficial exchange except the interference of government. So, while the birth of a free society would bring temporary hardships to many, the period of adjustment would be fairly brief. In the end, all would be better off than they had been when ruled by government (with the possible exception of such parasites as Presidents, White House advisors, and Pentagon Generals).

---

[1]For this and other examples of ridiculous government waste, listen to "Hayfoot, Strawfoot," an LP record by Willis Stone, available from Key Records, Box 46128, Los Angeles, California.

But what about government obligations such as the national debt—who will see that they are met? Those who ask this question have never stopped to analyze what is meant by "government obligations." Morally, the government is no more than a well-organized band of robber barons. In order to maintain itself in power, it borrows money, grants special privileges, and makes promises to certain groups and individuals. But where does it get the money to pay its debts and keep its promises? By the theft of taxation. Obviously, the victims of a hoodlum gang cannot be morally required to give up their honestly earned money in order to pay debts incurred by the gang in its attempts to stay in power over them. No government obligation of any sort is morally binding on the citizen-subjects (or former citizen-subjects) of that government. Those who voluntarily loaned money to the government were at fault for sanctioning and supporting the activities of the hoodlum gang, and justice demands that they must take their losses and make the best of it.

Of course, many who have "loaned" money to the government, expecting to be paid back later, have had no choice in the matter (Social Security is the prime example of this point). Others who have never voluntarily paid into government treasuries have been made dependent on governmental welfare payments when political meddling strangled the economy and denied them decent jobs. These people are among the most tragic victims of the power-grabbers. But to continue collecting money by force in order to make payments to them would simply be to perpetuate the system which enslaved them in the first place. In a newly born laissez-faire society, these people would have to either find jobs (which would be plentiful after the adjustment period) or depend on private charity. This may seem harsh, but it is far less terrible than what will happen to the poor, the sick, and the old if we allow government to continue in power until it brings us to economic collapse and mass starvation.

When considering the hardships which people such as Social Security recipients would undergo during the transition to a laissez-faire society, it is well to remember that most of these people are guilty of at least passively consenting to the politicians predations. If enough of them had raised a protest a few decades ago, we wouldn't be facing this governmentally induced crisis today. People who meekly consent to wrongs because no one else is objecting to them, instead of identifying and condemning the corruptions, are filling up a reservoir of hardship. If the dam breaks and they are engulfed in the flood, they shouldn't be too surprised. The hardships, after all, are partly due to their guilt of consent.

One of the most important considerations raised in connection with the abolition of government is what should be done with government wealth and property. As far as monetary wealth goes, this is no problem . . . since the government doesn't have any (as a look at the national debt figures will show). The government does, however, possess a tremendous amount and variety of "property" in the form of land, buildings, roads, military installations, schools, businesses such as the Post Office, Government Printing Office, and hundreds less well-known, prisons, libraries, etc., etc. Though these items are in the temporary possession of whatever bureaucrats happen to be in charge of them, they are not actually *owned* by anyone. "The public" is unable to own them, since nothing can be owned by a collective myth like "the people." Politicians and bureaucrats don't own them for the same reason that a thief doesn't rightfully own the property he has stolen. "Public property" is actually unowned potential property.

Since valuables in the possession of government are not actually owned, it would be perfectly proper for anyone to take possession of any piece of "public property" at any time that the government became too weak or careless to prevent him from doing so. The man who took possession of a piece of former "public property," claiming it and marking it as his own for all to see, would become the rightful owner of that property.

It has been proposed that the process of disposing of "public property" should be made orderly by selling the items to the highest bidder, rather than simply allowing them to be claimed by any comer. The money thus collected, it is held, could then be given back to the taxpayers in the form of income tax rebates, or it could simply be destroyed (assuming it to be in the form of paper currency or similar fiat money) in order to reverse the process of inflation and restore some value to the dollar.

Several objections can be raised to this plan, however. First it would be next to impossible to prevent a great deal of graft as the money from "public property" sales rolled in. Given a stream of money, a bureaucrat can always figure out a way to divert some of it into his own pocket, and who would there be to police the bureaucrats and politicians except other bureaucrats and politicians? Second, this system is definitely biased toward large firms and wealthy individuals. This would not be objectionable if the rich were rich largely because of their own merit and the poor were poor solely because of their incompetence and laziness, as would be the case in a long-established laissez-faire society. But in our governmentally controlled society, many of the poor are poor because bureaucratic regulation and taxation robbed them of a chance, and many of the rich are rich because of political pull.

Finally, selling "public property" to the highest bidder would inevitably involve a long delay before many of the items could be put to productive use. This delay would make the transition period to a laissez-faire society longer and more difficult, since a delay in production means a delay in available jobs and in produced items to consume. And if the process were not to be dragged on indefinitely, many items would have to be abandoned, to be simply claimed in the future (how many people do you know who want 100 acres ten miles from the nearest road in the middle of the Mojave Desert?). Of course the politicians would try to keep the sale business going indefinitely, in order to prolong their power and would thereby make themselves harder to get rid of.

From a moral point of view, items which aren't owned can't be rightfully sold, anyway. Sale is one means of disposing of property, and property is that which is owned. If something isn't owned, it can't be sold, and "public property" isn't owned by anyone, either the public or the politicians.

It has been objected that if "public property" were thrown open to ownership by anyone who claimed it, there would be a welter of confusing, contradictory claims, and possibly violence and bloodshed. It is true that this might happen initially, especially if government lost its power to hold onto its possessions all at once. Societies have survived a sudden flood of claims to some particular wealth on a smaller scale (gold rushes being a notable example). While there is a great deal of confusion and some injustice in the beginning, things usually settle down in a fairly short period of time, especially when there is a large amount of desirable, potential property to be claimed, as is the case with present "public property." And, it must be noted that such a situation of conflicting claims would certainly stimulate the growth of private enterprise services of protection, defense, and arbitration. This positive side effect would help the infant laissez-faire society get underway and gain strength quickly.

It has also been objected that if anyone could lay claim to any piece of former "public property," many valuable items might be claimed by undeserving bums and bureaucrats. Again, it's certainly true that this might happen in many cases. But the operations of the free market always penalize the incompetent, causing them to lose properties which they are incapable of operating effectively. If a drunken bum claimed the Chicago Main Post Office, what would he do with it? If he lacked the skill to operate the facility, he would have to simply hold on to it while someone else started a profitable private mail service in some other Chicago building, or he would have to sell it. If he sold it, it would then be put to productive use and he would be left with a sum of money to squander on liquor. Either way, the market would soon reach a condition of maximum productivity and the fate of the bum would become irrelevant to everyone but himself.

But, while incompetents would be shunted aside by the workings of the free market, those with ability and initiative would be given a chance to make their fortunes, regardless of their previous social and financial status. Not only would this wide-open claiming system at last give worthwhile opportunities to the poor and victims of discrimination, it would also help counteract the effects of eliminating welfare and government jobs.

There would certainly be difficulties and temporary dislocations involved in making the transition from government slavery to laissez-faire freedom, but they could be overcome by free men acting in a free market. And when the transition has been made, new opportunities would open up for everyone. There would be more and better jobs, better pay, a multitude of new ideas, inventions and business opportunities, and countless chances to "strike it rich." Inflation could not threaten society, because there would be a sound monetary system. Consumer goods would multiply, living standards rise, and the hopeless and degrading poverty of today's slums become a thing of the past. Most important of all, there would be freedom. No one would be taxed, or regulated, or forced to live his life according to someone else's standards. No one would need to fear that his peaceful and private pastimes would bring the police with a warrant for his arrest. No one would be forced to bow to the whim of a power-hungry bureaucrat.

On the other hand, if our society continues to be governmentally controlled, we can expect a steady increase in economic troubles, unemployment, inflation, crime, poverty, and, eventually, a complete collapse of the governmental monetary system, bringing widespread starvation. We can also expect a steady decrease in our government-permitted "freedoms" as more and more bureaucrats find more and more ways of taking care of us and exercising power over us.

A laissez-faire society is worth the thought, effort, and struggle necessary to achieve it, because *liberty is the answer to all of our societal problems.*

16
The Force Which Shapes The World

But a discussion of how government could be dismantled and how free men could then build a laissez-faire society out of the pieces still doesn't answer the question, "How do we get there?" Politicians are politicians because they enjoy wielding power over others and being honored for their "high positions." Power and plaudits are the politician's life, and a true politician will fight to the death (your death) if he thinks it will help him hold on to them. Even the gray, faceless bureaucrats cling to their little bits of power with the desperate tenacity of a multitude of leaches, each squirming and fighting to hold and increase his area of domination. How can we successfully oppose this vast, cancerous power structure? Where can we find a force strong enough to attack, undermine, and finally destroy its power?

Some people, gazing up at the fearsome might of the American Leviathan, have decided that our only hope lies in an eventual armed revolution. So they work to recruit revolutionaries, provoke a spirit of aggressive hostility toward The Establishment and promote violent confrontations with government representatives and police. Most of these people are quite sincere in their desire to increase liberty by overthrowing a government which insists on taxing us, regulating us, and "taking care of us" until it smothers us. Many of them even realize that we can't have real freedom so long as we have any government at all. But few, if any, of them have thought through the necessary implications of violent revolution.

Armed revolutions, whether they occur on a massive, organized scale or as disconnected, hit-and-run confrontations, are very destructive. Quite apart from the immorality of destroying the private property or life of an individual who has not aggressed against you, destruction is foolish and short-sighted. It often takes years to build what it may take only moments to destroy; and once destroyed, an object can never again be of benefit to anyone. Destruction reduces the total amount of goods available to everyone and, hence, reduces the welfare of every individual in the society (naturally, the poor feel this welfare reduction first and worst). The destroyed object can

The Force Which Shapes The World 161

be rebuilt, but only at the cost of much time, money, and intellectual and physical effort. It usually will not be rebuilt at all until the destruction is over so that the builders feel it will be safe. Meanwhile, the economy (which means all the individuals who try to improve their lot by trading goods and services with others) is weakened. To weaken a healthy economy would be bad enough, but to bleed our economy—which is already tottering on the brink of collapse—is suicidal folly.

Not only is violent revolutionary action destructive, it actually strengthens the government by giving it a "common enemy" to unite the people against. Violence against the government by a minority always gives the politicians an excuse to increase repressive measures in the name of "protecting the people." In fact, the general populace usually joins the politicians' cry for "law and order."

But far worse than this, revolution is a very questionable way to arrive at a society without rulers, since a successful revolution must have leaders. To be successful, revolutionary action must be coordinated. To be coordinated, it must have someone in charge. And, once the revolution has succeeded, the "Someone in Charge" (or one of his lieutenants, or even one of his enemies) takes over the new power structure so conveniently built up by the revolution. He may just want to "get things going right," but he ends up being another ruler. Something like this happened to the American Revolution, and look at us today.

Even if a revolution could manage to avoid setting up a new ruler, the great mass of people themselves would probably call for one. Revolution causes confusion and chaos, and in times of distress and disorder the first thought of the majority of people is, "We must have a leader to get us out of these troubles!" When people cry frantically for a leader, they always get one; there's no shortage of men with power-lust. Furthermore, the leader they get will be a dictator with power to "restore law and order" in accordance with the citizens' demands. Unless people know what laissez-faire freedom is (and that's the only kind of freedom there is), and unless they know that it is far preferable to a system of governmental slavery, the odds are that any violent revolution will only pave the way for a new Hitler. Then we will be far worse off than we are now, because we will be saddled with physical destruction and its resultant poverty, with economic collapse, and with a dictatorial state with popular support.

Knowing the dangers and drawbacks of violent revolution, a few advocates of laissez-faire have proposed that we get "our people" into government and dismantle it from the inside. The difficulty with this proposal is that only men of integrity, who have no desire to rule over others, could be trusted to dismantle government instead of joining the power elite once they got into official positions. But men of integrity could hardly be expected to make the sacrifice of wasting their lives in government jobs, surrounded by looters. And once again, if people didn't understand the desirability of a laissez-faire society, dismantling the government might only confuse and alarm them into calling for new leadership.

It has also been suggested that the way to win out over government in the long run is to withdraw all sanction from it and refuse to have any dealings with it; to avoid voting, accepting government subsidies, or using government services. The problem here is that government can compel us to deal with it, either by force of law or by holding a monopoly on some vital service. You may refuse to vote, but try refusing to use the government roads and mail system, to pay taxes, or to be drafted! Withdrawing our sanction from the looters by refusing to deal with them would be a very effective tactic . . . if the looters would permit us to do so!

Despair has caused some to decide that the battle, at least in America, is already lost, and that our only hope of some freedom for our own lives lies in building a new society on some remote island or in retreating into a wilderness to escape "Big Brother." Settling and industrializing a small island outside the tax-grip of any government (if such a place could be found) might be an interesting and even profitable venture, but it's no way to defeat governments. As soon as the free island became an attractive enough prize, some government would gobble it up. Founding a free island is not a step toward victory—at best, it's merely a postponement of defeat.

Similarly, a well-prepared wilderness retreat could be a life-saving shelter in case of a really severe socio-economic breakdown, but "opting out" is no way to defeat governments so we can have a free and secure world to live in. A retreat is just what its name implies—retreat, not victory.

The advocates of revolution, of dismantling the government from within or refusing to deal with it, or of "opting out" have failed to realize that if one wants to change society, one must first find out what makes society the way it is. Society is nothing more than a group of individuals living in the same geographical area at the same time. The values and the actions of each of these individuals are determined by the ideas he holds—by what he believes is right or wrong, beneficial or harmful for himself and others. This means that the customs, institutions, and life-style of any society are determined by the ideas held by the majority of influential people in that society. Just as the form of a man's life is the result of the ideas he holds, so the form of a society is the result of the ideas which prevail in that society.

Ideas, even seemingly insignificant ones, can have earth-shattering results when they are widely believed in a culture. For example, in the Middle Ages, a minor religious dogma held that cats were agents of the devil. Since religion was a very important factor in almost everyone's life at that time, almost the whole society participated in the religious duty of killing cats. As the cat population dwindled, the rodent population increased rapidly. The rats carried the fleas which carried the germs which caused the Black Death. Between one-fourth and one-third of Europe's people died and almost one-half of the people of England died within two years, all because of one stupid, bad idea (though a seemingly harmless one)!

Good ideas can be just as powerful as bad ones. The realization that diseases are caused by micro-organisms and not by demons, the will of God, or the bad night air, has saved more lives than the Black Death destroyed. This one good idea has improved the health and increased the life-span of every one of us. The partial realization that man has rights which no government is entitled to take away led to nearly two centuries of the greatest progress and happiness men had yet known.

Mistaken ideas kept man cowering in superstitious fear of the gods . . . smeared stone altars with human blood . . . caused living children to be thrown into sacrificial fires. Correct ideas—the result of reason—have freed man to stand proud and erect . . . to understand nature instead of fearing it . . . to achieve a better life for his children instead of sacrificing them to the gods of his insane fears.

Ideas are the forces which shape our lives and our world!

But because ideas are invisible, most people think of them as unimportant (if they think of them at all). You can see a city, but you can't see the multitude of plans that had to be drawn for each building, each street, each park. Nor can you see the millions of ideas that made possible the electricity, the automobiles, the supermarkets, the lawnmowers, the playground equipment, etc., etc. It's easy to observe a government (the bureaucrats won't let you ignore it), but you can't see the idea that makes it possible—*the belief in millions of minds that it's right for some men to govern, or coercively rule over, others.*

Because the forms of men's lives and of their societies depend on what they believe, *ideas are the most powerful force in the world.* If you want to get a man to change his life-style, you will have to get him to change his ideas about what sort of life-style is possible to and desirable for him. Similarly, if you want to change a society, you will have to get the majority of influential people to change their ideas about what their society can and should be.

In a cannibal society, the reason men eat human flesh is that it is considered proper, or perhaps even necessary, to use human beings for food. In order to get rid of the cannibalism, it is only necessary to change the prevailing idea that eating people is proper or necessary. In a governmental society, the reason some men rule over others is that the vast majority of opinion-molders in that society consider it proper or even necessary for men to be ruled by force. In order to get rid of government it is only necessary to change the prevailing idea that men must or should be kept in some degree of slavery by their rulers. In a society dominated by the idea that no man has a right to govern anyone else, government would be impossible—no would-be ruler could muster enough gunmen to inforce his will.

Not only can a society be changed by changing the ideas which prevail in it, *this is the only way it can be changed* (except by enslaving, impoverishing, or killing all the members of the society in order to forcibly prevent them from living in the way their ideas dictate). Government is only the concrete expression and result of the prevailing idea that it is right for men to be governed by force. At present, the American government has the sanction and support, or at least the apathetic acceptance, of the majority of its citizen-subjects. So long as the majority of men believe that government is right and/or necessary, they will have a government. If their government is destroyed before they understand the desirability and practicality of freedom, they will rush to set up a new one, because they believe they must be governed in order to have a civilized world. Until we change this idea, we can never have a free society.

Bringing about a laissez-faire society by changing the ideas which prevail in our culture may seem like a difficult, centuries-long task, but opinion-molding isn't really that hard. In any society, only a very small minority—perhaps one or two per cent—do any original thinking. A somewhat larger percentage act as transmission belts, passing the thinkers' ideas on to the rest of the population. The vast majority of the people simply absorb their ideas from the culture around them, accepting the word of authorities or the opinions of their social circle, with little question or thought. In order to change the ideas in a society, it is only necessary to change the ideas of the tiny minority of thinkers and then watch while they filter down through the commentators, writers, editors, teachers, and all the other "influential men," to be echoed by everyone else. It is the thinkers who control a society's future course—Presidents and other politicians are merely the actors who pass across the stage, mouthing the lines which they have absorbed.

Furthermore, it isn't even necessary to change the opinions of the men who are our present thinkers. Today's opinion molders are the remnants of a confused, exhausted, cynical past. Once, their ideas of a big, fatherly government watching over its citizens, regulating their economic affairs, protecting them from fear, want, hunger, pornography, liquor, and marijuana, and insuring their "general welfare" seemed new and promising. Now, however, the mess of poverty, slavery, and conflict resulting from their belief in forced welfare, forced socialism, and forced morality is beginning to become apparent to all. These thinkers of the past have not only failed to solve our problems, they've made them incalculably worse, and because the mess is beginning to stink so badly, their time is running out. They'll have to make way for a new breed of thinkers—for the libertarians (mostly young people) who don't have much influence yet but who will have in just a few years. Many of the thinkers of the future are already beginning to realize the meaning and necessity of freedom. When enough of them understand laissez-faire, the future is ours!

The idea we have to spread is very easy to understand—it is simply that government is an unnecessary evil and that freedom is the best and most practical way of life.

Throughout history, most men have considered government to be a given fact of life—as unavoidable as devastating storms and fatal illnesses. Of the few who thought about it at all, most concluded that, while government might be evil, it was a necessary evil because the nature of man demanded that he be ruled . . . for his own good (!). And the majority of men went along with this in an unthinking way because having a leader seemed to eliminate the awful need of being responsible for their own lives and decisions in an uncertain world. So the fear of self-responsibility became a fear of freedom, and rulers encouraged this by vesting government with all the authority, legitimacy, pomp and tradition they could muster, while keeping the populace ignorant and superstitious. We can still see this fear of self-responsibility in the demands for laws to protect the people from gambling, drugs, prostitution, misleading packaging, "unfair competition," guns, "sub-minimum" wages, monopolies, and countless other imaginary menaces.

But government means some men governing—ruling over—others by force, and this is what we must tell the people we want to convince. When some men rule over others, a condition of slavery exists, and slavery is wrong under any circumstances. To advocate limited government is to advocate limited slavery. To say that government is a necessary prerequisite for a civilized society is to say that slavery is necessary for a civilized society. To say that men cannot protect their freedom without a government is to say that men cannot protect their freedom without a system of slavery. Slavery is never either right or necessary . . . and neither is that form of slavery called government. We must tell people that government isn't a necessary evil; it's an unnecessary one.

We must also tell them that freedom, because it is the right way for men to live, is practical. A laissez-faire society would work, and work well. The social problems that perplex almost everyone are the result, not of too much freedom, but of government meddling in our lives with its compulsions, prohibitions, and ever-growing taxes. We must tell people that a laissez-faire society wouldn't degenerate into chaos, that instead it would solve most of our problems. And we must be ready to show just how such a society would maintain itself and why it would solve the problems.

There are an infinite number of ways to tell people about liberty—as many ways as there are individual ideas about how to do it. We can do everything from talking to friends to writing articles and giving speeches, to organizing huge street demonstrations against government injustices. Government has a great deal of *power* over us, but it doesn't have any *right* to dictate our actions. This means that, so long as we are careful not to initiate force against the person or property of any innocent bystander, we may oppose government in any way which we consider practical and reasonably safe. If we were in Russia or China, our tactics would probably have to be quite different, but in America people are used to a large measure of freedom of speech, so such activities as the publication of this book are *permitted* and still safe.

Fighting government with ideas of freedom has an interesting built-in safety factor—most of our politicians and bureaucrats, like most other people, can't see the importance of ideas. What counts with them is votes, tax money, and political deals. Such esoteric things as philosophical concepts about the nature of a free society will never become visible to them until the votes, the revenues, and the law enforcement begin to be effected; at which point it will be too late to stop the idea of freedom. If you throw a bomb, the police will come after you and the terrified public will cry for "law and order." But if you disseminate a constructive idea, people who are receptive will catch it, understand it, and pass it on, while the power structure will blindly ignore it.

To understand the importance of spreading the idea of freedom, think of what would happen if a majority (or even a large minority) of the people in America came to believe that government was an unnecessary evil and that freedom was the best and most practical way of life. Already, even with the support of most people, government bureaus are beginning to creak and falter and break down under the weight of their own incompetence. The Post Office cries for help, the courts have such an incredible backlog that "the right to a speedy trial" is a mockery, jails are packed, roads are crowded, schools never have enough money, and inflation spirals. Government is inadequate to cope with the complexities of modern life, and it's becoming apparent to all but the willfully blind. Along with this private businesses are beginning to grow in areas which were formerly the exclusive domain of government. The private mail delivery company, booming in spite of being forbidden to deliver first class mail, and private arbitration services and protection agencies are a hopeful beginning.

In a few years, government will be even more overburdened, confused, and more obviously inadequate. The progressive breakdown of many more "governmental functions" will be opening the way for daring entrepreneurs to gain a foothold and offer superior services to the public. What if, at the same time, millions of Americans lost all respect for government? What if they saw government for what it really is— an annoying and dangerous band of looters, power-mad bureaucrats, and publicity-hungry politicians? What if the government, which is supposedly founded on the consent of the governed, no longer had that consent. What if the governed by the millions refused to be *guilty of consent* any longer?

If millions of Americans no longer regarded government as necessary, they would revoke "the consent of the governed." Then, with the strength of numbers, it would be quite feasible to refuse to deal with government and to openly disobey its stupid and unjust laws. What could the bureaucrats do if 50% of the population ignored all trade restrictions—including tariffs, price controls, minimum wage laws, sales taxes, and even oughtright prohibitions? What if they simply bought and sold whatever they pleased, from gold bullion to bricks, for whatever prices and under whatever conditions they wanted, regardless of political regulation? What would the Internal Revenue Service do if three million of their subjects simply didn't bother to send in any income tax forms, and what if fifty thousand employers stopped bothering to deduct withholding taxes?[1] What could the army do with a million men who refused to be drafted? What could they do

---

[1] "In a recent conversation with an official at the Internal Revenue Service, I was amazed when he told me that, 'if the taxpayers of this country ever discover that the Internal Revenue Service operates on 90% bluff, the entire system will collapse'." This statement was made by U. S. Senator Henry Bellmon of Oklahoma, as quoted from the printed copy of hearings in the Senate Finance committee on October 2, 1969.

if most of the men in a regiment just quietly quit and went home, leaving their officers red-faced and screaming behind them?

Such mass scale, passive disobedience to unreasonable laws wouldn't need to be organized if the majority of people saw government for what it is and believed in freedom. It would start secretly and quietly, with individuals doing things they felt they couldn't be caught for. (In fact, it already has started.) But as disrespect for government increased, the practice of ignoring laws would become increasingly open and widespread. At last it would be a great, peaceful, de facto revolt, beyond any power to stop.

If faced with such a massive, peaceful revolt, the government would have only two choices—to retreat, or to try to impose a tighter police state. If the politicians decided on retreat, they would be forced to sit by and watch their powers crumble away, piece by piece, until their government collapsed from lack of money and support. If they tried to impose a police state, they would arouse not only the original revolters but most of the rest of the people as well to open rebellion. The bureaucrats would find it very hard to whip up any popular support against people who had done no damage to any innocent person but were obviously only living their own lives and minding their own business. At each new repressive measure, the looters would find their popular support ebbing away, their armies and police forces torn with dissent and bled by desertion, their jails too full to hold any more rebels.

In such a crisis, the politicians would almost certainly vacillate. They have enough trouble making up their minds in ordinary dilemmas. This policy of vacillation would shake the tottering government apart even more surely and quickly, leaving the stage open for freedom.

We can bring about a laissez-faire society, but only through the tremendous, invisible power of ideas. Ideas are the motive power of human progress, the force which shapes the world. Ideas are more powerful than armies, because it was ideas which caused the armies to be raised in the first place, and it is ideas which keep them fighting (if this weren't true, political leaders wouldn't have to bother with their tremendous propaganda machinery). When an idea gains popular support, all the guns in the world cannot kill it.

Throughout history, the vast majority of people have believed that government was a necessary part of human existence . . . and so there have always been governments. People have believed they had to have a government because their leaders said so, because they had always had one, and most of all because they found the world unexplainable and frightening and felt a need for someone to lead them. Mankind's fear of freedom has always been a fear of self-reliance—of being thrown on his own to face a frightening world, with no one else to tell him what to do. But we are no longer terrified savages making offerings to a lightning god or cowering Medieval serfs hiding from ghosts and witches. We have learned that man can understand and control his environment and his own life, and we have no need of high priests or kings or presidents to tell us what to do. Government is now known for what it is. It belongs in the dark past with the rest of man's superstitions. *It's time for men to grow up* so that each individual man can walk forward into the sunlight of freedom . . . in full control of his own life!

SOCIETY WITHOUT COERCION

A New Concept of Social Organization

by

JARRET B. WOLLSTEIN

PUBLISHED BY THE
Society for Rational Individualism

Society Without Coercion. Copyright 1969 by the Society for
Rational Individualism.

Internal illustrations by Karen Gilstad.

TABLE OF CONTENTS

Preface ii
Introduction 1
1.0 THE NATURE OF MAN 2
    1.1 The Nature of Society 5
2.0 THE NATURE OF GOVERNMENT 10
    2.1 The Morality of Limited Government 13
    2.2 The Proprietary Community 17
    2.3 Arguments Against Anarchy 19
    2.4 Naming A Free Society 21
3.0 AGENCIES OF RETALIATORY FORCE 23
    3.1 Justice Agencies 25
    3.2 Police Forces 27
    3.3 The Court System 30
    3.4 The Penal System 32
    3.5 The Armed Forces 35
4.0 CREATING A FREE SOCIETY 39
    4.1 Alternatives to Governmental Services 40
    4.2 The Imperative To Act 41
Footnotes 44

PREFACE

This essay was originally planned to be titled "Government Without Coercion," based upon a speech of that name given by the author before Silver Spring SRI on February 2, 1969. However, since the announcement of that title, further thought and evaluation has led to several modifications and extensions of the original thesis. In particular, it has become obvious that the phrase "government without coercion" is largely a misnomer, and that in any case the topic could not be adequately discussed without consideration of the larger issue of "society without coercion."

"Society Without Coercion" includes all valid concepts planned for presentation in the essay "Government Without Coercion," and like that planned essay answers the question of how police forces, court systems, armies, etc. could be operated without any form of taxation or of charitable contributions. In addition, this essay also deals in much more depth than was originally planned with the topics of "the nature of man", "forms of social organization", and "the morality of limited government". Nothing valid, then, has been omitted, and much has been added.

Before beginning this essay the reader is cautioned to keep an open mind. Many of the concepts presented here, particularly those of financing and operating agencies of retaliatory force, will be new and strange to him, and he may at first be apt to reject them out-of-hand. However, familiarity or strangeness is not the criteria of validity of concepts. The inherent morality and practicality of society without coercion is not altered by the fact that the concept is presently largely absent from human consciousness.

The social systems predominant in the world today, and indeed all known major social systems which have ever existed, have been inherently coercive. This does not, however, mean that all must be so, or that the premises upon which they are based are valid. Indeed, the author seeks through this essay to take a major step toward the eradication of the virtually universal fallacies and myths which the domination of coercive social systems has perpetrated.

The purpose of this paper is two-fold: first to deductively demonstrate the general principle that *there is no valid need of man which cannot be met by voluntary cooperation, based on reason and trade*; second to suggest specific ways in which the agencies of retaliatory force of a free society could be financed and operated. The specific ideas for operation and financing are simply *one possible* application of the more general principle cited above; they are not the *only possible* such specific application. Indeed, having read this essay, the reader is apt to think of many alternative possibilities himself. This is in fact exactly what is hoped for: that the reader start positively and creatively thinking in terms of a society without coercion.

The specific proposals for the operation and financing of agencies of retaliatory force presented here are original with the author, and exclusively a product of his own creativity (expect where noted otherwise). However, it is highly probable that many of these ideas have been discovered independently by others. The main distinction of this essay, then, is that it formally presents *many ideas* of social organization *as an integrated concept*.

In addition to the specific conception of agencies of retaliatory force, the proof of the impossibility of one individual being able to determine the rational self-interest of another in the general case, and most of the theory of property presented here are original with the author. Finally, I take full credit for the concepts presented here for creating a free society.

The general principles presented and applied in this essay are based upon the ideas of two major theoreticians: Ayn Rand, founder of the philosophy of Objectivism, and Ludwig von Mises, founder of the Austrian school of economics. In particular, the section on "the nature of society" draws heavily upon principles elucidated by Ayn Rand. I would then like to acknowledge these two major intellectual sources, without whose works the composition of this paper would have been highly improbable. In addition, I would like to thank Mr. Roy A Childs, Jr., of Buffalo, New York, a philosophy student with a brilliant future, whose extensive correspondence with me led to the correction of a number of myths which I held concerning the nature of government.

Jarret B. Wollstein

Silver Spring, Maryland; August 1969

SOCIETY WITHOUT COERCION

INTRODUCTION

Since time immemorial men have sought the ideal of a peaceful, prosperous and just society; a society in which they could be free to produce and act without the fear of force being initiated against them by their neighbors. Many sincere and intelligent men have attempted to create such a society; but despite their efforts, for the over two thousand centuries of human existence, the realization of that ideal has eluded all. Strife, poverty, slavery and fear have been the continual lot of the overwhelming majority of men throughout history; and even today, in the age of the space ship and cyclotron, it still is so. In the year 1969 over one-half of the population of the earth is enslaved by totalitarian dictatorships, which differ in principle in no important way from the despotisms of ancient Egypt and Rome. Of the remaining half of mankind, half again know continual hunger; and of all of earth's teeming billions, there is scarcely a one who will not at some time know the violence of his neighbors.

Strife, poverty, slavery and fear have been such common features of human existence that it is easy to mistake them for the natural state of man, and many have done so. Yet there is in human nature a seldom realized, but vitally real potential for creativity, achievement and happiness capable of creating a society peaceful and prosperous beyond the wildest dreams of poets and prophets. We see the embryo of that potential in the gleaming towers of industrial America, in the concerts of the musical masters of the eighteenth century, and in the love for a person who personifies the highest of our values. With this limitless human potential for achievement and happiness why is it, then, that in the history of society we most often find personified the lowest of man's vices, rather than the highest of his capabilities? What prevents man from achieving the best within himself? What specifically is it in the organization of society which reduces most men and nations to emaciated skeletons of what they might and ought to be?

While the specific factors are many and complex, the general answer is simply the initiation of force -- the act of taking life or property which belongs to another, without his consent. The name of the form of society which initiates or tolerates the initiation of force is the coercive society, and the alternative to it is a society without coercion. We will now begin by examining the nature of man, human action and society.

1.0 THE NATURE OF MAN

The dawn of man and the pageant of human history began in the primeval night of tropical Africa. At a time at least as distant as 2 million years ago, and perhaps as distant as five millions years, the first man-ape took an evolutionary step which forever set him and his species apart from all other creatures of the earth: he began to think. The content of that first thought men may never know, but its significance they can never successfully evade. By thinking, by looking beyond the undifferentiated whole of emotive reaction and by seeing beyond the unintegrated quanta of discrete, unrelated entitites which comprised the sentient universe of the brutes about him, man-ape became man; and an evolution of mind was begun whose final consequences we can not know even today. By thinking, that first genius of prehistory left forever the garden of innocence of his predecessors, and opened for his race the twin paths to heaven and to hell -- paths leading to worlds of mind beautiful beyond ecstasy and ugly beyond horror. Both would be the solitary earthy dominion of man, the rational animal.

The rational animal alone of all of earth's species was confronted with alternatives of existence: to be man or not to be, to think or not to think, to create or to loot. For all of the other animals of man's world, only one mode of existence was possible -- the animal; and only one means was available to achieve it -- force. For other creatures the environment and the law of the jungle were absolute and incontroversial. They could be successful or not in the bloody contest for a static food supply and in the unending battle against the elements, but they could no more change those conditions of existence then they could change the sun. For the animal, the physical environment is a metaphysical given. But for man, it was and is different.

Man could either reduce himself to the animal's mode of survival and submit to his environment; or he could soar beyond the timeless cycles of animal existence, by first understanding his environment and then controlling it. Man could either realize that rational potential inherent in his nature, or he could renounce it and return to the primeval slime from whence he came. Man could either obey the law of the jungle mindlessly, or he could use his mind to consciously comprehend it and thereby escape it. The latter choice, the choice to think or not to think, would be with man for the uncountable centuries of his existence.

In order to fully realize his human potential for creation, man had to renounce the animal's unthinking mode of survival and act not on the range-of-the-moment, but on the basis of long range principles. The basic discipline which provides such principles is ethics: "...a code of values to guide man's choices and actions -- the choices and actions which determine the purpose and the course of his life.[1]" Ethics, properly conceived, is neither a subjective whim of man, a divinely ordained set of rules, nor an arbitrary group of social conventions -- ethics objectively are a practical guide to human action and life on this earth.

The full ethical implications of the fact that man is a rational being were not realized until millions of years after his inception. Despite the attempts of the intellectual giants of scores of human civilizations, the riddle of what principles of morality constituted a valid guide to human action remained for Ayn Rand[2] and her revolutionary philosophy of Objectivism to solve in the twentieth century.

The basic principle of the Objectivist ethics is that man should act in accordance with his nature to maintain his life as a rational being and achieve his own happiness. By saying that man *should* act in accordance with his nature, Objectivism simply recognizes the fact that man *must* do so in order to survive as man, i.e., as a rational being. Not to act in accordance with his nature means for man to risk destruction, physical and psychological.

To act in accordance with one's nature means to pursue one's own *rational self-interest*. This entails holding one's own life as one's highest value and using reason to integrate and evaluate the material provided by one's senses. Secondly, it means to act to produce the necessities and luxuries of human existence. Unlike other animals, the wealth available to man is not a static quantity, determined solely by his environment. For man, wealth is a dynamic quantity proportionate to his ability to create and produce. Man is not limited to picking fruit from trees and vegetables out of the ground; he can also cultivate and increase the productiveness of the earth immeasurably.

However, even with his ability to increase the wealth available to him, the individual by himself is still in little better shape than the animal to survive if he must produce each and every necessity of his existence himself. If the individual is solely dependent upon his own resources for survival, there will be many tasks which he will have to do, but which he will only be able to do poorly. It is highly improbable that any single individual could be very proficient at everything. In isolation, then, the individual faces a constant battle for survival which will consume most of his energies and time, leaving little opportunity for abstract thought and the creative use of his mind. At most, if he wins the battle, the individual can expect to exist at little more than a subsistence level of survival. In order to use his abilities and energies to their maximum advantage, the individual clearly needs to be able to draw on more than his own productive abilities in isolation.

The solution to man's "problem of production" is clearly to somehow to gain access to the production of others. There are two basic ways in which the individual can do this. Either he can seize the productivity of others by force, or he can acquire it through voluntary exchange. If an individual chooses the first alternative, and seizes the productivity of others, he has in fact chosen a sub-human, animal mode of survival and evaded what human productivity requires. To be productive, man must have some incentive to produce. *Before any goods can be looted, they must first be created*. If a man is denied the enjoyment of his own productivity, then he will have little incentive to continue to produce. Thus, the looter ultimately defeats his own purpose. By seizing today what another man has produced yesterday, the looter discourages him from producing tomorrow. Therefore, the consequences of seizing the productivity of others is to undermine and destroy the basis for human wealth. The second alternative is to trade with others.

Trade is the exchange of ideas, services, goods or other values, by the voluntary consent of two or more individuals, for the purpose of mutual profit. For a transfer of values to be properly called trade, rather than theft, it is necessary and sufficient that all parties to an exchange own the goods which they are trading, that they

understand the conditions of the exchange, and that they participate freely. When
men deal with each other through trade, all parties to an exchange profit; that is,
their physical or psychological well-being and happiness are increased by the transaction. If their well-being and happiness were not enhanced, there would be no
reason for them to expend the effort necessary to engage in exchange. Since all parties to voluntary exchange profit, there is, in a community of trade, constant
incentive to increase one's production and to trade with others -- always seeking
the greatest value in exchange for one's own possessions. In the competition for
the values offered by others, men are required to ever increase the efficiency and
sophistication of their own productivity (if they wish to maintain their clientele).
Thus trade sets into motion the process of rising technological advancement and
efficiency; as well as continually higher human health, security and happiness, which
are their consequence.

Thus far, we have only dealt with two specific forms in which the individual can
act to further his rational self-interest: productivity and trade. Let us now discuss the general concept of rational self-interest in more detail. *In general, to
act in one's rational self-interest means to make maximum use of one's skills, knowledge and opportunities in pursuit of one's own happiness, recognizing the nature of
one's self and one's environment.* There are several types of actions which are demonstrably in the rational self-interest of *all* men, such as production and trade. However, there is no general solution for the problem of determining the rationality of
each specific choice and action of an individual. In fact, it can be conclusively
proven that it is impossible to make such a determination today. The reason stems
from both certain facts of man's nature, and from the present state of knowledge in
neurology.

First observe that man is a *self-modifying organism*. This means that the same
"stimulus" presented to him today and tomorrow can elicit different responses because
man's future action is modified by his past experiences -- that is, man changes as a
result of experience. This means that *time itself is a variable in human action.*
Now the second fact to remember is that the nature of thought and the structure of
the brain are largely unknown today. The internal circuitry, as it were, of man's
mind is largely unknown. For these reasons, *it is now socio-metaphysically impossible* (i.e., impossible given the nature of reality and of present knowledge) *to predict exactly what the individual will do in the future, even assuming that somehow
the totality of his past behavior is known.* I will now prove this fact.

The impossibility of one man absolutely predicting the future actions of another
can be expressed in terms of what is called the "black box problem" in physics. In
physics, the question arises: given a box containing unknown internal circuitry, can
one determine the nature of that circuitry and hence its action on future input signals, given also correlated past input and output signals? In simple language, knowing what went into and came out of the black box in the past, can one know what will
come out in the future if one knows what is going in now? The answer is that one
cannot know if the black box contains self-modifying circuits -- in the terminology of
cybernetics, if it "learns". This fact can be and has been mathematically proven.

Since man's mind does contain "self-modifying circuitry" and its complete structure is unknown, it is therefore socio-metaphysically impossible to completely predict
the future actions and knowledge of another man, even knowing the totality of his
past environment and actions and his present environment. Until the nature of the
brain and the mind become complete known, there will remain a large element of un-

certainty in one's knowledge of the present thought and future actions of others.

The individual himself is, of course, not nearly so constrained. He can know much more exactly what he is thinking at the present time, through introspection, and much more exactly what he will do in the (at least immediate) future from past experience and from knowledge of his present values. For these reasons, it is possible for the individual himself to determine his rational self-interest.

Moreover, since it is socio-metaphysically impossible for any person other than the individual himself to be aware of his own needs, knowledge, desires and capabilities at any given time, it follows that it is socio-metaphysically impossible for one individual to really determine the rational self-interest of another. For this reason, the individual should be free to think, choose and act in pursuit of his own rational self-interest. To interfer with this freedom is to thereby prevent the individual from *achieving* his rational self-interest and thereby to interfer with the maintenance of his life qua man. This is the actual reason why coercion is irrational and immoral, and why man should be free[3].

1.1 THE NATURE OF SOCIETY

Human society is a group of men related by inter-dependence, involving communication, commerce and/or purposeful physical contact. Society provides man with a vast variety of benefits which are summarized by the two cardinal values of *trade* and *protection from risk*. We have already discussed the value and virtue of trade. Let us now consider the nature of social protection from risk.

Social protection from risk is basically the use of accumulated resources to minimize dangers to oneself. There are four major sources of risk which an individual might encounter in his environment: *(1) natural violence, (2) human violence, (3) individual ignorance and (4) future uncertainty*. The individual is protected from *natural violence*, e.g., dangerous beasts, the elements and other natural forces, by the existence of protective social artifacts, such as houses and "hunting parties". The individual is socially protected from *human violence* within a particular community by custom, laws and police forces; and through armies he is further protected against violence from other communities. The individual is protected from many of the dangers of *his own ignorance* by being able to draw on the accumulated knowledge and experience possessed by his society. In more primitive societies this knowledge and experience is transmitted by means of a *verbal tradition* (i.e., by word-of-mouth and by tales) and by the immitation of others. In more sophisticated societies, it is transmitted by written records and by formal instruction. Finally, the individual is socially protected from much *future uncertainty* by social bonds (e.g., friendship and contracts) which make the assistance of others available to him in the event of his own failing. Thus in a primitive society, the young traditionally care for the old, and in a modern society a large number of insurance schemes are available which enable the individual himself to provide for possible future sickness and injury, or for old age.

Despite these tremendous benefits which society can offer the individual, for the rational man, society is not an end in itself, but simply *a means to the end of his own happiness*. Society is nothing but a group of individuals, and only the individual can strive toward ends. To speak about the nature of or the ends of a given society is only to speak about the nature and ends of many or most of the individuals who comprise it. Society has no independent existence, purpose or value outside of the existence, purposes and values of the individuals who comprise it.

The rational man values society not simply because he happened to be born into it, or simply because he is accustomed to living within it, but because in society he *may* achieve an expression and realization of self far beyond his possible attainment in isolation. Indeed, society is not by necessity of value to the individual, nor does the rational man feel compelled to live in the society into which he was born. If a society acts to enslave its members, to compel them to act to achieve goals desired by *others* rather than goals desired by *themselves*, the individual in society may experience a degradation and destruction of self impossible in isolation: witness the level of human existence in the slave states of Communist China and Soviet Russia. Society is, then, not an unqualified value to man, regardless of its form. What society is to the individual -- implement or impediment, fulfillment or abnegation, heaven or hell -- is determined by its fundamental form. There are two basic forms which any society may take: voluntary (or free) or coercive (or slave).

A free society is founded upon the concept of respect for the integrity and the rights of *the individual*. Its guiding sociological principle is *voluntary association among men*. *Voluntary association* is the principle that men should be free to form those relationships which they choose, and that all social organization should be a consequence of such voluntary commitments. The principle of voluntary association is a recognition of the fact that since only the individual can know his own rational self-interest, man is an end in himself, and not a means to the ends of others. The concept of voluntarism also means that the individual should be free to think, dress, eat, live, mate and act as he pleases, so long as he does not violate the rights of others.

A right is a claim made by the criteria of innate possession, creation or earning. To recognize the rights of the individual is simply to recognize a fact of reality. Fundamentally, the individual owns his own self (body and mind) because this is in fact what is meant by the concept of "an individual" -- a unique, self-determining entity. Then, using his body and mind, the individual can also come to own *property*. Property is a relationship between an individual and an entity. It is a relationship created through the actions of the individual with respect to an entity, and consists of the right of use, control and disposal of that entity. The major form of establishing such a relationship in modern society is through work and trade.

Any entity which an individual owns by right, he may be said to have a *property right* to. Property rights are the application of the right to life to the material objects of man's world. Property rights consist of the recognition of the fact that by acting on entities man is the cause of lasting alterations in them, and by this act acquires the right to use and dispose of them.

Formally, *property* may be defined as *any entity which the individual owns (i.e., can use and dispose of) by right*. There are two classes of property: physical and intellectual. *Physical property* is any physical entity (e.g., land) claimed by right; and *intellectual property* is any mental entity (e.g., a concept) claimed by right.

An individual comes to own *previously unowned property* (physical or intellectual) essentially by use -- in the terminology of John Locke, by "mixing his labor with it" If a persons uses an entity without lasting alteration of its form, the individual may then be said to own it during the time of use. For example, when an individual walks across an unowned field or throws a rock into a pond, he may be said to own these entities respectively during the time it takes him to walk across the field and the time it takes him to throw the rock. If a person in using an entity causes lasting alterations in its form *which are of value to him*, the individual then owns such entities in perpetuity. For example, when a farmer tills a particular tract of land, and builds a house and barn on it, he comes to own it permanently -- he has caused a lasting alteration in the property.

An individual may obtain ownership of *previously owned property* by either receiving it as a gift from the previous owner or by trading with him. Initially, the child will receive food, clothing and shelter as a gift from his parents. Later, in an advanced industrial country, he will trade his labor for a salary by working for a business. When individuals trade values which they own by right, the exchange if moral and proper, and requires the sanction of no outside party. When trade is conducted freely, all parties to it profit and (so long as fraud is not involved) exploitation is impossible. It is a commonly held myth that when an individual buys a good, the seller profits, but the buyer does not. This notion is completely incorrect. If the buyer did not value the good which he purchased *more* than the money which he possessed, there would have been no reason for him to buy the good. In a (non-fraudulent) voluntary exchange, both the seller *and the buyer* necessarily profit.

In a voluntary exchange, the individuals involved have a right only to what they have agreed to trade. For example, a worker in a factory only has a right to his salary -- he cannot morally claim that his working there somehow gives him a right to control the factory's production. Conversely, the employer only has a right to require that his employees work the agreed hours -- he cannot morally attempt to require them to work longer than they have agreed to work. Similarly, a student only has a right to demand that the school which he is attending provide him with the education which he contracted for -- he does not have a right to demand that he or his representatives plan the college curriculum, any more than the administration has a right to plan his sex life or choose his major.

When individuals trade values which they own by their voluntary consent, the exchange is thereby moral and proper, consequently neither requiring nor permitting any intervention by a third party. It is, for example, immoral for an outside party to tell an employer that he cannot hire a man for less than a certain amount (which is precisely what the government does with its unjust minimum wage laws).

Once the relationship of property is established, the individual's right to his property is therefore absolute and inalienable, as absolute and inalienable as the actions which originally created the property. The name of the economic system which recognizes the property rights of men is *laissez-faire capitalism*. *Laissez-faire capitalism is an economic system in which all property is owned by the individuals who earned it, trade is conducted by the mutual consent of the individuals who wish to participate in it, and force and fraud are barred from the market.* To interfer with the freedom of the market is to interfer with the freedom of the individual to use his own mind and body for goals which he himself sets.

In essence, the rights of the individual consist of the rights to life, liberty and property. It is important to point out that there is and can be no conflict between these three rights, for they are in fact all simply different names for the basic human right to life. An often heard platitutde today is that "human rights (meaning: the rights to life and liberty) are *more important* than property rights" For example, it is asserted that apartment or motel owners do not have a right to discriminate on the basis of race, and that the human rights of tenants *take precedent* over the property rights of realtors. This is an absurdity. Property rights are nothing but a sub-class of human rights. To prevent a man from setting any conditions which he wishes on the use and disposal of his own property is not to set the principle of human rights "above" the principle of property rights, but to place the desires of one group (in the example used above, the would-be tenants) above the rights of another group (in the example used above, property owners). The individual has a right to set *any conditions* which he wishes on the use and disposal of his property, be that property his wages or his skyscraper. Those conditions may be rational or irrational, a man may refuse to rent to Negroes or rent only to Negroes -- but whatever the conditions, they are the owner's to set.

Property rights are not contingent upon the amount of property involved. In the above example, the would-be tenants have no more right to force an unwilling realtor to rent an apartment to them, than does a realtor have a right to force unwilling tenants to move into his apartment. Both realtors and tenants have an inalienable right to use and dispose of *their own* property. The property of the would-be tenants is their money; the property of realtors is their buildings -- but the rights of both are the same: to control their own possessions. There is no conflict between human rights and property rights because they are one and indivisible. To deny a man his right to property, meaning his unabridged use and enjoyment of his own property, is to deny him that portion of his life, meaning his labor and thought, which went into his creation or earning of the property. Since men are material beings, without property rights, no other rights are possible.

Notice that the concept of rights applies fundamentally to *actions* rather than to *entities*, or to put it another way, to the pursuit of ends rather than to their (guaranteed) atteinment. To have a right to act is not to have a right to have one's success guaranteed. All actions involve risk -- in general the risk of failure. To have a right to life therefore means only to have a right to pursue life, not to be guaranteed that one will be provided with food, clothing and shelter in order to live. To have a right to liberty means to have a right to speak, move, create and in general to act. It implies no guarantee that one's actions will be successful. To have a right to property means to have a right to attempt to trade, earn, profit and control that which one owns. It does not mean that one can demand that others guarantee one's success or provide one with all of the property which one desires. Thus men do not have an inalienable right to purchase the goods owned by others. They only have a right to attempt to do so, and to demand that they not be interfered with if those others prove willing to trade.

There is the widespread misconception today that man's rights consist of the right to specific entities; e.g., a job, an education or an income. This is totally false. All entities are the property of their owners who have the exclusive right to decide how to use and dispose of them. Only the employer has the right to decide whom he will hire; only the administrator has the right to set entrance requirements to his college; and only the worker has a right to dispose of his own income. To claim a right to a job, an education or an income is to claim that the owners of these specific entities -- factories, schools and salaries -- do not have a right to them. But there can be no right to the unearned. An individual has a right only to *his own* life, liberty and property. To claim a right to another man's life, liberty and property is to evade and contradict the meaning of the concept of rights itself, and therefore to invalidate the moral basis for one's own claim.

The foundation of a free society is thus the inalienable rights of the individual to his own life, liberty and property; voluntary association; and the free market. Accordingly, the negation of a free society is the violation of man's rights, forced association between men and the suppression of free trade. All of these manifestations of a coercive society can be summarized by a single concept: the initiation of force.

To force is to cause an individual to act against his own judgment or to unwillingly (i.e., under the threat of harm or misinformation) surrender a value.[4] A value is any possession of the individual, including his life, property and state of health. There are two types of force: initiatory and retaliatory. To *initiate* force is to use it for the first time; for example, to attack a person. To defend oneself against an attacker is to use *retaliatory force*. The murderer, the thief, the looter, the embezzler, the dictator and the soldiers of an attacking army are all examples of initiators of force. The policeman (ideally), a businessman who defends his store from looters, the innocent victim who defends himself from a mugger, the husband who protects his wife from a rapist and a defensive army (one whose function is to protect a society from invaders) are all examples of persons who are using retaliatory force.

In the same manner that we may distinguish between *individuals* who initiate and retaliate against force (or identically, who violate and defend man's rights), we may also distinguish between societies which tolerate and which do not tolerate the initiation of force. The former we will term a coercive society; the latter a non-coercive society.*

The distinguishing characteristic of a coercive society is the violation of man's right by the initiation of force. Thus some man or group of men in a coercive society will dictate to others what they will and will not do, under pain of deprivation of property, imprisonment, injury and death. It does not matter whether the coercive individuals or groups identify themselves as bandits, the Mafia, the church, the party, the government, chief, Pharaoh, king, high priest or president. What is important is whether or not they initiate force. If they do, they are all simply criminals, regardless of their aliases and pretentions.

It is important to note that while men usually recognize criminal acts when they are committed by *an individual, in the name of his own interest*, they often fail to recognize the very same acts for what they are when they are committed by

---

*At this point a word of caution. When we say that a society is coercive or non-coercive, we do not of course mean that every individual in a society is coercive or non-coercive. Clearly this is seldom if ever the case. Rather what we mean is that through either custom, law, or default; within a given society, the initiation of force is frequently sanctioned or tolerated, or it is not. Thus the concepts of coercive and non-coercive societies refer to general characteristics of groups rather than to the universal behavior of their members.

some large gang, in the name of "social justice" or "the common good". Not only are acts thus committed not recognized for what they are, but they are even often regarded as just, proper and praise-worthy! Thus when a man breaks into a store at night by himself and steals its goods, he is recognized as a thief, but when a gang does the exact same thing during the day, calling itself the "Welfare Rights" association and calling their action a "protest against social injustice" they are excused or even lauded.

However, morality and man's rights are not a question of the size of one's gang. The same actions which are wrong for a single individual by himself, are just as wrong for a group of individuals in a gang. Theft, murder and assault are wrong whether these acts are participated in by one man, calling himself "Jack the Ripper", or by a million men calling themselves "the government". The social criteria of moral action is respect for the rights of man. No individual or group, minority or majority, church or state, has the right to initiate the use of force.

The possibility that man's rights may be violated, the existence of persons and groups who see initiatory force as an acceptable means to their ends, create the necessity for *agencies of retaliatory force*. Man has an objective need for such agencies: to protect the Negro from the white racist, to protect the businessman from the thief; in general to protect the innocent victim from the criminal.

Historically, several agencies of retaliatory force have been used, from the vigilantees of the Old West, to the sophisticated police forces of modern States. However, since such agencies deal in force and become proficient in its use, there is always the danger that they will cross the line from retaliatory to initiatory force and become even worse violators of man's rights than the threats which they were initially formed to combat. The largest agencies of force which have ever existed, and therefore potentially the greatest violators of man's rights which have ever existed, are modern governments.

2.0 THE NATURE OF GOVERNMENT

Government is, by definition, a "social monopoly of force." The greatest instrumentalities of force which have ever been assembled, the police forces and armies of the world, are at the disposal of governments. With these great agencies of force at their disposal, the potential ability of governments to violate the rights of the individual is accordingly great and indeed it is easy to see that they have done so. Whenever one thinks of the worst injustices in history -- massive wastes, confiscatory taxes, purposeless wars, great depressions, slavery, concentration camps and genocide -- one inevitably finds that such injustices were either a direct or an indirect result of governmental action. At the same time, governments usually meet valid and basic needs of human society (although almost never in a valid way). Thus governments also provide water power and roadways, prevent fraudulent business practices, combat air pollution, quell riots, protect patents and copyrights, capture criminals and defend their citizens against foreign invaders.

Yet even in doing so, governments also almost invariably violate the rights of their citizens. What is it, then, that differentiates the proper from the improper actions of governments?

What determines what is proper and improper for governments to do are, in essence, the same principles which differentiate the proper from the improper actions of the individual. Despite the lofty pretentions of most governments, the fact remains that they, like any other group of men, are nothing more than a collection of *individuals*. The "rights of a government", like the rights of any other association of men, can be morally no different than the rights of the men who comprise it. All that which is immoral for men acting individually is equally immoral for men acting in association. There is nothing which a government *can* morally do, which individuals by themselves *cannot* morally do. The group is ethically no different from the individual.

Consider the following situation: During the course of a day, one man approaches a second and demands of him that he surrender a portion of his income, on the grounds that the claimant needs the money more and knows better how to spend it than does the second man. If the second man refuses to surrender his money, then the first man attempts to take it by force. If the second man continues to protest and resist, the first man then shoots him. Now who would call the first man anything other than a thief and murderer? Who could regard the second man as anything but an innocent victim? The first man is clearly immoral and the second is clearly blameless.

Now let us suppose that instead of being one man, the would-be thief is a part of a larger gang, which calls itself "the Mafia." Now if the Mafia proceeds to rob the second man as did the lone criminal, would their actions be any the less criminal simply because there were five or ten of them instead of only one? The only rational answer is that their actions would not be any different, that robbery is robbery and murder is murder whether it is being committed by a single thief by himself, or by a thousand acting in concert.

Finally, let us say that our original thief is a member of a very large gang, that he in fact claims to be a representative of a group called "the Internal Revenue Service" and that this group is further empowered to seize money and property by an even larger group which is called "the Government". Instead of calling himself a criminal, our thief calls himself a "tax collector", and instead of saying that he is taking money and property for himself, he claims that he is collecting it for "the poor". Now how, I ask, is this "tax collector" any different from the lone criminal or a member of the Mafia? Like the criminal, the so-called "tax collector" is taking money or property which does not belong to him, for a purpose which his victim does not choose to voluntarily support (for if the victim voluntarily supported the tax collector's cause, there would be no need for him to forceably seize his money or property). Like the criminal, the tax collector will seize the man's property if he does not surrender it to him, and like the criminal the tax collector (or his agents) will kill the man if he attempts to protect his own property.

It is irrelevant whether a man steals by his own authority or with the sanction of a million others, whether he takes money for himself or for "the poor", or for any other group which did not earn it. Theft consists of taking a man's property against his will, regardless of the beneficiary. If the individual has an inalienable right to his own life, liberty and property, then morally his life and property are his own to do with as he pleases. It is just as immoral for a government to attempt to tax his earnings, regulate his business or draft his sons as it would be for some isolated individual acting on his own authority to do so. The association of men into a group called "government" does not free them from morality or sanction actions otherwise immoral.

It is also irrelevant whether the tax collector's victim has some of his property returned to him in the form of road usage, postal services, police protection, etc., or not. Since it is government, rather than the individual, which is deciding what is to be taken and what is to be given, the individual's control of his own property has still been lost. The return of the tax collector's victim's property in the form of certain governmental services is not trade but theft. In *trade* exchange is conducted by the *mutual consent* of the individuals who wish to participate in it, *according to their own terms*. In *taxation* the individual's property is taken from him *without his consent* and services *may be* returned to him *according to the government's decrees*. For this reason, the only thing which one can call taxation, the foundation of modern governments, is theft.

Now that it has been made clear that the same moral law applies to governments as applies to individuals, we can begin to innumerate the actions of governments which are clearly immoral. Firstly, any actions committed by governments which force the individual to act are immoral since they are violations of his human right to life and liberty. Thus, in modern times, forceable participation in social security or medical care programs, conscription, forced housing and public accomodations laws and compulsory attendance at public schools is immoral. Secondly, any interference with actions conducted by the mutual consent of the individuals involved is immoral. Thus laws prohibiting certain forms of sexual intercourse, laws against drugs and anti-abortion laws are immoral. Thirdly, any interference with free trade is a violation of man's right to property. Thus anti-trust laws, censorship, gun-registration and minimum wage laws are immoral. Finally, the deprivation of the individual of any value, physical or mental, is immoral. Thus taxation, welfare programs, rent controls, the regulation of currency, zoning, subsidies and tariffs are immoral.

To put it on a more personal level, whatever else it should do, a government can not morally tell a middle-class office worker that he must pay 20% of his income to feed unwed mothers and ship computers to the Soviet Union, send his children to a school that will teach them that their father is a member of a corrupt and sinful generation, contribute to socialized medicine and censor his TV set. The government of a moral society could not tell a poor Negro willing to work for less than $1.60 an hour that he cannot work for that amount, even though his employer cannot afford to pay him more; tax his income to build space ships and to pay farmers not to work; force his children to fight in Vietnam; or destroy his home in the name of "urban renewal." Government also cannot properly tell a corporation president that he must force his employees to join a union, cannot build a new factory without government approval, must pay 52% of his profits to subsidize Appalachia and build dams in the Tennessee Valley, cannot merge with GM, and cannot charge less than his competitors. In general, government can not morally coerce, threaten, harass, intimidate, investigate, conscript, regulate, censor, compete with, tax, subsidize, insure, license, inspect, indoctrinate, spy on or murder its citizens. In other words, whatever else it does, the government of a free society does not itself act as a criminal in the name of its citizens, or try to judge and live their lives for them.

What then are the functions left which government might conceivably engage in? The answer is *those which deal exclusively with the use of retaliatory force*, for government to essentially act as a "policeman of man's rights." This is exactly the limitation of functions which philosopher-novelist Ayn Rand proposes. Miss Rand defines what she considers to be a proper government as "an institution that holds the exclusive power to *enforce* certain rules of social conduct in a given geographical area[5]", in essence, a social monopoly of *retaliatory* force. This is what we will call a *limited government*.

It would seem that the limited government advocated by Miss Rand would restrict its functions to primarily those now conducted by the Judicial Division of the U.S. Government. Specifically, the primary functions of a limited government (and its associate implementory agencies) would be as follows: (1) the passage of laws defining and dealing with the use of initiatory and retaliatory force (the Legislative Branch); (2) the administration of such laws (the Executive Branch); (3) the registration of patents and copyrights (the Bureau of Patents and Copyrights); (4) the enforcement of contracts (Contract Enforcement Division of the Justice Department); (5) the prosecution of fraud (Anti-fraud Division of the Justice Department); (6) the investigation of crimes and the arrest of criminals (police forces); (7) the prosecution of criminals and the adjudication of the differences between men (court system); (8) the punishment of criminals (penal system); and (9) the protection of the society from foreign invaders (armed forces). We will now consider the morality of such a limited government.

2.1 The Morality of Limited Government

Although such a limited government as described above would be a tremendous advancement over all of the political forms which man has ever known, there are still a number of questions which arise concerning its morality. First there is the question of how its national boundaries are properly determined and what makes its laws (e.g., its constitution and procedural rules) binding upon a society. Second, there is the question of whether a limited government can require men to patronize its services or participate in its activities. Lastly, there is the question of how a limited government can morally prevent competition with its own functions; i.e., how can it maintain its "social monopoly of retaliatory force?"

Historically, national boundaries have been finally decided by force -- the power of a ruling elite to maintain dominion over a given territory, against domestic and foreign challenges to their authority, by virtue of force of arms. If there was a dispute over which national group controlled a given piece of land, differences were settled by going to war, victor take all. Similarly, national laws were historically decided by force -- the power of the ruling elite over its citizens. The state and its government then emerged, in general, not as the product of rational thought and voluntary agreements, but primarily as a consequence of simple brute force. The United States is only a partial exception to this rule. It is true that America originally offered *groups*, such as the Puritans or the Germans or the Catholics, if not *individual members of such groups*, a place where they could live according to their own beliefs. However, throughout its history, in the Indian Wars, in the Mexican-

American War, in governmental sanctioning of slavery, and in hundreds of other instances, the boundaries and the laws of the United States have been based upon force. The most that can be said for the United States is that it was, in the 19th Century, the freest country of the modern world, and is still, in the 20th Century, *among the freest*.

If one recognizes that the rights of the individual, including his property rights, are inalienable, then the only way in which social boundaries could be properly formed is by individual property owners voluntarily coming together to form a community whose boundaries are defined by their holdings. If within the perimeter formed by such holdings there existed an individual who did not wish to be a party to the community or consider himself a member of its "state," then he morally would be free to do so; and the external community would not have a right to force him to pledge allegiance to their national territory, flag or goals. In a free society, each individual is in fact an autonomous state in himself, free to associate or not with a larger group. In a free society, cooperation between men, and hence the geographical boundaries of social groups, is a product of voluntary association.

Applying the social principle of voluntarism to an existent nation-state such as the United States, we find that its present political boundaries are essentially the arbitrary product of the coercive organization of the state, rather than the product of a voluntary association of men. Consequently, there is no reason to consider present U.S. boundaries as either necessary, or as necessarily proper and just.

In addition to having a right to associate himself with a larger group, in a free society any individual would also have the right to *dissociate* himself from a formal society at any time (so long as he did not in the process violate a prior agreement). At no time can it be assumed that simply because a present political boundary exists, that men are morally obligated to respect it. It may be impractical and irrational not to respect existent political boundaries; but there is nothing sacred about them, especially not today when virtually all societies are coercive.

Similarly, there is nothing sacrosanct about the laws of today's societies. As we have already seen, most of the activities of the government of the United States are clearly immoral and a violation of the rights of the individual. Since the individual *always* has the right to retaliate against those who initiate force against him, there is no obligation on the part of the individual to obey most existent laws. Indeed, since the draft, censorship and a host of other laws threaten the very physical and intellectual existence of the individual, draft evasion, undergound presses and a host of other illegal acts are thoroughly moral and proper.* There is simply no obligation on the part of the individual to obey laws simply because the laws exist. If the individual's rights are violated by laws, he is morally justified in regarding the unjust laws as a ciminal invasion of his privacy and in retaliating accordingly.

There is, however, one type of law which is morally binding on all men -- objective law. An *objective law* is one which is based on the objective facts of reality and on principles derived from those facts. In general objective social laws are those which

---

*Whether they are to the individual's rational self-interest is another question, the answer to which depends upon many specific situational factors, such as the probability that the individual will be penalized for engaging in them or that his later success will be jeopardized by such acts.

prohibit the initiation of force and protect the rights of men. Laws against theft, rape, embezzlement, arson, larceny, assault, fraud and murder are examples of objective social laws. The individual is bound to obey objective social laws in the same way in which he is bound to obey objective physical laws: both are statements of facts of reality whose attempted evasion will be to the detriment of the individual. Just as an individual risks *physical destruction* when he tries to evade the law of gravity by attempting to fly by jumping off a cliff and flapping his arms, so an individual risks *psychological destruction* by attempting to build a fortune on stolen money. Both the would-be flier and the would be "robber baron" are attempting to defy objective conditions of their environment. This can only result in the attainment of the opposite of what they seek. Thus, the would-be flyer falls to the ground rather than rises in the air, and the would-be entrepreneur finds that his property mocks him rather than gives him happiness.

If the "constitution" of a society consists of a statement of objective law which prohibits the initiation of force, then it is objectively valid and morally binding on men -- all men, in fact, and not just the men of the particular society for which it was written. However, if the constitution of any society (other than a proprietary community, which will be discussed in sub-section 2.2) attempts to do more, for example, to prescribe political forms for the society, such as elections, and a division of powers, then that constitution is not binding upon men in those aspects. The reason that a constitution is not binding upon men in those respects should be obvious. How for example, can some group of men, declaring themselves to be the "representatives of the people" require that men vote every 4 years, or indeed at all? What principle of objective justice requires men to pledge their allegiance to the national political structure simply because they were born in a land where the structure exists?

This leads us to the second question about the morality of a limited government: To what extent, if any, can such a government require men to participate in its activities? Remember first, that a free society is a voluntary association of men, according to their own terms, for their own ends. Thus a free society cannot compel men to vote in its elections, register their inventions with its bureau of patents and copyrights, or make them patronize its courts (unless they have committed a crime). A free society can only prohibit initiatory force. In essence, a free society is one in which *participation* is also free. If an individual wishes to live in the territory of a given society without participating in its institutions and programs, that is his right. So long as he respects the rights of others, he is totally free to do as he pleases. So long as he violates none of his past agreements, his future choices are his to make.

Finally, we come to the crucial question of "how a limited government can morally prevent competition with its own functions; i.e., how can it maintain its 'social monopoly of retaliatory force'?" Let us first consider this issue in terms of a specific case. What happens if, for example, a group of men living within a "limited government" United States of the future decide that the state's police force is inefficient and that they could do a better job themselves. They then proceed to create their own "agency of retaliatory force" by hiring detectives and guards, and advertising their services on TV and in the newspapers. Let us assume that they proceed unhampered by government for awhile and build up a sizable business through their competency. After a few months this private police force is serving thousands of citizens and is so competent at their task that they make fewer false arrests, catch more criminal, prevent more crimes and charge less proportionately for their services than does the state police force. Eventually, the state of course notices this "private defense company." What are they to do now? The state has two basic alternatives: it can either leave the new free market defense company alone to prosper or fail, as dictated by its future actions, or it can decree that the defense company has usurped a rightful function of the state and order it to cease operations under penalty of fine, imprisonment or death of its managers and employees. Now if the state does the former, if the state adopts an attitude of laissez-faire toward the *defense* company, then the state's monopoly of force will have been broken and it will no longer be a government at all in the sense of a "social monopoly of retaliatory force." However, if the state does the latter, if it attempts to intimidate or to physically destroy the new defense company, it has then initiated force against innocent victims (persons who have not initiated force themselves). It does no good to assert that the state's action is moral since somewhere along the line the private defense company might have violated someone's rights through an error on the part of one of its policemen. The state also makes such mistakes, yet the proponents of limited government do not advocate its dissolution for this reason. If policemen of a free market defense company err, they should be punished for their error, as should the policemen of a state police force. But unless that error is a matter of company policy, then the managers and the corporation itself cannot be morally prevented from doing future business by the state. In general, if a free market agency of *retaliatory force* obeys objective social laws, acts as a policeman of man's rights and gets its customers through their voluntary consent, it has just as much right to exist as do the agencies of retaliatory force of the nominal state.

In short, the state has no moral right to prevent competitive agencies of retaliatory force from existing. In a free society, men are at liberty to form those agencies of retaliatory force which they wish to form in order to protect their rights. The form, number and relationship between such agencies in any given geographical area can be variable. There may be one or many such agencies in any given area, and they may be functionally distinct or operationally integrated. What their form and number will be is for the free market to decide, *which means* it is for the voluntary judgment of each individual who participates in the market to decide. If the state intervenes, if it tells men that they cannot form such agencies under penalty of fine, imprisonment or death, then the state is violating the rights of men to associate freely, and has in fact assumed the status of a coercive monopoly.

In a truly free society there would then be nothing to prevent the formation of competing agencies of retaliatory force, nor would there be anything to fear from them so long as they operated on the basis of objective law. It is true that it is possible for such competing agencies of retaliatory force to violate the rights of the individual or to fight among themselves (as Miss Rand points out). However, it is not true that such *possibilities* are *probable*, or that the existence of such possibilities implies that competing agencies of retaliatory force are *inherently* immoral. *The moral determines the practical; not vice-versa. The concept of "practicality" only has meaning in relationship to specific ends.* Since morality is "a code of values to guide man's choices and actions -- the choices and actions which determine the purpose and the course of his life,6" it is morality which enables man to select his ends; and because ends determine means, the moral determines the practical. Q.E.D.

Competing agencies of retaliatory force are practical because they are moral; they are not "immoral" because they are "impractical." Moreover, it is also possible for government to violate the rights of the individual, and in fact every government in history has done so *on an incredibly vast scale*. The gas chambers of Nazi Germany, and the rolls of Vietnamese dead of Welfare Statist America are a mute and tragic testimony to the human destruction wrought by governments. There is no such evidence that competing defense agencies would wreak similar carnage. Governments also fight among themselves, as R.A. Childs points out[7], but when they do what occurs is not termed a battle, but a war; and the victims are numbered in the millions rather than the hundreds.

There is nothing innately necessary or moral about a limited government. What defines the morality and practicality of any organization of retaliatory force in a free society is not whether its agencies are one or many, but whether they are just and objective. A "social monopoly of retaliatory force" whose existence depends upon the initiation of force is worse than a contradiction in terms -- it is an epistemological absurdity. Since a "limited government" cannot, by definition be limited to dealing solely in retaliatory force, we necessarily conclude that limited government is (with the sole exception noted below) inherently immoral and must be rejected by any advocate of human freedom and justice in favor of competing agencies of retaliatory force.

2.2 The Proprietary Community

The one exception to the logically necessary fact that even "limited government" is inherently immoral is the concept of a proprietary community. A proprietary community is one in which some single individual or corporation owns a given tract of land and establishes as conditions of purchasing land from them that (1) the purchaser upon residency subscribe only to some designated, monopoly agency of retaliatory force and (2) that the purchaser not sell his land to anyone who does not agree to the same proviso. There could also be "democratic" procedures for the election of administrators and legislators of this community, with the participation of the members of the community either invited, or even required (again, as a condition of land purchase).

Since the proprietary community is formed by the voluntary consent of the individuals comprising it, without the initiation of force, it is a society without coercion. And since there is a monopoly agency of retaliatory force, it has a government. In the proprietary community we may then establish a *government without coercion*. Government financing in such a community could be conducted in a number of ways including (preferably) the free market methods described in section 3, or by the simple (if uneconomical) expedient of required "citizenship dues" paid to the government (naturally as a condition of land purchase). Since the financing of all those agencies of retaliatory force which today roughly are included in the U.S. Justice Department is described in section 3, I will not repeat myself here. However, I will make a number of suggestions concerning a method other than dues (or voluntary "taxes" -- they amount to the same thing) of financing the administrative and legislative branches of the government of a proprietary community.

If our proprietary community is truly a non-coercive society, the function of the legislative and administrative branches of its "limited government" would be limited to, respectively, the passage and administration of laws defining and dealing with the use of initiatory and retaliatory force. For example, these branches might concern themselves with such things as (1) search and seizure, (2) arrest, (3) numbers of and forms of police forces, (4) judicial appointments, (5) declaration of war and (6) patents and copyrights.

The very simple way to pay the salaries and expenses of the administrators and legislators of such a limited government without even "voluntary taxes" is by means of *voter's fees*. Since one would expect that both the number of such administrators and their constituency would be proportional to the population of their society, there would clearly be enough money from voter's fees to support them in any society. In the United States today, for example, (a very large society) since there are hundreds of thousands of persons who vote in state elections, and millions who vote in national elections, it is easy to see that a very modest fee indeed would pay the salaries of the various elected officials and their staffs. Thus, to take a specific example, if each of the over 70 million persons who voted in the Presidential election of 1964 ahd paid a fee of $1 there would have been enough money to pay the President's salary, the Vice-President's salary and the salary of 1,500 aides at $20,000 per year each; and there would still be $10 million left over to maintain the White House and the President's plane.

A similar minuscule fee of $1 per candidate could be charged for voting in Senatorial, Congressional and state and local elections. It would be difficult to imagine someone who could not afford to pay $1 every few years. If there were such persons, I suppose that in the interests of "participatory democracy" they could earn the money by sweeping up voting booths.

Although this suggestion and the implementation of the proposals listed in section 3 could occur in a proprietary community and thereby produce a non-coercive society with government and without taxation, there are a variety of reasons which make the existence of competing agencies of retaliatory force probable in a free society, as well as desirable.

The major objection to a democratic proprietary community is that *universally, voting behavior appears to be a manifestation of "wish fulfillment."* Demonstrably people vote for programs that they would never voluntarily support if they had to take the money out of their own pocketbooks. The U.S. space program is a good example. Apparently what happens is that when people vote they forget the fact that *they* will have to pay the costs of any program enacted by government, and in doing so they must forgo alternative uses of their money. Instead they seem to believe that when government undertakes a program *somehow they can have their cake and eat it too*; that is, they can have the *benefits* of government programs, without having to pay any of the costs. This, of course, is totally absurd. Nevertheless, the dichotomy between political and economic behavior is so wide that no other conclusion is possible. Since the political process encourages and permits this and many other forms of irrational human action, I suggest that the whole process be scrapped in favor of truly free market *competing agencies of retaliatory force*. Before considering in detail how such agencies could function, let us first consider the morality and "practicality" of what we will, for the moment, term an "anarchist" society.*

---

*The phrase "anarchist society" is not the contradiction in terms which it might at first appear to be to some persons. All <u>anarchy</u> means is "the absence of government", not the absence of social order (which is in fact epistemologically impossible). Anarchy also does not necessitate social chaos as we will demonstrate in the next section.

2.3 Arguments Against Anarchy

Men live by myths, and the twentieth century American is no exception. From birth to death men live believing in absurdities which even the most cursory investigation would have disproven. Most twentieth century Americans believe that God exists, that psychoanalysis works, that the United States is a free country and that government is necessary in order to insure social order. It is this latter myth which we will be primarily concerned with here.

The belief that government is necessary to insure social order is a pure superstition, based upon a psycho-epistemological process different in no important respect from the Medieval belief in goblins and witches. The Medieval peasant invested the abstractions of evil and "things that go bump in the night" with an irrational anthropomorphism and power, and similarly most twentieth century Americans (unfortunately including Ayn Rand and most otherwise Objectivists) invest the abstractions of goverment and political authority with a similar aura of supernatural power.

At the outset let it be made clear that government is nothing but men acting in concert. The morality and value of government, like any other association of men, will be no greater and no less than the morality and value of the men comprising it. Since government is nothing but men, its inherent authority to act is in no way greater or different than the authority to act of individuals in isolation. If it is moral for government policemen to arrest suspect criminals, it is also moral for "private policemen" to do so. If it is moral for government to try and imprison men, then it is also moral for non-governmental corporations to do so. Government has no magic powers or authority not possessed by private individuals. Let he who asserts that government may do that which the individual may not assume the onus of proof and demonstrate his contention.

The basic reason why a social order could and would arise in the absence of governments (as they are known today) is the fact that man has an objective need for social order and protection from initiatory force. This objective need would create human associations producing order in society. The morality and permanence of these associations will be determined by the morality and rationality of the men creating and working in them, as is the case for any social institution.

Perhaps the strongest attack on "anarchism" -- certainly the most vitrolic -- was made a few years ago by Ayn Rand. In her article on "The Nature of Government" she states:

> A recent variant of anarchistic theory, which is befuddling some of the younger advocates of freedom, is a weird absurdity called "competing governments." Accepting the basic premise of the modern statists -- who see no difference between the functions of government and the functions of industry, between force and production, and who advocate government ownership of business -- the proponents of "competing governments" take the other side of the same coin and declare that since competition is so beneficial to business it should also be applied to government. Instead of a single, monopolistic government, they declare, there should

be a number of governments in the same geographical area, competing for the allegiance of individual citizens, with every citizen free to "shop" and to patronize whatever government he chooses.

Remember that forcible restraint of men is the only service a government has to offer. Ask yourself what a competition in forcible restraint would have to mean.

One cannot call this theory a contradiction in terms, since it is obviously devoid of any understanding of the terms "competition" and "government". Nor can one call it a floating abstraction, since it is devoid of any contact with or reference to reality and cannot be concretized at all, not even roughly or approximately. One illustration will be sufficient: suppose Mr. Smith, a customer of Government A, suspects that his next-door neighbor, Mr. Jones, a customer of Government B, has robbed him; a squad of Police A proceeds to Mr. Jones' house and is met at the door by a squad of Police B, who delcare that they do not accept the validity of Mr. Smith's complaint and do not recognize the authority of Government A. What happens then? You take it from there.[8]

Once one gets past Miss Rand's typically vitriolic rhetoric (which only indicates that Miss Rand is quite hostile to what she mislabels as "competing governments") one finds that she has essentially one argument. Miss Rand asserts that what is properly designated as "competing agencies of retaliatory force" or a free market of justice would not work because the competing agencies would end up protecting criminals and shooting it out with each other. One can only term this a straw man argument.

The situation which Miss Rand "describes" is patently absurd. If competing agencies of retaliatory force protected criminal they would not be competing agencies of retaliatory force at all. Rather they would be criminal gangs, plain and simple. Further it would be sheer insanity for individuals "subscribing" to competing criminal gangs to live on the same "turf." In this respect, Miss Rand is correct. However what I and every other advocate of a society without coercion are advocating are *not* "competing governments" (a misnomer) or "competing criminal gangs" (an ethical monstrosity) but "competing agencies of retaliatory force," which Miss Rand has in fact not dealt with at all.

In the situation described above, in which neighbors subscribed to competing police departments, what is certain (if they were in fact police departments operating on the basis of objective law, rather than criminal gangs operating on the basis of mob rule -- which is what Miss Rand described) is that Police B would accept the validity of Police A, or in fact the validity of any reputable police department and cooperate with them in the arrest of Mr. Jones. Police B certainly would not protect Mr. Jones from justice if there was objective evidence that Mr. Jones had committed a crime, nor would Police A proceed to attempt to arrest Mr. Jones unless there were such evidence. In this manner, objective law would eliminate coercive "shoot-outs."

Once competing police departments began to function, standard operating procedures would be created to deal with such cases. At least two possible procedures come to mind: Either by stipulation the police department to which a man subscribed would be the only one which could incarcerate him; or, by stipulation, the police department where the complaint was filed would incarcerate him. In the extreme there would be little motivation for policemen to put their lives on the line for a suspected thief, and if competing police departments operated as Miss Rand falsely pictures, then they would quickly go out of business due to the attrition rate of policemen killed in the "line of duty."

This is only one of the flaws of Miss Rand's argument. Other problems include her failure to explain exactly how government can morally outlaw competing agencies of retaliatory force, or what it is that prevents the state police from shooting it out with the county police in similar situations. Clearly both Miss Rand's premises and logic are in error in this case. But we do not have to rely solely on speculation to demonstrate the practicality of "anarchism." There does in fact already exist a country with operating competing agencies of retaliatory force -- the New Hebrides.

In an article appearing in the Spring 1969 issue of *Innovator* and entitled "The New Herbides as a Libertarian Retreat Area," William Danks (SRI Local Representative for Hawaii) reports:

> The islands of the New Hebrides are administered by the world's freest and most anti-statist form of government. Under the terms of a 1914 protocol a joing French and British Condominium was established, giving each government equal powers of administration, but denying soverign territorial right to both. There are three court systems -- British, French, and Joint -- as well as both British and French police systems. Interestingly, there are no reports of murder or armed robbery with violence on record under either system. (p. 7-44)

Having briefly refuted the main myths involved in arguments against "anarchism," let us now go on to something more constructive and do what Miss Rand claimed was impossible: concretizing the operation of what are properly termed *carfs* (short for <u>c</u>ompeting <u>a</u>gencies of <u>r</u>etaliatory <u>f</u>orce). But first we should consider the proper name for a free society.

2.4 *Naming A Free Society*

To name the social system of a free society is not as nominal a task as at first it may appear to be. It is not only the existence of *complete* social freedom which is absent from today's world, but also the idea of such freedom. There is, in truth, probably no word in the English language which properly denotes and connotes the concept of the social system of a free society.

A number of persons who have recognized the fallacies in the advocacy of not just *this or that government*, but who have also recognized the inherent "contradiction in government" itself (such as Murray Rothbard and Karl Hess) have decided that since *archy* means rule, or the presence of government -- which they are against -- they will designate their sociological position as *anarchy* -- no rule, or the total absence of government. This decision is unfortunate, to say the least, since it embodies several epistemological fallacies. Firstly, the term anarchy is a negative term; to say that one is "for" anarchy is only to say that one is *against* government. It is not to say *what are* the positive social forms which one advocates. This may be perfectly fine if one, in fact, advocates no positive social forms. However, if one advocates *freedom* and its economic expression laissez-faire capitalism, the designation "anarchy" or "anarchism," of itself, will hardly suffice. Secondly, anarchy merely means "no rule" not "no coercion." It is perfectly possible to have an anarchist "society" with coercion initiated by random individuals and robber gangs. So long as these persons do not claim legal sanction or create formal and enduring institutions, one would have a very coercive "anarchist society." Further, it is possible for there to be an anarchist society in which no force was initiated, although due to the personal irrationality and mysticism of its occupants, no rational person would want to live in it. For example, imagine a society occupied exclusively by non-violent schizophrenics, or equivalently, by Zen Buddhists.*

Less important, but also significant, is the fact that the term "anarchy," in present usage,has come to mean not only "no rule" but also has come to imply 'social chaos and senseless violence.' This *is* a corruption of the original meaning of the term, but nevertheless it makes the word "anarchy" an impediment rather than an implement to communicating the concept of a free society. When one wishes to defend in principle and implement in reality a free society, it is irrational to deliberately choose a term which one knows will alienate, at the outset, persons with whom one eventually intends to deal.

Another term has been suggested by Robert LeFevre, advocate of the free market and founder of Ramparts College in California. Mr. LeFevre rejects the term "anarchy" primarily because of its past close association with collectivism and, recognizing the fallacy of "limited government," proposes in its stead the word "autarchy," meaning "self-rule." Again this term suffers several epistemological faults. It fails to state *how* one should rule oneself, and in fact says nothing about the nature of social order.

Next we have the term "voluntarism," also advocated by many proponents of the term "anarchism." This expression is superior to the term "anarchy" in that it does exclude coercion from its subsumed concept of social order. It is therefore acceptable for this communicative purpose. However, several necessary differentia in the valid concept of a free society are still lacking. Conceivably one could have a "voluntary" collectivist society (at least for a while), in which individuals voluntarily became slaves, as well as a voluntary individualist society, in which the individual is his own master. Consequently, this term is not fully satisfactory.

A phrase in increasingly popular use which I advocate as the best presently available specification of the socio-economic position of persons advocating a society of consistent rational freedom is "anarcho-capitalism." Here the prefix "anarcho" indicates the lack of coercive government, and the word "capitalism" indicates the positive presence of free trade based upon respect for man's rights. This term is not ideal: the prefix "anarcho" has negative semantic value, and the term "capitalism" is intimately associated with the present American statist mixed economy. However, it would seem to be the best term which we now have, and consequently we will use it (and in more limited contexts "voluntarism") in the remainder of this essay.

---

*See also the cover article in the July 18, 1969 issue of *Life*; "The Youth Communes."

3.0 AGENCIES OF RETALIATORY FORCE

The agencies of retaliatory force of a free society are those whose primary concern is the deterrence and prosecution of those who initiate force. These are the same agencies listed as the implementory agencies of a free society, with the exception of a legislature and administration, whose functions are taken over by the managers and employees of the various free market justice companies; particularly by judges and by a new class of professionals -- ethical scientists. We will consider these agencies in five classifications for analytic purposes: (1) *justice agencies*, which include patent and copyright registration agencies, contract registration agencies and anti-fraud companies; (2) *police forces*; (3) *courts*; (4) *penal institutions*; and (5) *armed forces*. The division of these agencies of retaliatory force into these five classifications is not meant to imply that they are necessarily functionally or administratively separate from each other, or from other free market institutions (such as insurance companies). Indeed, since one class picks up where the other leaves off, so to speak, it is highly probable that in a free market, several of the various classifications of agencies of retaliatory force would be combined within a single corporation. However, we will discuss them as basically distinct activities, since these classifications provide a convenient epistemological partition.

The major question which we will deal with in this section is how these agencies could be financed and operated in the free market. Although the author is clearly of the view that government is objectively undesirable and generally inherently immoral, it should nevertheless be pointed out that these financing proposals could also be implemented in the context of a Randian limited government, which also rejects taxation.

The concept of organizing and financing agencies of retaliatory force without any form of taxation or charitable contribution, presented here represents a fundamentally new concept in social organization. All large societies which have ever existed have been coercive at least in regard to their operation and financing of courts, police forces and armed forces. All large societies which have ever existed have relied on taxation, conscription, and in a word, force, to maintain the apparatus of the state police forces. If a free society is ever to be achieved it is this coercive state apparatus which must be replaced by truly voluntary institutions. The theoretical base for such institutions has been laid by Ludwig von Mises and Ayn Rand. The concrete, practical base will be established here.

The general answer to how such agencies could be financed in the free market is in fact very simple. Protection from initiatory force is an objective and basic need of man; a need just as objective and basic as his need for food or air. A man can no more exist in an environment where he is apt to be the victim of capriciously initiated force, without recourse, than he can exist naked on the moon. Because man has an objective need to be protected from initiatory force, he is naturally willing to provide for such protection. There are two ways in which he can do this. Either the individual himself can proceed to undertake his own defense against and arrest of criminals, or he can delegate this activity to an outside agency. The latter alternative is by far the more preferable. As in every other area of economic activity, specialization and division of labor in agencies of retaliatory force are of tremendous benefit to the individual. The untrained man who personally attempted to catch a thief who had robbed his house would almost certainly find that his economic and psychological loss (e.g., forfeited wages and mental anguish) would be greater than his probable "gain" in the form of recaptured goods, in the unlikely event that he was successful. For the rational man who has been victimized by a criminal, the much more sensible course is to delegate the protection of his rights to a specialist. Thus the emergence of agencies of retaliatory force in a free market, in the absence of government, is epistemologically certain. The basic principle is: *Need generates demand, making funds available.*

There is a second important question concerning the operation of agencies of retaliatory force: What is to be the source of their monetary support? Is it to be taxation, charitable contributions or subsidies from say the steel industry? Although any of these means might, after a fashion "work," they are all objectively undesirable. As we have already pointed out, taxation is theft, clear and simple, and no end can morally justify it. Charity and subsidies from unrelated industries are undesirable because they break the economically rational and controlling link between *services and support*. No one would suggest that in a free market steel companies should be subsidized by farmers or visa versa. Properly, in a free market each company would be expected to pay its own way. If a company provides goods and services which people really need and desire, they should have no trouble doing so. When support follows from services, an agency gets exactly what it morally deserves, meaning *what it has earned*. But when this economic link is broken, be it by taxation or by charity, no one can then tell what the services of a company are really worth; and when income is guaranteed, no one really cares. When an activity is removed from the market, waste and bureaucracy begin. Police forces should then not be financed by neighborhood donations, state lotteries or charity bazaars. Penal systems should not be subsidized by courts, or by dairy farmers or by humanitarian societies. Each and every agency of a free society ought to pay its own way: SUPPORT SHOULD FOLLOW FROM SERVICES RENDERED.*

The third basic question which arises concerning agencies of retaliatory force "unconstrained" by a central legislature or administration is "What is to guarantee their objectivity and morality?" First of all it should be pointed out that a person is simply deceiving himself if he thinks that central legislatures and administrations per se guarantee anything. As has already been stated, governments are responsible for the greatest atrocities in human history. The only thing which will guarantee the morality and objectivity of anything is the rationality of man. If men operate on the basis of objective morality, they will cooperate and solve their problems rationally and peaceably. If men act on the basis of subjectivism and irrationality, there is in fact no way at all to guarantee any of their actions. In any event, at best a person can only guarantee his own actions -- no man can guarantee the actions of another. And it is only on the basis of a rational philosophy that one can even hope that men will act rationally and peaceably. A collective, specifically a legislature or administration, is no better than the philosophy of the men who compose it. The free market alternative to such universally coercive institutions is a community of law and legal scientists.

A *community of law* is a given geographical area whose inhabitants act on the basis of the same morality and principles of social action. The essence of such a community is communication. When rational men are aware of ideas of others which are demonstrably true and significant, they will act accordingly. Hence in a free society, different judges belonging to separate court systems would read each other's decisions and journals and adopt those newly discovered principles which were correct and superior to past procedures. Legal societies would exist for this particular purpose. Since the laws of a free society would be objective, they would be *capable of scientific proof*.

---

*This is, of course, not to say that there is anything wrong with loans to start new enterprises or similar forms of assistance. It is only to say that over the long run, a business should pay its own way.

Many persons who reject the possibility of a purely voluntary community of law do so simply because they do not recognize what objective morality really means. By objective moral principles it is possible to precisely answer sociological questions which are now arbitrarily decided by the majority vote of legislatures and by the whimsical decrees of bureaucrats. Anarcho-capitalist agencies of retaliatory force would adopt statute laws by the same process that modern scientists adopted the theory of relativity -- by a process of objective validation and proof. No one had to force the *physical* scientists *of today* to accept this new principle of *physics*, and similarly no one would have to force the *legal* scientists *of tomorrow* to accept a new principle of *justice*. Both, as men of reason, accept the evidence of their senses and the judgment of their mind. Just as force is an anathema to progress in science, so force is an anathema to progress in justice. Progress and truth depend upon the uncoerced judgment of men -- they do not depend upon the decrees of bureaucrats and legislatures.

Of course, in a free market of justice, there might be those who dissented from the judgment of others. But just as innovation and invention in the physical sciences does not depend upon or require total agreement among engineers, so justice and social order in a free society do not depend upon total agreement between legal scientists. For a free society to exist, for free market justice agencies to successfully coexist, it is not necessary that men agree completely about everything, but only that they agree about fundamentals -- meaning basic philosophy. In time, truth will prevail if men are free.

Let us now consider in detail the possible form and financing of the agencies of retaliatory force of an anarcho-capitalist society.

3.1 Justice Agencies

What we have designated as *justice agencies* include bureaus of patents and copyrights, contract enforcement and fraud prevention. *Bureaus of patents and copyrights* are institutions for the registration and recording of new scientific inventions and intellectual creations. These agencies could be easily financed through registration fees. Thus every time someone wished to register a claim, he would pay a fee first for a patent or copy search, and then another payment for the registration of his claim and the maintenance of his file; this would contrast with the current procedure of tax subsidization of these functions, and only nominal payments made by persons registering claims. The lower the fees of a free market bureau, the better its services; the more people would patronize it and the more profits it would make. Profitable bureaus of patents and copyrights also imply competition, and competition in turn leads to innovation. Thus one would expect a great deal of technological progress associated with free market bureaus. Specifically, one would expect that free market bureaus would provide modern electronic information storage and retrieval devices, rather than present antiquated card files.

Naturally, in an anarcho-capitalist society, there would be several such bureaus. Wouldn't this make information searches difficult and confusing? Not at all, if one remembers the technological progress which accompanies capitalism. Despite the fact that patent and copyright searches would have to be made with each existing agency in order to be certain that a given device or literary creation had not been registered previously,* the total time of making several searches with firms using electronic

---

*Unless a person could prove that he had discovered a given physical or literary device independently. See my article "Intellectual Property Rights and Social Action" in the April 1969 issue of <u>The Rational Individualist</u>.

information storage devices would be far less than the time involved in making a single search through endless rows of file cabinets. In this manner, a competitive free market system of patent and copyright registration would be far superior to a coercive system.

It is also quite probable that electronic links would be established between the different agencies for the same reason that the telephone systems of a free society would be interconnected*: it is to the rational self-interest of the bureaus to do so. One bureau of patents and copyrights would then accept "information calls" from other bureaus in order to gain access to *their* files. Next, let us consider contract protection agencies.

The concept of a contract protection agency was (to my knowledge) originally suggested by Ayn Rand. As a free market agency, a *contract protection agency* would be a company whose function was to insure the millions of credit transactions which take place daily. The great majority of large purchases made by Americans today -- homes, automobiles, washing machines, color TV sets and so on -- are *credit transactions* in which a downpayment is made followed by monthly installments for anywhen from a few months to forty years. A contract protection agency would provide services to both the seller and the buyer in these transactions. For the seller, the contract protection agency would act as a combination insurance company and collection department, paying the seller the value of the contract outstanding if the buyer defaulted on his payments. The contract enforcement agency would then collect from the buyer, through the courts if necessary. For the buyer, the contract protection agency would insure that a seller lived up to his part of the credit contract, making repairs on a new car, say, for its warranty period. For these services, contract protection agencies would charge appropriate fees.

The third justice agency to be considered is the "anti-fraud" company. This would be a firm which investigated charges of fraud against individuals or corporations, attempting to get the persons involved to cease their fraudulent activities and to pay damages for the injuries which they had caused. An anti-fraud company is an extention and free market counterpart of the government's new "Department of Consumer Protection." Initially, anarcho-capitalist anti-fraud companies might attempt to procure cooperation from a person or firm which had committed fraud by simply pointing out to them that they had done so, and requesting that they pay the damages which they had caused. Failing this, the anti-fraud company might then threaten advertising the immorality of the concerned individuals or company (thereby causing them economic and social loses) or threaten to take legal action against them. Finally, as a last recourse, formal charges would be made, and the case (if accepted) would go to court. The anti-fraud company would finance its activities through fees collected for their services, and perhaps through the receipt of a portion of the damages awarded in successful cases which they brought to court.

Let us now move on to the more controversial issues of free market police forces, court systems, penal institutions and armed forces.

---

*See my article "'Public Services' Under Laissez Faire (IV) -- the Telephone System," which appeared in the May 1969 issue of The Rational Individualist.

3.2 Police Forces

Today there is the commonly accepted, but completely fallacious idea that somehow police protection, access to courts and even legal counsel is a "right" of citizenship in the United States. However, there is no more justification for such services being provided "free" (i.e., through taxation) than there is for color TV sets to be provided for each and every person in America at "public expense." Either a person has a right to his own life, liberty and property, or he does not. If he does, nothing can justify forcing him to subsidize another person for *any* purpose, including for the purpose of police protection. Either a person has the responsibility of maintaining his own life, or he does not. If he does, then he must earn the necessary funds himself to pay for the necessities and luxuries of his own existence.

In a free society, police protection, like every other service, would be available on a contractual basis, only to those who were willing and able to pay for it. There are four main ways in which an anarcho-capitalist police force could be financed: (1) through service contracts (similar to insurance); (2) through specific investigatory fees; (3) through special contracts; and (4) through fines. We will now discuss each in turn.

Service contracts would be the major source of revenue for a laissez-faire police department. A *service contract* would simply consist of a contractual agreement between a police department and an individual, whereby the police department would agree to provide the individual with certain services (e.g., investigation, physical defense of his property, etc.), should he need them, in exchange for a yearly premium. These policies would work essentially like insurance. Virtually everyone in a given society would subscribe and pay the yearly premium in order to be assured that, *should the need arise*, police protection would be available. Nonetheless, during any given year, only a small fraction of the total number of policy holders would actually need major police services. Therefore, the cost of police protection would be effectively spread over a large number of subscribers.

Let us take a concrete example. Suppose the cost of an average police investigation in Brandenberg was $5,000. If an individual needing police protection had to pay this cost all at once, he probably could not afford it. However, instead of paying such a large "specific investigatory fee," the individual will almost certainly be a subscriber to police protection, as will millions of others. Say there are 1000 subscribers in Brandenberg paying $100 a year each, making the total income for this small, local police department $100,000 per year. During the course of any given year, it is unlikely that more than four or five persons out of this 1000 will need police protection. If their investigations cost $5,000 each, this makes a total investigatory cost of $25,000 per year, leaving $75,000 for other police functions. Since the individual only pays $100 a year, he has in fact received $5,000 worth of benefits (so to speak) for his comparatively nominal fee. This is exactly how insurance works: on the principle that only a fraction of policy holders will ever collect at a given time, while many more are paying premiums.

The second form of police income is even simpler to explain. In the rare case that an individual needed police protection but had not entered into and did not now want to enter into a long term contract, or in the case of an individual requesting special services (such as perhaps hunting for a missing person), there would be *specific investigatory fees*. Again, these fees would be rather high, compared to the normal contractual agreement, but in some cases persons would find them worth paying.

The third form of police income would be *special contracts*. Thus, for example, a company owning a major turnpike* would probably contract with a private police force to patrol their highway, since it is to their rational self-interest to prevent reckless driving and other acts which would discourage use of their road and thus decrease their profits. Or similarly, a private factory might hire police to guard their facilities.

Finally, police forces in a free society could be financed through receipts from *fines*. As a contractual condition of procuring police protection, individuals could empower police departments to collect fines for misdemeanors which one committed. This would also save costly court expenses for both the justice company and for the private individual.

Let us now consider how anarcho-capitalist police forces might operate.[9] There are two basic operational types of crimes: those reported (or discovered by police) after the fact, and those reported (or discovered by police) during the fact. In the former case, police procedure would be quite clear. A family, upon returning from an outing, which discovered that their house had been robbed, would call the police and report the fact, as they would today. Then (unlike today) the police would *first* check to see if the family was signed up with them and entitled to this form of assistance by their contract. This could be done virtually instantaneously through electronic information retrieval systems. If the family was signed up and entitled to this type of assistance, a policeman would be dispatched and would proceed with his investigation. If the family was not signed up, or not entitled to this type of protection by their contract, a police force salesman would probably be sent out along with an investigator. The salesman would explain to the family, which has now become a high risk, how they could extend their contract to cover this situation if they were already signed up, or he couldexplain to them the forms of contract now available to them if they were not signed up, or he could simply tell them the cost of the specific investigation which they were requesting if that is all they wished to pay for. Naturally, if they had not already contracted for the type of police service which they were now requesting, they would have to pay more for it at this time than they would have had to pay if they had been covered by a service contract; just as a person must pay more for auto insurance after he has had an accident than before. However, the important point is that in after the fact cases it is clearly possible to verify whether or not a family had signed up with the police, and if not, to assess the appropriate fees.

Crimes discovered *during the fact* by police present a somewhat different situation. If a policeman comes upon a person being assaulted by a mugger, he does not, of course, have time to verify whether or not the person attacked is signed up for police protection, even if this would only take a few minutes. If the person were signed up, he would probably be somewhat annoyed that the policeman stood around checking his identity while he was sustaining mortal injuries. If he were not signed up, the police force might be losing a good prospect. For these reasons, among others, a policemen encountering such a situation would as a matter of course immediately come to the apparent victim's aid. Of course, the person being attacked does not have any

---

*Roads in a free society would, like everything else, be privately owned. For a description of the financing, construction and maintenance of roads without taxation or eminent domain, see my article "'Public Services' Under Laissez Faire, parts VI and VII -- the Roads" which appear in the July and August 1969 issues of The Rational Individualist.

"right" to demand that he be protected, any more than he has a right to demand that he be fed when he is hungry. Both police protection and food are commodities which one has to purchase in a free market. The fact that a person may be an innocent victim does not alter his obligation of providing for his own life.

There are, however, a number of reason why a policeman would automatically come to a person's aid in such a situation. First, as mentioned above, the victim might be a present client. Second, the victim would be a good *potential* client. Third, it is to the policeman's self-interest to see that criminals are countered, since this increases the profits of the police department, or more directly might increase his own salary. (Conceivably raises and promotions would be based on how well a policeman performed his function of protecting men from criminals.)

Now what happens if the victim is not in fact a client of this or of any other police department in the *during the fact* case. Again, there are two possibilities. First, the person might have called "Help, police!" If he did so, he has then in fact made a verbal contract for police assistance, just as you make a verbal contract to pay the check when you walk into a restaurant and order a meal. In this case, the policeman would send the victim a bill and expect him to pay. In the second case, the person *does not* call "Help, police!," but is simply lying there, bleeding while the mugger is beating on him. In this case no verbal contract exists. However, for the reasons mentioned above, the policeman *would* come to the person's aid. Being rational, the police force would also send this person a bill which he would be *requested* but not *obligated* to pay. Since the police have just saved his life, there is a good chance that he would pay. Or, if the police force were smart, they would send out a salesman and attempt to sign him up. Since he had just benefited from their services, it would seem quite likely that he would at least take the "special budget protection package." If he did not, the small expense of saving his life could be easily financed out of general police receipts, and surely no one in Brandenberg would complain about the policeman spending a few minutes of his time to save an innocent victim's life.

There is, finally, at least one other way in which police protection might be financed. Since the investigation of crimes, the protection of property and other such activities are actions necessitated by criminals, it would seem logical to make *them* pay at least part of the cost of such operations. *Thus, one of the debts of the criminal to "society" in a free community might be to pay back the cost of the investigation which he necessitated.*10 In this manner, police protection for the poor might be financed.* It will be interesting to see, if we ever create a free society, just which method of financing -- service fees or criminal payment -- would work out best.

Before going on to the courts and penal system of anarcho-capitalism, I will consider one more issue connected with police departments: arrests. Some libertarians assert that arrest is inherently immoral because it is in fact the initiation of force against persons whose guilt has not been proven "beyond a shadow of a doubt." There is, however, a very simple epistemological justification for arrest in a free society. It is as follows.

Necessarily man acts on the basis of his knowledge. At best man can be *epistem-*

---

* A second obvious method of financing police protection for the deserving poor would be through charity -- either from private agencies, or from the police department itself.

ologically certain, i.e., certain in a given context of knowledge. Man can seldom, if ever, be *metaphysically certain*, that is certain that there exists no alternative in the universe to his judgment. To be metaphysically certain, in most cases, requires omnisicience, which man clearly does not possess. Man can generally only be certain that he has examined all relevant facts available to him, and integrated them without contradiction; what *is* relevant is again dictated by his state of knowledge.

Knowledge of the truth of propositions is not an either/or condition, a dichotomous function. Knowledge is a continuous function, varying from, at one end, complete ignorance to, at the other end, complete (epistemological) certainty.

In assessing the guilt or innocence of a man accused of committing a crime there exists, accordingly, an *epistemological evidential continuum*, varying from *possibility of such guilt*, to *certainty of such guilt*. At different levels on the evidential continuum, different actions are appropriate. Thus, when one suspects that a man might *possibly* be guilty of a crime, it is proper to question him. When one has evidence that a man is *probably* guilty of a crime, it is proper to arrest him. And when one is convinced that a man is *certainly* guilty of a crime, it is proper to punish him. In general, the appropriate action with respect to suspected criminals depends upon the amount of evidence which one has. Arrest is then justified when guilt is probable.[11]

Now this does not of course mean that the morality of one's actions finally depends upon the contextual validity of one's judgment. Whether one was right or wrong in questioning, arresting or imprisoning a man depends upon whether he had in fact committed a crime. If in a free society the police arrest or the courts convict a person who later turns out to be innocent, they would be required to make restitution for their errors equal to the damages and inconvenience which they that caused him (unless the person had contractually freed them of this obligation).

There are two ways in which an anarcho-capitalist justice system could deal with police and judicial error. Either the police force of a free society could have its clients contractually agree to be subject to arrest when *the police* (or a magistrate) judged the evidence to be sufficient (thus freeing them from the obligation of making restitution if they arrested a person who later turned out to be innocent); or they would agree to make restitution if they made a mistake. Of the two possibilities, I prefer the latter. If the police or courts make a mistake, they should pay for it. In a free market of justice, police making many errors would thus quickly be eliminated by bankruptcy. Let us now consider the court system of a free society.

3.3 The Court System

At least three of the four major methods of financing which could be used by a free market police force could also be used by a free market court system: (1) service contracts, (2) fees for individual cases and (3) revenue from damage awards.

Just as police protection in a free market would generally be provided through *police service contracts*, so access to the courts would generally be through *judicial service contracts*, which made litigation available to policy holders. Failure to take out such a policy would mean that litigation would only be available at greater increased costs later. This form of financing and contractual relationship is identical to police service contracts, so we will not discuss it further. Similarly, revenue from damage awards in the court system would parallel fines as a form of police income. In court cases, a proportion of damages awarded in civil suits could be retained by the court to pay for some or all of its costs.

In the case of court and police services not covered by service contracts, the question arises "What specific amounts would be charged for a given case or investigation?" A case (or investigation) concerning the same issue could take a highly variable amount of time to deal with, depending upon specific circumstances. It might often be impossible to forecast in advance all of the costs involved in any specific judicial action. How are court fees, then, to be assessed in advance? The answer is simply that they would not be. One would only be billed later, as one is for treatment by a hospital for a major illness -- unless, of course, the expenses had been previously covered by one's judicial service contract. If the additional fees were very high, provision might be made for time payments -- sort of a "Go to court now, pay later" plan.

Let us next examine several specific issues relating to the operation of free market courts. First there is the question of how evidence, witnesses and jurors to be obtained in an anarcho-capitalist court system. Necessarily the concept of subpoena must be generally rejected. An individual has no inherent duty to appear in court or to supply evidence, simply because he or it are needed. How then are such obviously necessary items to be procured?

The simple answer is to make the provision of evidence, testimony or jury duty a condition of judicial service contracts.[12] Those persons who did not agree to this condition would be denied access to the courts as plantifs. Since most persons would sign service contracts (since it is to their rational self-interest to do so), the great majority of members of a free society would therefore be contractually required to provide the requested facts and services to the courts.

An alternative method of obtaining evidence, witnesses and jurors would simply be to pay for them. Even today, after all, it is not uncommon for evidence to be bought. This would take care of procuring facts and witnesses in most cases where they were not contractually available. It would also probably be much more desirable to have professional jurors, the legal scientists whom we spoke of previously, than randomly selecting untrained citizens.

At this point, one might ask if mercenary jurors and witnesses would not be likely to accept bribes from the prosecution or defense, thus corrupting and frustrating justice. The answer is no, since they would probably be hired and paid by the court itself, rather than by attorneys. Indeed since they would probably work in the same courts regularly, they would be particularly immune from the "temptation" to accept bribes, because they would lose their jobs and jeopardize their entire career if they did so. As legal scientists, one would also expect professional jurors to have quite a bit of professional integrity. In the case of paid witnesses, fraud could be deterred by establishing penalties (including imprisonment) for violation of "witness contracts" with the court.

Another question arises concerning the court system: If a person is being tried for a crime, to which court system does he go to -- his own or that of the person brining charges against him (assuming that they were different)? I would suggest that it be his own court system. I see nothing harmful in allowing a man the right to decide, to some extent, the statutes to which he is subject.

Wouldn't the existence of somewhat different statutes create legal chaos? Not at all. Today there are different statutes in different states, so that one must, for example, know what state he is in, in order to know the traffic regulations to which he is subject. Similarly, in a system of competing court systems, one would have to know what justice company a person was subscribing to before bringing a borderline suite against him.

Remember: it is only in details that the justice companies of a free society will differ. They will operate by the same general principles, or a free society will in fact not exist. The fact that judges and professional jurors read the same professional journals would guarantee that if they acted on the same principles they would follow the same statutes (generally).

However, in regard to many forms of *personal contracts*, a free society would be radically different from today's societies. In a free society all that would be required for a contract to be legally valid would be for the parties to it to understand its conditions and agree to them voluntarily. This introduces the possibility of great diversity in personal contracts. The marriage contract is a good example. Today, the state proscribes the permissable forms and responsibilities of marriage for both parties; and those permissable forms and responsibilities are largely uniform. In an anarcho-capitalist society, bigamy, group marriage, two-year renewable marriage contracts, marriage contracts in which the wife agreed to be responsible for the children in event of divorce and innumerable other types of legally formalized inter-personal relationships would be judically protected.

3.4 The Penal System

The penal system goes hand in hand with the court system. Let us now consider the nature of criminal justice in a free society. Again, a radical departure from present practices and customs is necessary. Today's penal system is based on an objectively immoral and archaic concept of justice: punishment. Webster's first definition of *punishment* is "to cause (a person) to undergo pain, loss, or suffering for a crime or wrongdoing." This concept of "justice" is immoral because its primary focus is upon *harming the criminal*, rather than *providing retribution for the victim*. It is archaic because it is nothing but a restatement of the *Old Testament* concept of "an eye for an eye, a tooth for a tooth," which overlooks the fact that putting out the eye of the criminal does not restore the eye of his victim. The proper focus of justice is upon the victim.

In this context, there are three proper functions of a penal system: retribution, removal and rehabilitation. Let us begin by considering the most important, a concept which is all but totally absent from today's "justice" system: retribution.

The basic principle of objective justice is that when one commits a crime, one incurs a debt to the victim (or to his heirs) equal to the amount of damages which one has caused. In a word, the basic concept of objective justice is retribution. The damages involved in a crime are manifold, including at least: (1) *direct losses* from the crime, such as the loss of money, property, etc.; (2) *indirect losses*, such as the time value of one's money (i.e., interest) and opportunity loss; (3) *physical and mental inconvenience* caused by the crime (e.g., time lost in talking to the police and in going to court); and (4) *personal expenses incurred by the crime*, e.g., legal fees. All of these are costs which the criminal should be required to pay since he necessitated them.

The first consequence of the implementation of the principle of retribution is that, unlike today, crime in a free society would become quite unprofitable. Today it is literally possible a bum to steal $50,000, hid the money, turn himself in to the police and receive a sentence of two years in jail. At the end of two years, he has officially "paid his debt to society" and is released. He can then dig up the $50,000 and, if he is careful, spend it. Our criminal bum has thus earned himself $25,000 a year, making theft quite profitable for him. Under a system of objective criminal law this would be impossible. In a rational society, if a man stole $50,000 he would by that act be liable for a debt of $50,000 *plus all other costs generated by his crime*. If he were caught, he would have to work until he paid back that debt. So if our bum still had possession of the $50,000 when he has caught he would hardly be inclined to keep it while working in prison for 50 years at $1,000 a year. There would simply be nothing for him to gain by doing so, and in fact he would have much to lose.

A thief in a sane society would immediately return all of his stolen loot which he still had in his possession, thus immediately providing at least partial restitution for his victim. The difference outstanding between the amount which he had stolen (plus the other costs engendered by his crime) and the amount that he could pay back immediately would probably be paid by an insurance company; which the thief would in turn pay back. Thus the victim would not have to wait any time at all to have his property returned. The use of the intermediary of an insurance company to pay back the victim would also be to the rational self-interest of the criminal since it would greatly lower the amount of extra compensation which he would have to pay for the time value of the stolen money and for opportunity loss. Since under a system of objective criminal justice a thief would have to pay back *more* than he had stolen, it is clear that thievery in a free society would be quite unprofitable. We will later establish that this is the case for other crimes as well.

The principle of retribution explained here provides a method of making an exact calculation of what should be required of a criminal. If a man steals $50,000 he owes that amount (plus other damages), and not a dollar more. Compare this exact concept of justice with today's capricious system where the degree of "punishment" for the same crime can vary drastically from state to state, and from time to time, but is uniformly arbitrary. Can there be any doubt as to which system is the more objective and rational. I think not.

One may also ask what debt the murderer incurs. First, there is a debt to the victim's heirs. Thus if the murder victim had been supporting a wife and two children and was intending to do so for another 20 years, the criminal would be required to continue paying their support. The richer a person, the greater his productive ability, the greater the debt a criminal would incur in killing him. However, in some respects the debt created by a murder is irretrievable. There is no way of paying back a victim (or his heirs) for lost pleasures and lost dreams. The murdered than has, in this respect, an *infinite debt* to his victim. The best way of paying this debt might be for provision to be made in statute law for individuals to specify what they want done with their killer if they are murdered. This would constitute a recognition of the fact that a man has an inalienable right to act, and that he can require those who interfer with his ability to act to carry out his will which he can no longer carry out in person. Hence a murdered poet might prescribe that his assassin work the rest of his life to earn money for struggling poets. There is also the possibility of a murder victim prescribing insidious punishments for his killer -- such as being "boiled in oil," sold into slavery, being used for "humanburgers," or being used for medical experimentation. I need not comment on the deterrent effect of allowing men to prescribe such punishments for their murderers.

The concept of retributory justice coupled with modern science also permits a fairly straight-foward answer to the question of what debt a person incurs when he injurs another person, say by shotting him through the lung. The simple answer is to require him to be a donor for an organ transplant. In this case one's assailant would be required to contribute one of his lungs to a central organ bank, and one in turn could draw a lung out of the bank. (The intermediary of a central organ bank is introduced to insure that one "gets fitted" properly.) Thus rather than putting out one's assailant's eye if he puts yours out, you simply take his as a replacement.

Retribution is, however, only the first of the three proper functions of a penal system. The other two are removal and rehabilitation. *Removal* is the limitation and control of the actions of an individual to insure that he pays back the damages that he has caused (or that he act according to the will of his victim). The degree of removal, like the degree of retribution, is not a constant, but a variable whose value depends upon the specific nature of the crime and of the criminal. Thus in the case of a "three time loser," removal from society should be complete to insure that the malefactor pays back his debt. Conversely, in the case of a person who had just gotten into a fight which resulted in only minor injuries to his victim, the degree of removal might be zero. At one extreme there would, then, exist penitentaries such as we have today, completely separated from the rest of society, and at the other extreme there might simply be parole boards which the criminal would check with infrequently. Between these two extremes there are many other possible forms of removal. Let us now consider them in more detail, and in doing so we will see how penal institutions in general might be financed.

Where removal is complete, prisons should be established as self-supporting communities -- farms, in the event that little commerce with the outside world is desirable. Today such totally removed institutions are irrationally operated on the basis of equalitarian socialism. All criminals are given the same trivial wages, regardless of their crime or their productive ability, and are provided with free room and board. The work which criminals do is often a game, of little productive value; and there is no possibility for advancement. This state of affairs is largely responsible for the failure of our prisons to rehabilitate criminals. It is imperative, therefore, that capitalism be imported into the prisons.

Prisoners should be paid market wages for their work, and they should be able to advance in their jobs according to their competency. Thus the more productive a prisoner was, the faster he could pay off his debt. The prisoner would in turn use his wages, after a portion was deducted pay off his debt, to buy food, clothing, shelter and entertainment. Just as in the outside world, those who did not work would not eat. Conversely, those who were highly productive would be able to buy better goods than those who were not very productive.

For those prisoners who had little or not skills, and for those who wished to increase their skills (and thereby increase their productivity and *decrease* their time in prison) there could be job training programs and academic courses. The cost of these educational services prisoners could also pay for out of their future wages.

Where removal need not be complete, even more possibilities exist. "Prisons" could be factories or sections of factories in cities. Prisoners could be daily bused from special dormitories to the factories during the day, and back again at night.

Under such a system of profit-making prisons, rehabilitation would be automatic. With the exception of "crimes of passion," most persons commit crimes because they believe that theft, murder and other criminal acts are the easiest way of achieving their ends. Among other things, they lack confidence in their ability to earn the values which they desire. A penal system operated as described above would create an environment in which a prisoner could not support his life by crime and would have to work to earn his living. In this respect only would a prison be essentially different from the outside society. Moreover, the more a prisoner worked, the sooner he would be free. Such an environment is ideally suited to teaching men the value of work and to create or restore their confidence in their ability to support their own lives.

3.5 *The Armed Forces*

Undoubtedly one of the most difficult questions for advocates of freedom to answer has been "How could the armed forces be financed without taxation?" At the present time, defense and defense-related expenditures in the United States account for nearly one-half of the Federal budget. Since it is wishful thinking to imagine that Soviet H-bombs and Chinese mass armies would cease to be threat if laissez-faire capitalism were established in the United States in the foreseeable future, very large expenditure for defense will probably still be necessary in a free society. Further, unlike the police forces and courts, which provide services primarily for *individuals*, armed forces provide services primarily for *large groups*, such as an entire society. How then can one rationally assess and collect the billions of dollars necessary for such services which apparently effect an entire economy?

It should first be noted that the armed forces of a voluntary society, like all of such a society's institutions of retaliatory force, would differ greatly from the present coercive counterparts. The function of the armed forces of a free society would be defensive: to protect that society from those seeking to enslave or destroy it. The armed forces of a free society would not protect non-communist dictatorships from communist dictatorships, nor attempt to prevent valid revolutions against totalitarianism. An anarcho-capitalist armed forces would in fact be the compatriot of all peoples who sought to destroy the greatest manifest threat to their lives: *the coercive state*. The armed forces of a free country could morally seek only the defense of men from those who initiated force against them, and its primary concern would be with the members of its own society.

The next question which occurs is how are such armies to be raised. The only possible answer for any advocate of man's rights is that they be raised *voluntarily* through contractual agreements between men. The armed forces of an anarcho-capitalist society would be composed of paid professionals dedicated to the cause of human freedom.

The immorality of the draft is obvious. Not quite so obvious is the fact that it is also completely unnecessary and impractical for the defense of a free society. The reason why the draft is unnecessary can be summarized by a single sentence: *Men defend that which they value, and there is no purpose in their defending that which they do not value.* Thus if men value the society of the United States of America, they will defend it *freely*. If they do not value it sufficiently to do so, then what person or group can morally claim that they should be forced to defend it? All that can be claimed is that some men (e.g., the voting population of a country) should have the "right" to *force* others (e.g., the out-numbered and non-voting young) to fight their battles for them. But this is nothing but the purest hypocrisy. Such a moral position has never been, and could never be justified by anyone. A draft is involuntary servitude, and involuntary servitude is slavery, plain and simple. The enslavement of some men to defend the lives of men who are too cowardly to defend themselves is the lowest kind of moral cannibalism.

The draft is impractical because one cannot temporarily enslave some men in order to secure their own long-run freedom, or in order to maintain the freedom of others. Slaves simply make inefficient soldiers for they have no incentive to be efficient. And how can one possibly convince them that they should fight for the freedom and rights of others when their own freedom and rights are being denied *en toto*? Moreover, there are many other inefficiencies which result from conscription as it exists today: high training costs engendered by large turnover rates, the occupational inefficiency of two-year soldiers and the negative motivational effect of paying America's defenders less than Job Corps Trainees from the slums. Consider further the blatant diseconomies of forcing highly trained, individualistic scientists and professionals to do menial work in the name of "democracy" and "impartiality." Then there is the destructive psychological effect of attempting to turn free men into robots, capable only of obediance and not of thought or independent judgment. Finally, there is the loss in productivity to the external community, which Professor Milton Friedman calls a "tax in kind,"[13] of removing such highly productive men from society.

The draft is clearly totally at odds with objective morality and the requirements of a free society. The soldiers of a moral society would necessarily be fully-paid professionals. Let us now turn to the topic of financing and operating an anarcho-capitalist armed forces.

Apparently the greatest obstacle to operating an armed forces without taxation is the great sums of money involved. Over 80 billion dollars has been allocated for the current fiscal year (1969-1970) to U.S. defense spending. Where would all of this money come from without taxation?

The first fact to point out is that the armed forces of a free society would not be nearly as expensive as the armed forces are today; neither absolutely nor relatively. Since the armed forces of a free society would be a *defensive* organization, rather than a "world policeman," cost of operation would be for that reason alone much lower. In the extreme, such incredibly irrational wars as Vietnam (where we witness the spectacle of the first Orwellian continuous war, destroying thousands of American lives and draining billions of American dollars) would be impossible. In a rational world no one would volunteer for such a war. Immediately, then, we would have a savings of $40 billion a year. In addition, the absolute cost (all things considered) of professional soldiers would also be much lower for the reasons given above. These are two factors contributing to a lower *absolute cost* of the armed forces in a free society.

To understand how a lower *relative cost* would occur, consider the social context in which the armed forces of a free society would exist. Under laissez-faire capitalism we can anticipate a rate of economic growth *at least equal* to that of the American industrial revolution, or about two to three times as great as our declining rate of growth today. Such a rate of economic growth would produce, after a few decades, undreamed of heights of productivity and affluence. For example, a growth rate of 5% per year, lasting 20 years, would increase the 1968 GNP* of the United States of $800 billion more than 2.6 times to $2.13 trillion. *Any socialist country would be literally unable to copy, steal or mimic the technology of a laissez-faire America fast enough to even begin to match this rate of technological progress.* Such an incontroversial lead in technological development would make the cost of maintaining an effective deterrence relative to the GNP, a fraction of what it is today. (Even now, the semi-free United States spends only one-half as much as the Soviet Union on military armaments, expressed as a per cent of the national GNP.) In such a context, a multi-generation advance in weaponry over the rest of the world would not be long in coming. For example, an *effective* ABM, or orbital continuous beam laser emplacements might be developed. The inherent dynamism of laissez-faire capitalism would then create a relatively inexpensive armed forces. With this background, let us now examine in detail how financing without taxation could be effected.

First consider just what and whom it is that needs defending, or, conversely, think of the primary objects of attack by totalitarian states. In order of decreasing primacy, targets in the nuclear age are: (1) centers of social organization and control: administrative facilities of agencies of retaliatory force and communications and transportation facilities; (2) offensive and defensive military facilities (missile bases, ships, radar installations, troop concentrations, etc.); (3) industry; (4) food sources; and (5) population centers (i.e., cities).

Now the basic answer to the question of how the armed forces of a free society could be financed is that these subdivisions of society would provide for their own defense, in proportion to the degree of threat which they perceived as confronting them. Larger corporations might do so by building armaments; smaller firms could contract for defense with special "protection companies." In those cases where industries were geographically concentrated, making them logical objects of enemy attacks, it would become rational for them to join together in special associations and mutual assistance pacts to, for example, purchase and maintain missile sites to deter attacks against them. Center of social organization, agricultural communities and population centers could do likewise. (Protection companies would naturally provide for their own defense.) The major instrumentalities of the armed forces of a free society would then consist of indigenous defensive installations, purchased from any one of a variety of contractors and maintained by personnel hired specifically for that purpose. In a phrase, the answer to the problem of defending a free society from external attack is a *non-coercive* "military-industrial complex."

Troops could be raised in a variety of ways: private contracts, special training of police to create "standby reserves" or special organizations which trained citizens interested in participating in the armed forces. The "armed forces" of a free society, unlike today, need not be a monolithic organization with tin soldier regimentation. Such forms of coordination and cooperation between different groups as might be necessary would arise, when objectively necessary, through cross-organizational military associations -- similar to the associations which unite the private volunteer fire-departments of America.

---

*GNP: Gross National Product, the theoretical total value of all goods and services produced in a given society in a given year.

It should be emphasized that the major form of financing the armed forces of anarcho-capitalism -- *protection contracts* -- would not be charity, in the sense of men contributing arbitrary amounts to vague causes, without receiving any tangible value in return. A free market in military defense would mean that men would only contribute to those forms of defense which directly contributed to *their* security, according to their perceived need for it.

There are also many other possible supplemental forms of financing for particular military activities. To give one example, consider military research. A simple form of financing this activity would be for a research company to issue special "defense bonds" to raise capital. The principal and interest on these bonds could then be paid back out of profits accrued from the sale of patents resulting from such research, or products developed with these patents -- the technological spin-offs.

Protection contracts could also be extended to cover American individuals or corporations living or operating in foreign countries. A three party contract could be concluded between, for example, an American company abroad, the foreign government (or defense corporations) and an American protection agency. The American protection agency, with the agreement of the foreign government would protect the American factory from hostile natives in return for a yearly fee which the industrial firm paid. Similarly ships could contract for naval protection, planes for air protection and so on. American military agencies could also contract with foreign communities to protect them from Communist invasion or local despots.

Finally, in time of war, a further method of military financing exists. During conventional wars, such as the Korean War, "war bonds" could be issued to finance military operations. These bonds could then be repaid when the army won by selling unowned land and government property in the defeated country. If the army did not win, it would presumedly go bankrupt; such as the risks of war.

This now concludes our discussion of the financing and operation of agencies of retaliatory force of a free society. In summary, justice agencies (e.g., patents and copyrights, contract protection and anti-fraud companies) could be financed by *service fees*. Police forces and courts could be financed by insurance-type *service contracts*. Penal institutions could be financed by making prisons self-supporting, profit-making institutions. Finally, the armed forces of a free society could be financed by *protection contracts* and *special bonds*.

We now know how and why a free society might work. However, rather than stopping here and leaving my concept of a free society without a means of practical implementation, I will now discuss how such a society could be created in reality, given the socio-political nature of the United States today.

4.0 CREATING A FREE SOCIETY

We are now living in a society very far removed from the free society possible and proper for man. Today association is not free but controlled, determined and coerced in a myriad of ways by government. Property is not fully private, but increasingly public. And force is rampant upon the land. In the United States today we are witnessing the conversion of welfare statism into welfare fascism. The process of censorship is already beginning, and it may not be long before men will not even be free to dissent.

Between our decaying freedom and total slavery stand only the remnants of individualism and a hand-full of Objectivists. As I see it, there are basically three alternatives which those of us who value their freedom have: (1) submission, (2) retreat or (3) activism. To submit is tantamount to accepting those forms of personal subjugation which already exist -- e.g., the totalitarian draft, confiscatory taxation, and fascist control of free enterprise -- as well as accepting those even more heinous forms which are yet to come. To submit is tantamount to surrendering one's life without a struggle. For any man who values his life, this is not an alternative at all.

The second alternative is to retreat, to form an Atlantis on an island somewhere in a remote region of the earth or preferably on another planet. Of course, retreat need not be complete: one could conceivably set up a society in the world somewhere which traded with other communities. However it must be pointed out that with populations below a certain "critical mass," there is an inverse relationship between contact with the outside world and internal security. Thus a society of 1000 Objectivists who set up their free community on say Cuba, and who traded with the United States, specializing according to their relative advantage in sugar cane and philosophical research, would be totally dependent upon the United States for their continued economic prosperity, and hence they would be potentially subject to control by the U.S. Government. Should Washington decide that such a community of radical individualists were a threat to the fascist "Great Society" (which ideologically they certainly would be), it would have the power of destroying the "free port of Cuba" by simply stopping trade with it or declaring an embargo.

At the opposite extreme, if 1000 Objectivists decided to form a free society in the remote regions of South America or Africa, being very careful to conceal the existence of their community and trading with no one, they *would* be able to obtain very high security; but their living standard would probably be very low. It is simply impossible for a small group of even the most productive men and women to duplicate the division of labor benefits and capital investment of a world-trading community of over one billion. In natural resources alone they would be drastically limited. Only when the standard of living of the United States radically declined would such a community be very attractive to many Objectivists.

The third alternative is to create a free society in the larger community of the United States. This necessarily could only be achieved through the general process of education. The reason why education is the only possible means to this end is that our present coercive state and our concomitant flagging freedom and prosperity are simply a consequence of the incorrect values and philosophy which people hold. Abolish the state (the main instrumentality of those values and that philosophy) overnight -- say through a violent revolution -- and the subjectivist and collectivist values which most Americans hold would remain, reassert themselves and recreate a society *just as coercive* as the one we have today; and probably even more so. Since values as the primary, and social forms the consequence, the *only* way to create a free society on a large scale is through education. However, a process of slow education, the gradual change of the philosophy of America is not an alternative open to us. Long before we could penetrate the established public school and political system with our ideas if we confined our actions to traditional forms of education, censorship will be imposed. Clearly an expedient to cultural change is needed.

4.1 Alternatives to Government Institutions

How often have you presented a brilliantly stated, logically air-tight thesis to a collectivist only to have him say "That's fine in theory, but in practice it wouldn't work." This of course is an absurdity, but it is next to impossible to convince most collectivists of this fact by purely forensic ability. Clearly, if we are to convince the great majority of American intellectuals, something more than "logical theorizing" is necessary.

What I propose is the actual creation of alternatives to government institutions -- initially schools, post offices, fire departments and charity; later, roads, police courts and armed forces. Libertarians recognize that government services are hopelessly obsolete and inherently economically unsound. With the present system, it is patently impossible to assess the costs of education and police investigations at all. Rather than trying to politically convince two hundred million Americans that this is so on the basic of rational economic theory, libertarians should instead demonstrate the fact by actually creating the far superior institutions of a free society. Fire departments, schools and post offices should immediately be set up by men and women who understand the free market and who are competent as businessmen.

One way to do this would be for rational businessmen to cooperate with libertarian students and theorists in order to establish such enterprises as *franchise operations*, using all of the skills of modern industry. Simultaneously, libertarians should act politically to free the market to facilitate these enterprises; meanwhile theoreticians should attempt to infiltrate the mass media, or start their own popular magazines and telecommunications facilities to emphasize to the American people that these institutions *are* working far better than their governmental equivalents; and then to explain *why* they are doing so. Such a dramatic demonstration of the efficacy of the free market might well accomplish what mere talk alone is unable to do: free America.

How can the men and women of America fail to understand the value of freedom in all areas of human enterprise when private post offices, roads and police are actually providing far better services than government is capable of delivering?

4.2 *The Imperative To Act*

"We are now witnessing the collapse of civilization. Collectivism and its many social manifestations, fascism, communism and welfare statism, are running rampant and virtually unopposed in the world today. Society and men may survive the coming armageddon, but freedom and the individual will not. This is the age of world war, world crisis and world statism. The present domination of collectivism heralds the beginning of a new dark age before the start of the twenty-first century -- *a dark age in which the dictators will be armed with nuclear weapons.*

"The only thing which can prevent the final fall of reason, freedom and civilization, *the only thing which can prevent you from dying in a totalitarian America*, is counteraction on a vast scale. The only philosophy capable of giving man and civilization a rebirth is Objectivism."[14]

There are two pre-conditions for the preservation of the partial freedom and prosperity which we now enjoy and the attainment of that state of existence proper to man. The first is the existence of a philosophical defense for freedom and man's rights. The second is the existence of men willing to act on the basis of those principles to preserve their lives and to create a free society. Both pre-conditions are necessary; neither one by itself is sufficient. The first precondition was provided (in essence) by Ayn Rand with the publication of *Atlas Shrugged* in 1957. The second pre-condition is yet to be established. *If freedom is to be won, and slavery to be averted, it is imperative that the second pre-condition be achieved -- that men aware of the issues involved, particularly the readers of this article, act.*

A free society will not be created by some nebulous "others," it will either be created by you or it will not be created at all. Freedom will not be won simply because "it is right," but it will be realized only when and if those who recognize that *it is right* take positive action. Those of you reading this essay who are going about your day-to-day routine as if collectivism did not exist, as if you were not immeasurably and increasingly diminished by the myriad of irrational laws governing your actions; you will be the ones responsible when the concentration camps come to America; and moreover, you will be the prime canididates for them. For too long you have sat in your discussion groups and talked about what is wrong with America; now is the time to do something about it.

Not only is it imperative to act; it is also immoral *not to do so*. Consistent with Objectivism, one has the moral duty to act to preserve one's own life and meet threats to it. The basic criteria of morality is to *act* in your rational self-interest. To merely abstain from initiating force against others is not to act morally. Under any circumstances, to be moral, one must postively act to maintain one's life. Today, to fail to act is to commit suicide.

Do not say that someone else will act for you. There is no one else. Do not say that you do not know what to do; there is not one else who knows better. Do not say that you are too busy with your daily routine. To be too busy to act against collectivism is to be too busy to live.

The irrationality of presently inactive Objectivists can best be described by means of analogy. It is as if one evening when your entire family were at home, everyone went about their normal routine, eating dinner, watching TV and doing homework, while outside the rest of the block was in flames and the fire was rapidly moving toward one's own home. True, your home is not yet burning; but the best possible way to insure that it will be soon, that you and all that which you value would soon be destroyed, would be to do nothing. Not to call the fire department, not to leave, but just to sit there as if nothing extraordinary was happening, would be the most blatant irrationality. So it is that thousands of Objectivists across the country go about their daily affairs, to all intents and purposes oblivious of the collectivist threat to their life. They may be aware of that threat in the abstract, but their failure to act on the basis of that awareness is effectively as bad as not being aware of that threat at all. Even worse, to be aware of a threat to one's life and yet to fail to do something about it is tantamount to choosing the immoral.

It does not matter whether one is inactive because one does not care to do anything about that threat, or because one does not know what to do. Not only do you have the responsibility to act, but you also have the responsibility to think. *You* must judge, plan and organize to realize that state of freedom which is proper to man. Perhaps twenty years ago one could justify going about a daily routine without acting against collectivism -- perhaps then. However such inaction is certainly not defensable today. The very things which you value so much that you are afraid you will lose through activism -- your job, your social activities, and your future -- these are the very things which you are sure to lose through *inaction*.

You are free to evade the fact that you are responsible for your own life, but you are not free to escape the consequences of that evasion. You are free to be fatalistic, but you are not free from the consequences of that fatalism. You are free to fail to act, but you will not be free at all if you do.

What can you do? Join SRI or a similar organization, or start one of your own. Participate in its projects; contribute to its functions. Don't abandon your children to the schools of the state -- start alternative schools of your own. Cooperate with others, explain to them the necessity of activism and get *them* working.

Do not be indifferent to the failure of others to act. When they so fail they jeopardize your own probability of success. If ten thousand of us act, freedom may be won; if only ten of us do, it probably will not. Do not fear to pass moral judgment on the inaction of others, or delude yourself into believing that the choice to act or not to act is a matter of individual preference. This is false. The same reasons which make action a moral necessity for you, makes it a moral necessity for others. The same reasons which make inaction immoral for you also makes it immoral for others.

Do not be overwhelmed by the magnitude ot the task before us. The state *is* powerful and much larger than we are at present, but it is also corrupt and inherently inefficient and appeals to the worst within men.

To win anything worth attaining we must be right, but to win anything at all we must also act. Like that first man of prehistory uncountable eons in the past, you have the choice to think or not to think, to act or not to act, to submit to the tyranny of your environment or to soar beyond it.

Man's fate for centuries in the future and perhaps for all time will be determined by what you do or fail to do today. Which shall the dawning of the twenty-first century herald: the begining of the first mature human civilization or the end of man? The choice is for you to make.

If you choose the former, if you choose to act to preserve your life, then join with us to create that society as far beyond twentieth century America as twentieth century America is beyond the caves: SOCIETY WITHOUT COERCION.

FOOTNOTES

[1] Ayn Rand, "The Objectivist Ethics," The Virtue of Selfishness (New York, 1964), p. 13.

[2] Ayn Rand is a Russian-born philospher and novelist. Her major works include the novels Atlas Shrugged and The Fountainhead, and the books Capitalism: The Unknown Ideal and Introduction to Objectivist Epistemology. She is presently editor and publisher of a monthly journal of her philosophy -- The Objectivist.

[3] In the argument stated in the text we asked what could be predicted about human thought and action assuming that one could know in totality and detail the neurological structure of the human brain and the nature of all environmental stimuli and correlated human response. Let us now ask if these variables in human action could in fact be specified at any time, even in the remotely distant future. To this question the answer would appear to be that metaphysically it is possible, but epistemologically it probably is not. Consider the kind of scientific description that would be necessary in order to predict in detail and precision the actions of any given human being. First, the general structure of the human brain would have to be specified exactly. Second, the specific structure of the brain of a given individual under study -- its differences with the general structure and the functional importance of those differences -- would have to be known. Third, a suitable encoding system would have to be found for all environmental stimuli effecting the individual; such specifications to precisely describe not only discrete stimuli and their psychological effects in isolation, but also to precisely describe their nature and psychological effects as complex patterns. Even the question of whether environmental stimuli are to be treated as discrete or as patterned is itself a function of the state of human consciousness: i.e., an individual may focus either upon discrete objects in isolation from others, or he can focus upon an entity as a part of a larger pattern, or he can focus upon an entity's relationship with other entities, and so on. The possibilities are virtually infinite. Fourth, the incredibly complex effects of the environment on man, and the effects of man on the environment would have to specified. The position, relationship between, pattern of and perceived significance of every object which our subject encountered, would have to be specified before one could precisely begin to attempt to predict his thought and action.

If the determination of the four factors listed above is metaphysically possible, it is highly unlikely that it will be achieved before the sun of the earth goes nova, obliterating the environment being specified and hence frustrating the successful specification of human action and thought. We therefore reassert that given the nature of man and his universe, the complete description and prediction of the thought and action of an individual is virtually impossible. Since knowledge must precede control, the successful control and coercion of another individual (i.e., control and coercion without violation his rational self-interest) is virtually impossible. Hence man should be free.

[4] After Ayn Rand.

⁵Ayn Rand, "The Nature of Government," The Virtue of Selfishness (New York, 1964), p. 107.

⁶Op. cit.

⁷R.A. Childs,"An Open Letter to Ayn Rand: Objectivism and the State," The Rational Individualist, 1:10 (August, 1969), pp. 4-12.

⁸Op. cit., pp. 112-113.

⁹At this point I would like to thank Mr. Sheldon Wasserman for his suggestions made to me in 1967 of how a free market, fee-paid fire department might operate. I have here applied his concept, plus many of my own, to police departments.

¹⁰Thank you, Donna Rasnake, for reminding me of this possibility.

¹¹This analysis is based upon principles elucidated by Dr. Leonard Peikoff in his speech "Certainty Without Omniscience" delivered at the First (and last) Regional Conference on Objectivism, held at the University of Virginia at Charlottesville, April 30, 1967.

¹²I would like to credit Mr. William Bobick for this brilliant suggestion.

¹³Milton Friedman, "The Case For A Voluntary Army," The New Guard, 7:5 (May, 1967), pp. 12-16.

¹⁴Jarret Wollstein, "Intellectual Property Rights and Social Action," The Rational Individualist, 1:6 (April, 1969), p. 24.

The Right Wing Individualist Tradition In America

An Arno Press/New York Times Collection

Bailie, William. **Josiah Warren:** The First American Anarchist. 1906.

Barber, Thomas H. **Where We Are At.** 1950.

Barnes, Harry Elmer. **Pearl Harbor After a Quarter of a Century.** Left and Right: A Journal of Libertarian Thought, Vol. IV. 1968.

Barnes, Harry Elmer. **In Quest of Truth and Justice:** De-Bunking the War Guilt Myth. 1928.

Barnes, Harry Elmer. **Selected Revisionist Pamphlets,** n.d. 1972.

Bromfield, Louis. **A New Pattern for a Tired World.** 1954.

Burgess, John W. **Recent Changes in American Constitutional Theory.** 1923.

Carroll, Charles Holt. **Organization of Debt into Currency:** and Other Papers. 1964.

Fleming, Harold M. **Ten Thousand Commandments:** A Story of the Antitrust Laws. 1951.

Flynn, John T. **As We Go Marching.** 1944.

Harris, George. **Inequality and Progress.** 1897.

Individualist Anarchist Pamphlets, 1867-1904. 1972.

Knight, Bruce Winton. **How to Run a War.** 1936. New Preface by Bruce Winton Knight.

Lane, Rose Wilder. **The Discovery of Freedom:** Man's Struggle Against Authority. 1943. New Foreword by Robert LeFevre. New Introduction by Roger Lea MacBride.

Left and Right: Selected Essays, 1954-1965. 1972.

The Libertarian Forum. 1969-1971. Murray N. Rothbard and Karl Hess, editors.

McGurrin, James. **Bourke Cockran:** A Free Lance in American Politics. 1948.

[La Monte, Robert Rives and H. L. Mencken.] **Men Versus The Man:** A Correspondence between Robert Rives La Monte, Socialist and H. L. Mencken, Individualist. 1910.

Montgomery, Zach[ariah], compiler. **The School Question:** From a Parental and Non-Sectarian Stand-Point. 1889.

Nock, Albert Jay. **Our Enemy, The State.** 1935.

Olds, Marshall. **Analysis of the Interchurch World Movement Report on the Steel Strike.** 1922.

Oppenheimer, Franz. **The State:** Its History and Development Viewed Sociologically. 1926.

Paterson, Isabel. **The God of the Machine.** 1943.

Phillips, C. A., T. F. McManus and R. W. Nelson. **Banking and the Business Cycle:** A Study of the Great Depression in the United States. 1937.

Schoeck, Helmut and James W. Wiggins, editors. **Scientism and Values.** 1960.

Scoville, John W. **Labor Monopolies or Freedom.** 1946.

Scoville, John and Noel Sargent, compilers. **Fact and Fancy in the T.N.E.C. Monographs.** 1942.

Snyder, Carl. **Capitalism The Creator:** The Economic Foundations of Modern Industrial Society. 1940.

Society Without Government: 1969-1970. 1972.
Tannehill, Morris and Linda and Jarret B. Wollstein.

Spooner, Lysander. **Let's Abolish Government,** 1852-1886. 1972.

Sprading, Charles T., editor. **Liberty and the Great Libertarians.** 1913.

Sumner, William Graham. **What Social Classes Owe to Each Other.** 1883.

Tolles, Frederick B. **George Logan of Philadelphia.** 1953.

Tucker, Benj[amin] R. **Instead of a Book:** By a Man Too Busy to Write One. 1893.

Vreeland, Hamilton, Jr. **Twilight of Individual Liberty.** 1944.

What Is Money? 1884-1963. 1972. Rothbard, Murray N. and I[saiah] W. Sylvester.

Williamson, Harold Francis. **Edward Atkinson:** The Biography of an American Liberal, 1827-1905. 1934.

Winston, Ambrose Paré. **Judicial Economics:** The Doctrine of Monopoly as Set Forth by Judges of the U.S. Federal Courts in Suits under the Anti-Trust Laws. 1957.